The Land Rover Experience

A user's guide to four-wheel driving

Second edition – October 1994

Tom Sheppard

Published by

This book deals with post-1986 model Land Rovers, Defenders, Discoverys and Range Rovers where details of controls and transmission are concerned and incorporates operational details relating to the significant changes made for 1995 Model Year. The vast majority of the book's advice and philosophy, however, may be applied to all Land Rover operations with appropriate discretion.

Published by Land Rover and distributed by Unipart to Land Rover dealerships.
Book trade: sold through WHSmith, distribution through Vine House Distribution.
Project conceived and directed at Land Rover by Roger Crathorne .
Written, designed and produced for Land Rover by Tom Sheppard, MBE, ARPS.
Illustration artwork by Mike Lister of Plum Advertising, London and Tom Sheppard.
© Tom Sheppard 1994

Photography
Land Rover: pp 4 up lt, 15 up lt, 22 lwr lt, 31 lwr lt, 36, 43 rt, 46, lwr lt on pp 57, 58, 71, 78; pp 86, 87, 89, 119, 142 lwr, 143. Drury Lane Studio Meriden: pp 3, 11, 20, 124, 134, 136. Tarmac Construction Ltd: p 10. Mike Hallett: p 101 rt. Superwinch: p 103 lt, lwr rt. Jardine PR: p 142 top.
All remaining photography: Tom Sheppard.

Acknowledgments
The author would like to express grateful thanks for their interest, help, and enormous patience with this and the First Edition to:
David Bowyer, Bradley Doublelock (Philip Hanson), Commercial Body Fittings (Mick Bowling), Dubai Equestrian Centre (Dervilla Campbell), Fortune Promoseven (Donal Kilalea, Jihad el Sibai), Fresh Tracks (Daniel Collins), Ib Kidde-Hansen, Michelin Tyres (Terry Khokhar, Alan Baxter), Paul O'Connor, Geoff Renner, Tom Robson, Superwinch (Terry Mason), Dariush Zandi.
And within Land Rover: Chris Batiste, Ron Brown, Tony Bourne, John Carter, Roger Crathorne, Bob Dillon, Neil Dodswell, Dave Drummond, Steve Earnshaw, David Fulker, Alison Grose, Mike Gould, Kate Higton, Colin Hill, Chris Hoyle, Roger Hughes, Phil Jones, Tony Northway, Adam Ormandy, Colin Parkes, Kieth Parsons, David Saunders, Chris Scaife, Graham Silvers, Harry Turnbull, Russell Turnham, Tim Vass de Zomba, Dick Woodhouse.
The pre-distillation analysis for Section 4.1 (On-road towing) was particularly demanding and special thanks go to Brian Bevan (The Motor Industry Research Association and IMechE paper C132/83), Professor Robin Sharp (Cranfield University), and Malcolm Burgess (Land Rover) for their help and patience.

The Land Rover Experience

Contents

...continued

The Land Rover Experience

...continued

The Land Rover Experience

...continued

The Land Rover Experience

Introduction

First-timers and fleet-users. This book is aimed at first-time four-wheel drivers and fleet users alike – a wide brief we hope is met by the headings and signposting within the book.

Aim. The aim of the techniques outlined in this book is to realise the fullest potential of your Land Rover product, to make your driving as safe and relaxed as possible, to ensure that in difficult conditions you get stuck as infrequently as possible, to ensure you hazard your vehicle as little as possible and that you damage it not at all – criteria equally important for private and commercial users. For this reason safety is emphasised throughout.

Book layout. Open the book at any page and scan along the top of the left and right hand pages. You will see the Section number, the Section subject and, on the right, the Sub-section number and title – for example, 'Section 5, Operations – recovery, 5.4. Winching'. The Sub-section numbering sequence – 5.1, 5.2, etc is a constant reminder of which section you are in. Cross referencing is by Section and Sub- section, not page numbers.

Headings, summaries, access. Each Sub-section (4.1, 4.2, etc) is divided into two or more parts each with a heading; every paragraph has a heading too and side-notes give a further summary. This way you can go straight to what you want, using the summary for reminders.

Short term use. Use this book like a tiny encyclopaedia. Use the index, glossary, contents pages (and contents summary on the rear fly-leaf), section headings and side-notes. Cross-referencing and a degree of repetition in the book will enable you to do this quickly.

Long term use. You will not carry all of this book in your head. Reading it, you will absorb the principles needed to become a sensitive and (therefore) proficient off-road driver. You will not only get to know the strengths and limitations of your vehicle but you will learn how to read the ground and apply the variations of technique you will encounter. Soon it will be instinctive; you will have written your own book.

Manual and automatic transmission. Many off-road commercial operators tend to favour manual transmissions, often for reasons of initial cost and commonality with earlier fleet vehicles. Because manual transmissions require more detailed description, the emphasis in this book should not be interpreted as favouring that technology. Automatic transmission has considerable advantages and, used on- or off-road, is very operator-friendly.

Additive experience. Many readers will already have experience in off-road operation and have developed their own techniques of doing things. We found, in the preparation of this book, that such inputs are always valuable and often apparently conflicting methods did not in fact conflict at all – they were just suited to subtly different sets of conditions. Experience was nearly always additive rather than reflecting opposite techniques; given common aims of safety and care of the vehicle the best course was usually self-evident.

Glossary, index, technical data. Some terms and usages may be new to you and a glossary (Section 10.1) explains many as well as giving some insight into how things work. The technical data section shows current vehicle specifications which inevitably vary world-wide; space does not permit them all to be shown. Those given are for the UK.

Foreword

Fragile earth – care for the environment

Philosophy

On/off-road vehicles are here to stay. Industry, civil engineering, the emergency services, the overseas relief agencies, agriculture and the defence Services would be severely handicapped and in some cases totally incapacitated without them. In many overseas regions such vehicles are often the only means of maintaining point-to-point land communications and transport.

And in the developed countries they have, in addition, found a niche in the automotive marketplace among those warming to their capabilities as the most practical of family hold-alls and maids of all work – the kind of vehicle that can tow a canoe-trailer to a mountain lake or do the school run and return with four children, a wet dog, a lawn mower and four sacks of compost picked up en route. As a bonus, these vehicles are also enormous fun to drive.

But their very popularity and versatility confers on us, as operators, users, and owners, a special responsibility towards the environment in which we live and they operate. The engineers and legislaroad enthusiasts have increased the potential for damage to vegetation, soil, water, wildlife and the solitude afforded by these areas.

We feel sure that all users of Land Rover products will wish to familiarise themselves with environmental principles.

'Torque gently' conveys both an exhortation to drive with a gentle right foot on the throttle (or brake) – as well as the implied suggestion also to 'talk gently' and not indulge in inappropriately 'macho' antics in our powerful machines.

Following the dual meaning will preserve both our vehicles and our environment for the future enjoyment of ourselves and others. Few, if any – in their heart of hearts – could disagree with such a philosophy.

...continued

tors continue their work in the pursuit of clean air; the latest diesels and catalyst-equipped petrol engines minimise atmospheric pollution.

We must also be certain not lastingly to damage the ground we drive on when off-road – especially vulnerable when wet. In so far as many of them will be new to the capabilities of their vehicles, recreational users must be especially aware of their responsibilities. There are currently many miles of off-highway road open to the public around the world. In recent years ever-growing numbers of off-

The freedom of the open countryside is made accessible through the capability of off-road vehicles. Take care of the countryside wherever you are. Where access is limited, close gates you have opened.

The Land Rover Experience

9

Practicalities

And few – applying little more than common sense and good manners – would not come up with the following list of practical points to remember when operating away from tarmac roads:

People and wildlife

• Allow wildlife priority over your own progress.

• Domestic animals too, especially horses and ponies, may be unused to the presence of vehicles in remote areas. Accommodate their nervousness; switch off and wait if necessary.

• Sheep that have strayed onto a track often run ahead of a vehicle rather than leaving the roadway. Be patient. Stop and let them disperse or pull over to let them by.

• Gamebirds and other wildlife often soak up the warmth of tarmac by sitting in the middle of country lanes or other clearings. Your vehicle may panic them into running across your path rather than away from you. Be prepared for this – and for the last minute appearance of a second or third bird from the hedgerow.

• Animals are often dazzled by headlights and may be unable to get away from the danger. Be aware of this; drive with extra care on unfenced lanes or open tracks. And that really does mean driving slowly.

• Be especially courteous and considerate towards walkers or riders – especially in remote areas. Like it or not, you have an ambassadorial role to play and inevitably, arriving in a comfortable offroad vehicle whilst others are progressing 'the hard way', you will, to a degree, be perceived in the idle villain's role!

• Always respect the privacy of other people; not always easy to assess, but many go to remote areas to savour the peace and solitude.

Access

• It is essential to be *certain* of your right of access to tracks and wild areas.

• A road marked on a map does not automatically confer a right of way. If in any doubt at all, ask – or refer to a highly detailed map such as one of the UK 1:25,000 series.

• Access rights to land for vehicles varies from country to country. Make yourself aware of the appropriate regulations for the country in which you are driving. Developed, highly populated or densely legislated countries usually have complex regulations. See Section 7 for an overview of UK access rights.

• Observe the Country Code – an encapsulation of common sense – whatever country you are in. Close gates you have opened.

Erosion

Four-wheel drive vehicles can contribute enormously to erosion when carelessly used off-road. Guidelines to min-

*If they can do it......
The example set – at
enormous monetary
cost – by local plan-
ning authorities and
civil engineers is all
too often overlooked
or taken for granted.
Before (above left)
and after (lower left)
shows the care taken
to landscape, replant
and minimise envi-
ronmental damage
even when a major
civil engineering pro-
ject such as the A55
Conway Crossing
tunnel in Wales is
involved. Enjoyment
of a 4x4's off-road
capabilities need not
be – must not be –
incompatible with
care for the environ-
ment.*

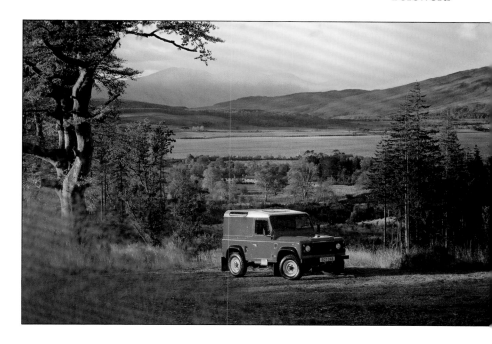

imise possible damage:

• New ruts form rain channels which cause erosion – especially where surface vegetation such as grass has been scraped away by spinning wheels.

• So keep off soft ground if possible – sinkage causes ruts.

• Do not spin your wheels on grass.

• Where a track exists, stick to it. Your wheel tracks away from it can tempt others to do the same and a another swathe of land can be spoiled.

• Travelling over open meadows with two or more vehicles, do not follow in each others' tracks. This will reduce the risk of forming ruts.

• Be doubly cautious when using mud tyres. Ideally they should be used only when deep mud is envisaged; they can quickly damage other ground.

• Use designated areas for training.

Litter

• Never leave litter under *any* circumstances.

• Take back what you brought with you.

Polishing your halo

Observing all the recommendations above will seem impossibly onerous the first time you read them. The second time you read them you will see just how much common-sense and simple courtesy is involved. The third time (and this may be a little later), you will start realising that that is what you actually *do* and will feel good about it.

Caring for the environment is far more important than the current fashion it may seem. We all share humankind's newly realised responsibility. Enjoy your driving!

Section 1

The ingredients

1.1. Why four-wheel drive

Halving the load

Terminology. It is worth an initial thought about what four-wheel drive or 4x4 really does do. Incidentally, '4x4', spoken as 'four-by-four' means there are four wheels, of which four are driven by the engine. So a normal car, be it front wheel drive or rear wheel drive, is a 4x2 'four-by-two' – four wheels in total, of which the car is driven by two. Some types of truck are referred to as a 6x4 – six (wheels driven) by four.

What it does – and doesn't do. A 4x4 does not double the power on the road; it takes the power you do have and spreads it between four wheels instead of only two. If a vehicle needs a certain amount of push (tractive effort or traction) to make it go at a given speed or traverse a certain type of terrain, a 4x4, by having twice as many driven wheels as a 4x2, will actually halve the tractive load on a given piece of ground and thus greatly reduce the chance of slipping, skidding or spinning wheels. Four-wheel drive is thus a considerable benefit to effective operation and to safety. If 4x4 is now combined with large wheels and large amounts of wheel movement on supple, well damped springs, the ingredients of an effective off-road vehicle, capable of operating on rough uneven ground, are starting to take shape.

Doubling the effect

Maintaining traction. Thus if conditions are such that an ordinary 4x2 car driving only one pair of wheels could spin those wheels and lose traction, a 4x4 will actually be twice as effective in using the power of the engine to maintain traction.

More from four. The diagrams sum up what we have been discussing. All over the world there are bits of ground – oily tarmac, icy roads, glazed snow, wet grassy fields – that will not support the tractive effort needed under certain conditions when power is put through one pair of wheels. Put that power through two axles – four wheels – thus halving the traction required of each wheel, and your 4x4 is likely to get you through – securely and under complete control.

'4x4' equals four-by-four equals four-wheel drive.

4x4 spreads power between four wheels, reducing risk of slip.

Where 4x2s slip a 4x4, demanding less of the ground, will grip.

Ground thrust

Direction of travel

4x2 – all the power on two wheels. High ground stress. Wheels may slip or spin.

4x4 – same power spread between four wheels. Half the ground stress. Double the traction.

Traction from the wheel at each corner of the vehicle is the overriding advantage of four-wheel drive on roads. Off-road it is even more important.

Even 4x4s have limits. Of course conditions may be so bad or the traction required so high that even a 4x4 spins its wheels or needs lower gears. These occasions are addressed later in the book but in general four-wheel drive enhances safety and effectiveness on and off road at all times. As we shall see, if you are driving any of the current Land Rover range and are therefore in four-wheel drive all the time then you are at a further advantage – always ready for the unexpected rather than having to assess the conditions and then select 4x4 with a separate control lever as is the case in some vehicles.

4x4 enhances security. Unlike many makes, Land Rover vehicles are in 4x4 all the time.

1.2. Traction – 4x4 and low range

Push with float; here we are looking at push. Rear axle of 4x2 vehicle (left) is asking twice as much shear strength from the ground as the 4x4 (right). Ground stress is further reduced by big wheels and low tyre pressures – permissible under certain conditions (see Section 8.2). Less ground stress equals less chance of slip and thus more traction.

4x2
Power shared by only two wheels

4x4
Power spread between four wheels

Traction is combination of four driving wheels, low gearing and lack of sinkage.

Ingredients of traction
Pushing backwards and downwards. Traction tends to be thought of as pull – farm tractors pulling wagons. In fact it is push – the bottom of the wheel pushing against the surface of the ground to move a vehicle forward under varying conditions. In perfect conditions of infinite grip one-wheel drive would suffice but where roads can get wet and slippery and where no-road conditions are muddy, four-wheel drive means three wheels can still push if one gets on a slippery patch.

Big footprint equals low ground stress equals more traction.

Push with float. Away from the perfect conditions of one-wheel drive, the real world where 4x4 is necessary is often soft as well. Spreading the weight over a bigger 'footprint' helps prevent sinkage. Big wheels have a bigger ground footprint than small ones and this footprint can be enlarged still further in emergency conditions by letting tyres down a little. (There are important speed and safety implications to this – see Section 8.2) In addition, big wheels give a smoother ride over rough ground.

Big wheels also give smooth ride, maximum ground clearance.

Ground clearance. Big wheels also ensure greater ground clearance over obstacles. Land Rover vehicles' beam axles keep this ground clearance constant – unlike an independently sprung front

end on other vehicles – and keep the tyres' tread always flat on the ground. The diagram below shows how.

Grip and gradient – enemies of traction. If poor grip can be overcome by driving four wheels instead of one or two and also benefit from bigger wheels, the other enemy of traction is gradient – uneven surfaces, steep hills (or heavy loads up not-so-steep hills). The extra traction you need for this comes from additional low gears – the other half of the traction equation.

Independently sprung axle (top) loses ground clearance on one-wheel bump. Land Rover's beam axle (below) less liable to lose traction through grounding. Tyres stay flat on ground.

Extra gears

Lower gearing. Extra low gears are just what are available on most 4x4s (but not all in the same gearbox). The transfer box on a 4x4 got its name because it is what transfers power from the normal gearbox to the rear axle *and* front axle thus making it a 4x4. But this extra transfer gearbox is also a two-speed affair with a high ratio and a low ratio.

Doubling the number of gears. The two-speed transfer box is a simple solution. It is 'downstream' of the main gearbox and by selecting low ratio it gears-down *all* the gears in the normal gearbox. In 'high' the gears are unaffected. So your Land Rover has a transfer box to effect the four-wheel drive function and additionally to provide what amounts to a complete set of very low gears so that five-speed box in effect becomes a 10-speed box. Making a single gearbox with ten forward speeds which could be successively selected would result in an expensive, heavy and complicated item.

Low ratio for heavy jobs. The 'low box' is selected for specific heavy duty tasks using a separate lever as we shall see (Sections 2.1 and 2.2).

All the tricks at once. A Discovery displays the attributes of an off-road 4x4 in a common combination – the gradability (ability to climb steep obstacles) afforded by the low transfer gears, the facility of providing drive to each wheel, the extreme wheel movement – see also Section 3.3 – and the benefits of the one-piece beam-axle.

Traction is power without slip. Big tyres and 4x4 minimise slip; a low ratio transfer box gives the 'power'.

Concept of transfer box in 1:1 high ratio (left) and low ratio (right) which gears-down the final drive to give more 'power' at the wheels. Note that the main gearbox is 'up-stream' – ie between the engine and the transfer gearbox.

Main gearbox

1.3. Permanent four-wheel drive

Why centre differential

Selectable 4x4. On some 4x4s the four-wheel drive function is itself selectable. Normal driving is done in two-wheel drive – as a 4x2 – and the driver has to decide when conditions require 4x4. In such vehicles the front and rear axles, which in fact revolve at slightly different speeds, are usually locked together when 4x4 is selected without any ability to accommodate the front/rear speed difference. The result is transmission 'wind-up' or tyre-scrub – most usually a combination of both; such vehicles can thus only be driven in 4x4 when off-road where the small speed differences can be accommodated by slight wheel slip; they should not be driven on a hard road with four-wheel drive selected.

Permanent 4x4. Since 1983/84 all Land Rover products have been designed with 'permanent 4x4' – the four-wheel drive function is engaged all the time and the front axle, as well as the rear, is driven. Two-wheel drive is not available. But as we shall see, there need be no wind-up or tyre scrub with your Land Rover vehicle.

Improved security, performance. Land Rover, pioneers of the first 'full-time' 4x4, the Range Rover, believe that the extra security and traction performance that result from permanent 4x4 is well worth the extra engineering involved. Such an arrangement also reduces driver workload and makes security and optimum performance an inherent feature of the vehicle rather than being dependent on driver use of a particular feature as in vehicles with selectable 4x4. With permanent 4x4 you are always ready for the unexpected.

Centre diff – the need. Extra engineering? In the same way as the wheel on

Concept of the centre bevel-type differential that divides engine power between front and rear prop shafts.

the outside of a turn travels farther than the wheel on the inside (photo opposite), so the front and rear wheels of a vehicle travel slightly different distances too – again due to the different tracks they follow in bends. So a 4x4 vehicle with permanent four-wheel drive needs a differential arrangement *between the front and rear axle drives* to accommodate the slight front/rear rotational differences – in the same way as there has been a differential between left and right wheels on the drive axle of just about every car since the turn of the last century.

Land Rover vehicles have one. All Land Rover vehicles made since their adoption of permanent four-wheel drive have a centre differential between the front and rear propeller shafts to even-out the drive torque between front and rear axles, preclude transmission wind-up and prevent tyre scrub.

Illustration right shows different track – and distance travelled – by front and rear wheels in a turn. Without a centre differential a permanent-4x4 vehicle would encounter tyre scrub, wheel slip or transmission wind-up. Need for <u>locking</u> centre diff is shown in picture above; a Discovery with centre differential deliberately (and incorrectly) left unlocked in demanding off-road conditions. Grip is markedly different front and rear, due to loose soil and weight transference to the rear; this allows front wheels to spin while rear wheels do not rotate.

Why lockable

Centre diff lock. Current Land Rover products not only have full-time four-wheel drive and a centre differential but that differential is lockable to enhance traction in difficult situations. It will couple automatically on Range Rovers (See Section 10.1, Glossary, Viscous coupling).

Why. The reason for making the centre diff lockable – ie the differential action is temporarily put on hold – is that traction conditions are often different front and rear. For example on a very steep slippery slope weight transference to the back axle may off-load the front wheels enough to let them lose grip and spin. Or there may be occasions when the front wheels are on a grippy rock and the rear wheels are on slippery mud. In these conditions locking the centre differential effectively locks the front prop shaft to the rear prop shaft and precludes lost traction through wheel-spin on either axle – see Section 2.3.

Where poor grip may permit excessive front/rear axle speed differences, centre differential is locked.

The Land Rover Experience

19

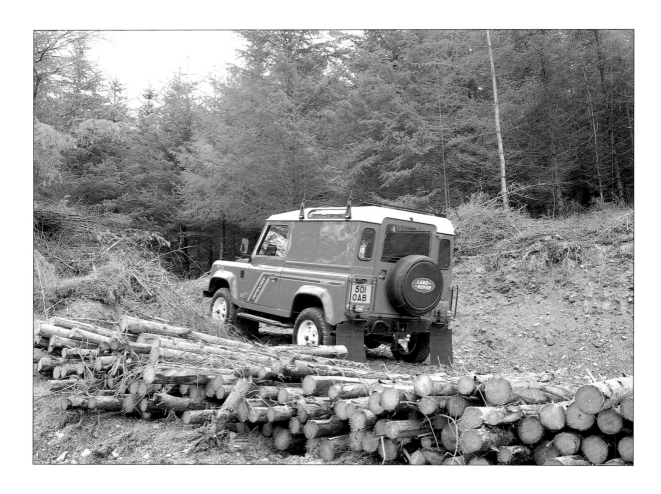

The Land Rover Experience

Section 2

Enhanced traction

2.1. Traction controls

Small lever beside main gear lever controls engagement of high or low ratio transfer gears, the concept of which is shown in the diagram at Section 1.2. Defender left, Discovery above; Range Rover automatic facing page (note thumb-button selector release).

Land Rover products have full-time 4x4 plus two-speed transfer box plus centre diff that may be locked.

Transfer lever

Traction aids – how and when. As a 'full-time' (permanent) 4x4, a Land Rover vehicle already gives you enhanced traction compared to vehicles driven by one axle only or compared to those with selectable or 'part-time' four-wheel drive. But as we have seen, your Land Rover has additional aids further to enhance its traction – a two-speed transfer gearbox and a lockable centre differential. This section is about how to select these functions and when to use them.

The 'little gear lever'. The small lever aft of the gear lever on Defender and ahead of it on other models is called the transfer gear lever since it controls the two-speed transfer gearbox – see diagram at Section 1.2 to refresh your memory on what the transfer gearbox does. You may hear the lever referred to also as the 'hi-lo' lever or the 'range-change'. If your vehicle has a transfer lever its function is the same on vehicles with manual and automatic gearboxes and is to select high

Transfer lever controls low/high ratio when moved fore and aft; shift only when stationary or under 5 mph. (See Section 2.4.)

Drawing shows range change concept for all these vehicles. Lever should normally only be moved when vehicle is stationary or moving slower than 5 mph. See Section 2.4 for when and how low range should be used.

range – normal on-road gears – when pulled fully aft, or low range (sometimes referred to as 'low ratio') when pushed fully forward. Normally these selections should be made only when the vehicle is stationary or when moving at less than walking pace (below 8 kph – 5 mph) though there may be occasions (see Section 6.1, 6.2.) when you may wish to (and can) go from low to high range at higher speed.

The new Range Rover. The 1995 model-year Range Rover (as distinct from the classic 1993 version) uses a different system for controlling the transfer gearbox in both manual and automatic transmission variants. In both vehicles the range change is effected electrically and the transfer lever has been eliminated; the manual gearbox vehicle has a fascia-mounted button to select low and high range while the automatic gearbox vehicle has an 'H-gate' transmission selector which combines both gearbox and range change command functions in the same lever. This is dealt with more fully on the next two pages and in Section 2.3.

Low range. Section 2.4 gives detail on when and how the low transfer gears should be used.

Centre differential lock. Centre diff lock is manually controlled by lateral movement of the transfer lever on Defender and Discovery (automatic diff lock on both models of Range Rover) and its use is covered in Section 2.5.

New Range Rover has electric range change – see next spread and Section 2.3.

...continued

The Land Rover Experience

2.1. Traction controls – contd

Electric range change

Same function, plus logic gates. On the New Range Rover the range change is effected electrically by pressing a button on the fascia in the case of the manual-gearbox model, or by use of the gear selector lever in the auto-transmission vehicle. In both cases a simple 2-parameter logic gate is employed:

Electric range change eliminates need for transfer lever. Operates by button with manual gearbox; through gear selector lever on auto.

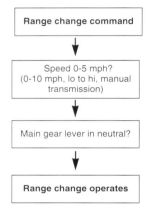

```
┌─────────────────────────────┐
│   Range change command      │
└─────────────────────────────┘
              ↓
┌─────────────────────────────┐
│      Speed 0-5 mph?          │
│ (0-10 mph, lo to hi, manual  │
│      transmission)          │
└─────────────────────────────┘
              ↓
┌─────────────────────────────┐
│  Main gear lever in neutral? │
└─────────────────────────────┘
              ↓
┌─────────────────────────────┐
│    Range change operates     │
└─────────────────────────────┘
```

Manual gearbox version – indications. The fascia button has a built-in light (LED) that works in conjunction with the instrument-pack Message Centre as shown in the table below to show the status with a reminder of why the change may not have taken place. Electric range change with auto transmission is covered in Section 2.3; when and how to use low range is at Section 2.4.

Both versions have speed and neutral logic gates. Message Centre and lights confirm status

Electric range change – indicators, <u>manual gearbox</u> version		
What you do	*Range change light (LED)*	*Message Centre indications*
Press once for 'LOW'	<u>Steady ON</u> - you are in low	'LOW', then 'L' prefix. eg 'L3' means low box 3rd
Press again for 'HIGH'	<u>Steady OFF</u> - you are in high	'HIGH', then no further indication except gear
	<u>Flash briefly</u> – shows one or other 'gate' criteria not met, ie	
	a. Speed above 5 mph	a. 'SLOW DOWN' shows for 4 sec
	b. Main lever not in neutral	b. 'SELECT NEUTRAL' shows for 4 sec

Electric range change button on fascia of manual-transmission versions of New Range Rovers (left). Note there is no normally selectable 'N' position in the transfer box on this vehicle. This can only be obtained (for dead-engine towing) by inserting a 5 amp fuse in position 11 in the under-seat fusebox.

Really steep slopes (right) call for all the traction controls – low transfer gears, centre diff lock, and a readiness to use the parking brake. As diagram shows (below), handbrake operates on propeller shaft so should not be used when vehicle is moving. Stopped on extreme slopes, vehicle should also be in gear with diff lock engaged.

Electronic traction control, handbrake

Electronic traction control – (ETC). ETC is an *automatic* feature available on all current ABS-equipped Range Rovers which inhibits wheel-spin by applying pulsed brake to a spinning rear wheel and thus enhances traction on ice, snow or in severe off-road conditions. Like ABS, it is especially effective in maintaining control when one side of the vehicle is on a more slippery surface than the other. A dashboard light indicates, purely for information purposes, when it is operating; there are no driver controls. A further note appears at Section 10.1, Glossary.

Handbrake – only when stationary. As it is adjacent to the transfer gear lever it is worth mentioning the handbrake at this point although it is not strictly speaking a traction control. The handbrake on Land Rover products acts on a drum on the rear propeller shaft immediately aft of the gearbox and as such it is extremely powerful. The handbrake should be regarded as a *parking brake only*. Use of this handbrake when the vehicle is moving at all will cause severe juddering shock loads and wind-up to the transmission. For this reason, except in emergencies, the handbrake should never be applied *until the vehicle is stationary*.

WARNING. Under no circumstances should you attempt to use it for trying to do 'hand-brake turns'.

CAUTION. Handbrake is a transmission brake; do not apply while the vehicle is moving. Use as parking brake only (except in emergency).

Concept of handbrake shown, with drum on rear propshaft immediately aft of transfer gearbox. When centre diff-lock is engaged handbrake effectively works on both prop shafts as they are then locked together.

The Land Rover Experience

2.2. Automatic transmission

Basic knowledge
Standard procedure. Adherence to
Driver's Manual techniques will ensure
competent, non-damaging performance
from a vehicle equipped with automatic
transmission off-road in high or low ratio.
The tolerance and smoothness of an auto
transmission, indeed, will often permit
operation in high ratio where off-road
conditions are not unusually demanding.
Standard operating procedure can be
summed up briefly:

1. The automatic gearbox is a ZF four-
speed unit with automatic lock-up on 4th
ratio above a certain speed to minimise
torque converter slippage.

2. **'D'** *enables* (ie permits the use of) all
four forward ratios. **'3'** enables the lower
three – ie it will use 1st, 2nd and 3rd but
not change above 3rd. Similarly **'2'**
enables 1st and 2nd only and **'1'** enables
1st-only. (The above and Items 3-5 below
refer to high range mode with the H-gate
auto selection arrangements on the new
1994/5 Range Rover; see Section 2.3.)

3. Select **'N'** on the main gear selector
before making a transfer box selection. If
it will not immediately engage, apply the
brakes, engage **'D'** briefly, go back to **'N'**
and try again. See Section 6.2 for low
transfer to high box on the move on
Discovery and old Range Rover.

4. If you are stationary for any length
of time, engine running, select **'P'** or **'N'**
rather than let the vehicle idle 'in-gear'
which will unnecessarily heat up the
transmission fluid.

5. If you are in **'P'** or **'N'** apply the
footbrake before selecting a forward or
reverse ratio to avoid creep.

6. Remember there is no 'gate'
between **'D'(or '4')** and **'3'** (ie the catch
does not have to be released) so for a sudden acceleration requirement and to force
a very rapid change-down all you have to
do is 'slap' the selector lever back into the

'3' position. This will give you quicker
response than a 'kick-down'.

Because of certain operating differences, the H-gate auto transmission on
the New Range Rover is dealt with in
detail at Section 2.3 but the basics above
are valid. You will find it useful, however, to absorb the operating philosophy
outlined here first.

Controlling the automatics
Automatic transmission off-road.
Though traditionally most off-road operations are carried out by vehicles with
manual transmission, this is no more than
a statistical fact rather than validating any
preferences. That there is considerable
advantage in the use of automatic transmission off-road is attested by the fact
that major power and other military users
specify it in their general service vehicles.

Advantages and disadvantages.
Whilst the most obvious advantage of
auto transmission is that of ease of operation for the driver – important for the military or public utilities user whose mind
will be on other things as well as driving
– there are also significant benefits in
terms of vehicle durability and protection
from driver mis-use and transmission
shock loads. Off-road performance can
itself be enhanced by an automatic's quick
seamless changes of gear in 'lift-off' situations – see opposite. The only disadvantages are higher initial cost and increased
brake wear though, as already indicated,
major professional users with cost-effectiveness in mind compare this with the
higher maintenance and repair costs of
mis-used manual vehicles and still opt for
automatic.

**Operating philosophies – knowledge
still needed.** A Discovery or any Range
Rover with auto transmission can be
operated on a minimum-knowledge basis
by, say, a fleet or pool operator with dis-

*Automatics for off-
road use have con-
siderable functional
advantages –
endorsed by major
military users.*

*Automatics off-road
can be operated in
two ways – mini-
mum knowledge or
advanced.*

*Auto transmission is
an elegant, least-
stress way of dealing
with on-the-limits
terrain. Knowing
how to get the best
from it is well worth
the trouble.*

Changing to low range (where selection is by manual lever), select 'N' on main selector before moving transfer lever. Perusal of overall gear ratios on auto (Section 9), explains why an automatic needs low range 1st for adequate down-slope retardation. For 'up and over' (right) use low range '3' for climb but slip into '1' for descent. For slippery 'forest floor' (above) low 3rd is best (see below) – with diff locked manually on Discovery.

parate drivers of differing experience; for these or the inexperienced a basic knowledge will suffice. On the other hand refinement of operating effectiveness and vehicle capability will result if time is taken to learn to get the best from the system – see Sections 6.2, and 6.3.

Gradability vs engine braking. In comparison to a manual transmission, you will find an auto has surprising gradability in high range but, particularly off-road, engine braking is inherently poor even in low range. You will need to engage '1' low range to obtain satisfactory engine braking on a descent. Note that if speed is too high this will not engage, even though it has been selected – see next paragraph.

Steep up and down. A steep climb followed by a steep descent sums this situation up well. Whilst you will probably be able to climb well enough in high

range on 'D', you will need low range '1' for the descent. To save doing a range change at the top of the incline the technique should thus be to engage low range before the obstacle, select '3' (see below why), make the ascent and, at the top, with forward speed at a minimum, pull the main selector back to '1' in order to get maximum retardation for the descent. If you are over the summit and select '1' with the speed too high, it will not engage; you will stay in 2nd or 3rd with little or no engine braking – see Section 6.4. for emergency procedure.

'Lift-off' elimination of wheel-spin. The reason for selecting '3' before a slippery ascent or other potential wheel-spin situation is that as soon as the wheels begin to spin the auto sensors will recognise the reduced torque and change up; this will tend to eliminate wheel-spin as soon as it occurs – in just the same way as you would lift off the throttle with a manual transmission to quench wheel-spin near the top of a steep loose slope. Selecting '3' rather than 'D' ensures change-up is not too high.

Muddy, 'forest floor' situations. The same applies for 'forest floor' slippery mud situations. Even though the main ratio actually in use may be 1st or 2nd, having the selector in '3' ensures that, as soon as wheel-spin and its reduced torque is sensed, the gearbox will change up to 3rd to eliminate spin.

The main off-road control you will use with auto is aimed at improving down-slope retardation.

Auto will change up to low-box 3rd on a loose slope better than you could on a manual. Use the facility and save wheel-spin.

2.3. H-gate automatic transmission

On New Range Rover selector lever has separate plane of movement for HI and LO; picture shows low range quadrant illuminated with 'Manual' mode selected – see text opposite below. Note there is no normally selectable 'N' position in the transfer box on this vehicle. TRANSFER NEUTRAL can only be obtained (for dead-engine towing) by inserting a 5 amp fuse in position 11 in the under-seat fusebox.

H-gate provides two-plane operating quadrant for selector lever – HI plane nearest driver, LO plane farthest away.

HI an LO quadrants are separately illuminated according to which transfer range is active. Use in conjunction with Message Centre messages.

Normal operation

The H-gate. In 'Normal' mode (see Mode switch, next column) the H-gate automatic transmission *functions* in exactly the same way as the unit controlled by selector lever and transfer lever. The difference is only the manner of control – an H-shaped operating gate with the selector lever able to move along either side of the H to give high range in the plane nearest the driver and low range in the plane farthest from the driver.

Transfer neutral. The 'crossover' from one plane to the other is at the **'N'** point of each operating quadrant; at the centre of that crossover line is the Neutral position for the transfer gearbox, not normally selectable – see caption above.

High range. Operate the selector lever in the plane nearest the driver to use high range gears. All the basics mentioned in the previous section (Section 2.2) in high range apply equally well to the H-gate transmission.

Low range. Operate the selector lever in the plane farthest from the driver to use low range gears. In low range, operation is also the same as standard automatics though there are, as a reminder about

climbing a steep slope in '**3**' and descending in '**1**', small pictograms in the 3 and 1 quadrant positions to indicate respectively steep ascent and steep descent.

Indicator lights

Indicators and Message Centre. As with the manual version of the New Range Rover, a combination of steady or flashing indicator lights and readouts on the instrument binnacle Message Centre give you information about the status of a range change. As before, in general a steady light means a completed range change whilst a flashing light shows a process is still under way.

H-gate lights. The illumination under each side of the H-gate selector quadrants is used as a 'Active range' and 'Target range' indicator. When high is selected (active), the quadrant nearest the driver is illuminated; when low range is selected, the quadrant farthest from the driver is illuminated. Following the philosophy that flashing means things are still going on, moving the selector lever across the bar of the H from high to low range will result in the high range quadrant lights remaining on and the low range (the target range) lights will flash until the range change is actually complete. When that happens, the 'low' quadrant light will remain on and the 'high' light will extinguish. LO to HI is a similar sequence.

Message Centre information. As with the manual gearbox version of the new Range Rover, the instrument binnacle Message Centre will show the transfer gear range you are in, eg going into low you will first get 'LOW', then an 'L' prefix to the gear number.

Mode switch

'Normal' vs 'Sport' or 'Manual'. The Mode switch, located beside the H-gate, may be pressed to turn normal high range

Electric range change logic sequence

HI to LOW selection
LOW quadrant light flashes
HI quadrant light still steady

↓

Speed 0-5 mph? — No? → Message Centre: 'SLOW DOWN' Reduce speed to under 5 mph

↓

Main gear lever in neutral? — No? → Message Centre: 'SELECT NEUTRAL' Move selector to 'N'*

↓

Range change takes place
LOW quadrant light steady.
HI quadrant light extinguishes.
Message Centre: 'LOW', then prefixes gear with 'L', eg L3 is third low range

* Whilst the selector lever must be in the 'N' position to move over to the LO quadrant, if you have then inadvertently moved down to, say, L3 before the range change is complete or before your speed is below 5 mph, then you will get this warning.

Electric range change will only change transfer ratios if speed is less than 5 mph and main gear selector is in neutral.

into 'Sport' and low range into 'Manual'.

'Sport' mode – high range. Pressing the Mode switch in high range gives 'Sport' mode which moves gear change points within the automatic gearbox higher up the engine rpm range thus achieving a more sporty acceleration profile without having to resort to kick-down or use of the selector to hold a given gear (though these facilities are still available).

'Manual' mode - low range. Pressing the same mode button when you are currently in 'Normal' low range turns the low range auto transmission virtually into a manual gearbox. Thus to select **'3'** when stationary in low range 'Manual' is effectively to start off in third gear and hold it until you select another gear. As will be seen in Section 3.2, 'Gentle right foot', there are times when off-road surface conditions are so slippery that you want the gentlest possible pull-away to avoid wheel-spin. Low range 'Manual' enables you to judge the best gear for these conditions and select it. In fact the gearbox does not actually start in third when low

range '3' Manual mode is selected since this would lead to excessive slip and temperature rise in the transmission fluid; however, it spends a very short time indeed in 1st and 2nd before going to (and holding) the gear you have selected.

Message Centre information. As with the manual gearbox version, the Message Centre will give an indication of the gear, the range and the mode selected. Thus low range third in manual mode will show as LM3.

Range change logic criteria

Speed and neutral – as before. The same logic will prevail as with the manual gearbox version with electric range change; that is, speed must be below 5 mph and the main gear selector must be in neutral before a change will occur. *Both criteria have to be met before the range change will take place.* The diagram above gives a visual summary of what happens in the case of a HIGH to LOW change; similar criteria and warnings apply in LOW to HIGH.

Press MODE switch and NORMAL HI becomes SPORT; NORMAL LO becomes MANUAL.

LO MANUAL effectively turns low range into a clutchless manual gearbox.

2.4. Low range – when and how

throttle opening or even at idling revs.

Low 1st – too low? Low range first, because of its enormous 'power' capability, is often too low for slippery surface conditions and it is easy for you to spin the wheels inadvertently through the application of more torque than the ground can take. It should be used when grip is very good, when momentum is not required and when there is little danger of spinning the wheels – mainly when considerable tractive effort is needed. Its particular application is in affording engine braking down very steep slopes (see Section 4.5, 'Descending steep slopes'.)

What to start off in

Low 2nd – rule-of-thumb. Second is a good rule-of-thumb starting-off gear for most low ratio situations – muddy conditions, steep slopes and the like even with a heavy trailer. Because tractive effort available is then more closely matched to what the ground will take, there is less risk of wheel spin and the lost traction that results. As indicated on the previous page, with automatic transmission select '3'; this can sometimes also be the solution with manual transmission where conditions demand the delicate touch.

Low 3rd, 4th, 5th – versatility. Third, fourth and fifth gears in the low range are good 'getting about' gears with manual transmission ('D' or '4' in auto) for the better parts of derelict mountain or desert tracks, for getting across the field, for forest tracks that are a bit tight for high range. They bring out the vehicle's versatility and the ease with which it traverses cross-country terrain; you can make a respectable speed in fifth or 'D', yet change all the way down to second when the going gets more difficult (see Section 4.2, 'Driving on tracks').

Low ratio gears the vehicle down by nearly 2:1 and provides enormous tractive effort.

'Power' and 'control'

Low range for *power.* As we have seen, selecting low ratio on the transfer box is not just another gear but affects *all* the gears in the main gear box (including reverse), gearing them down by nearly 2:1. The obvious uses of the low range are thus occasions when you want a great deal of 'power' or tractive effort – towing a car out of a ditch, ascending a very steep slope, getting out of deep mud or sand, pulling a fallen tree trunk out of the way.

Low range 1st gear provides superb control for slow, steady crossing of obstacles such as rocks and for brake-less descents; too low for inclines.

Low range for *control.* Less immediately obvious uses for the low ratio include the provision of control rather than high tractive effort. Examples of this might be steadying the vehicle on a very steep descent without use of the brakes or, classically, allowing the vehicle to crawl over rocks slowly, steadily, without jarring – and with your foot off the clutch pedal and without use of the brakes. Low box, first gear excels in this kind of exercise and can often be used with minimal

For most situations, start in 2nd. Use 3rd, 4th, 5th are for 'getting around' on rough ground.

Saharan boulders epitomise the 'control' case where low range 1st gear gives steady rock-crawling capability. 1st gear start is sometimes appropriate to heavy towing but higher gears provide general off-road flexibility (left). Avoid temptation to 'use clutch as another gear'.

Driver still the key. We shall see in the ensuing sections specific examples of what gears to use. And also that there is more to maintaining traction than just selecting a low gear; driver sensitivity is half the battle – see Section 3.2, 'Gentle right foot'. (Also Section 6.1, 'High/low range overlap'.)

Automatic transmission. As in high range, automatic transmission will start the vehicle in first gear and change up as far as it is permitted by the position of the gear selector lever – all the way up to 4th gear if it is in 'D', up to 3rd if the lever is at '3', no higher than 2nd if the lever is at

'2', and it will hold 1st for steep descents if the lever is moved back to '1'. You thus have total control – see also Section 2.2 and 6.2, all on the subject of automatic transmission. Section 2.3 deals with the specific features of 'Manual' mode low range automatic (H-gate) transmission on the New Range Rover.

Driver sensitivity – a gentle right foot – is still the main key.

2.5. Centre differential lock

Centre
diff
Low   locked
N   Centre
High   diff free

Diagram shows movement of transfer lever to select diff lock. Inset shows warning light – not present on Range Rovers which have automatic diff lock. Poor-traction low-box off-road conditions such as loose sand are invariably more effectively tackled with diff lock.

When to use diff lock

Poor traction overcome. As we have seen, the centre differential may be locked as required or, on Range Rovers, will lock automatically when this action is needed. The reason for the provision of the lock-ing facility on the centre differential which separates the front and rear pro-peller shafts is that there are a number of poor-traction situations when such a lock will enhance the vehicle's performance. See also Section 1.3, 'Permanent four-wheel drive'.

Range Rover's centre diff lock is automatic – actuated by viscous coupling (see glos-sary Section 10.1.).

Spinning wheels. Many will be famil-iar with the single spinning wheel of a conventional car on an icy road. This is the result of the drive wheels being on surfaces of different grip characteristics – one wheel on ice with the other on dry road. It is possible for the same situation – fore and aft – to arise in a 4x4; front axle on firm, grippy concrete while the rear axle is in mud – an extreme example but the principle applies to a greater or lesser extent in nearly all off-road situations.

On Discovery and Defender, select cen-tre diff lock when there is any risk of losing grip.

When to use diff lock. A simple rule-of-thumb is to use diff lock when you use the low range transfer gears on any loose or slippery surface. Use of low range gen-erally means that you are on difficult or uneven ground and wanting a high trac-tive effort. Such ground usually has uneven traction characteristics as well as an uneven surface and you will be need-ing all the traction (grip) you can get. Locking the centre differential will pre-clude loss of traction resulting from potential front/rear differences in grip.

High range diff lock? It is possible to engage diff lock in high range too. When, if ever, is this desirable? It will be useful to engage diff lock in high range when

Be sure to de-select diff lock when on a firm, level, non-slip-pery surface.

driving on potentially difficult surfaces such as wet grass, mud, loose or packed snow, or loose sand on tracks or in open desert.

When to de-select diff lock. It is important to de-select diff lock when on any hard grippy surface such as tarmac or concrete (wet or dry) whether you are in high or low range. The 'DIFF LOCK' warning light will illuminate when the diff is locked and should be a reminder to you. If you do not de-select on grippy surfaces the steering will feel stiff, there will be excessive tyre wear through scuff-ing and there will be transmission wind-up putting excessive strain on the trans-mission which may make it hard to use the transfer gearbox lever to disengage low ratio.

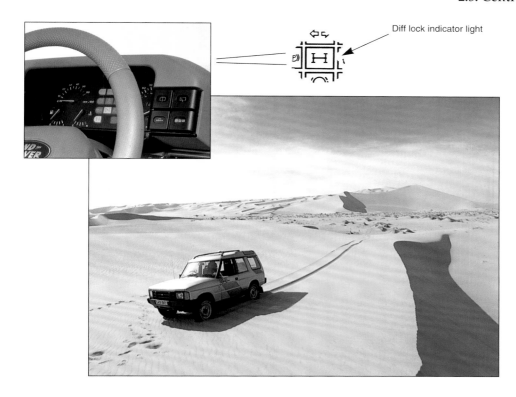

Diff lock indicator light

Controls and indicators

How to select and de-select diff lock.
On any Land Rover model where diff lock selection is not automatic the transfer lever can move side-to-side as well as fore and aft; move the transfer lever to the left to select diff lock – whether you are in high or low range. Make it a habit to briefly ease the throttle and dip the clutch as you do this – in case there is a transitory speed difference between front and rear axles at the moment when you select the inter-axle lock. Move the lever to the right to de-select diff lock; when the diff lock disengages the warning light will extinguish.

Diff lock indicator light actuation.
The 'DIFF LOCK' indicator will come on when the diff lock is actually engaged – not just when you move the lever to select it. Similarly it will only extinguish when the diff lock is actually disengaged. If the light is reluctant to go out after de-selecting diff lock some transmission 'wind-up' may be present. Reversing a few metres, then going forward will usually disengage diff lock , extinguishing the light.

Range Rover – automatic diff lock.
All current Range Rovers have viscous coupling unit (VCU) centre diff 'lock' actuation for which no manual selection or indicator light is required. A viscous coupling (see Glossary, Section 10.1.) sits across the two halves of the centre differential and when relative motion between the front and rear propeller shafts is sensed, the coupling becomes extremely stiff, effectively locking the differential.

To select diff lock, ease the throttle, dip the clutch, move transfer lever to left; move to right to de-select. (Discovery and Defender only – Range Rover has automatic diff lock.)

Diff lock light comes on only when diff lock actually engaged.

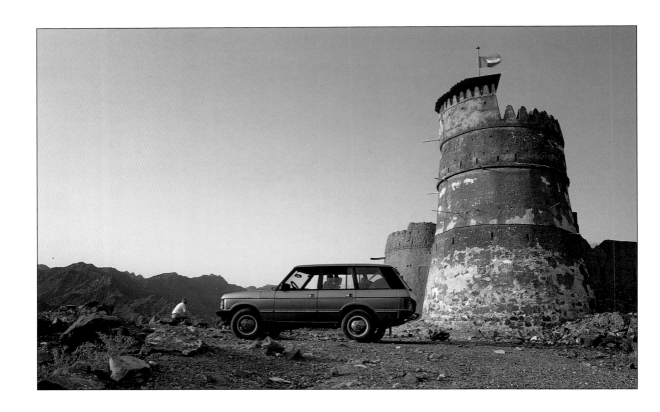

Section 3

Preliminaries

3.1. Mind-set

Smooth operation, making the vehicle flow over the ground – right – rather than jolt, is an indication of the required mechanical sympathy. Work your vehicle well (left) but take the drama out of your driving.

Be smooth and gentle with your vehicle. Using the power is not the same as being brutal.

Mechanical sympathy

Aim smooth. All machinery responds well to being treated with mechanical sympathy – even a vehicle with a reputation for ruggedness such as the Land Rover. There is more to this than just following maintenance schedules and keeping the oil topped up; that is vital but is not the whole user-interface picture. Smooth driving operation is the aim.

Be kind. Using the very considerable capabilities of your Land Rover product need not preclude your being kind to it. It is a very tolerant vehicle but clunks in the transmission, prolonged wheel-spinning, misuse of the clutch and harsh treatment of any of the controls, engine or suspension should be avoided. Specifically:

1. Transmission controls. (Gear lever and transfer box lever.) Moderate force and moderate speed is the best way to use these levers – firm and gentle. If it is difficult to engage low range, leave the transfer lever where it is, dip the clutch, engage first gear and let the clutch up slightly to reposition the gear wheels. Keep the clutch down and try again.

Avoid transmission clonks; let the clutch grip fully when it has to. Kill wheel-spin quickly.

Similarly, difficulty engaging first or reverse (or noise in doing so) may be eased by dipping the clutch, quickly engaging a higher gear (say, third) and then trying again.

2. Riding the clutch. Don't slip the clutch or 'use it as another gear'. Don't 'ride' the clutch either; by this is meant resting your foot on the pedal with slight pressure so as to be able quickly to disengage it. It is natural enough for a properly cautious or inexperienced driver negotiating a difficult piece of terrain to want to be able to use clutch and brake with the minimum delay but riding the clutch – in effect reducing the pressure of the clutch springs – will encourage clutch slip and cause premature wear. Have the clutch fully engaged and your foot clear of the pedal whenever possible.

3. Wheel-spin .... As we shall see in more detail, wheel-spin is lost traction and *prolonged* wheel-spin will scoop earth from under the wheels worsening the situation. It is not good for the transmission either. A fast spinning wheel suddenly getting grip can cause shock loading on the transmission and the possibility of transmission damage.

3a .... but.. There *are* circumstances – certain types of mud with the best mud tyres – when controlled, short-period wheel-spin will permit the tyre to cut through to drier ground and obtain traction where none existed before. The same approach in sand would be disastrous. So you must become wheel-spin-aware, know how your tyre tread is faring and, as we shall see, make judgements.

Pride – learn when to back off

Minimise the drama. Probably the most golden of the rules governing difficult off-road driving is to admit defeat early and reverse out. Good off-road driving is achieved with the minimum of drama. Huge water splashes, spinning wheels and flying clods of earth are rarely necessary. Even the best drivers perpetrate these fireworks occasionally if they have misjudged the terrain – and usually feel a little sheepish afterwards.

Back off, try again. Often such drama stems from fear of failure and then trying too hard. You will learn from this book, and with practice, that part of the learning process is acquiring the procedures for initially getting it wrong – typically the failed hill scenario (Section 4.4). You will learn that getting it wrong first time usually does not matter; you will learn to relax. When a very steep slippery climb stops your vehicle and the wheels begin to spin, back off at once; try again, possibly with a little more speed and in a higher gear. Holding the vehicle with uncontrolled wheel-spin will cause excessive damage to the ground, will usually worsen the vehicle's chances of making it up the slope and, in some cases, will cause a vehicle to slew sideways-on to the slope and possibly tip.

Wheel-spin alert! The same goes for stretches of deep mud or sand – though the two are quite different. If you do not make it through the patch first time and there is any *sustained* and ineffective wheel-spin, stop before you bog deeper, reverse out and try again using a different route or different tactics. Do not be too proud to admit that you got it wrong.

If it isn't going to go, reverse out while you can and try again.

Getting through second time is better than having to be towed out on the first.

3.2. Gentle right foot

Climbing slopes like this requires a very sensitive foot on the throttle. Paradoxically you may find you need to ease off the throttle at the steepest part – where risk of wheel-spin is greatest.

Wheel-spin, traction control

Reading the ground. You will have seen that effective use of the low range and realising the extraordinary potential of your vehicle depends a lot on a driver's appreciation of how much traction the ground itself will take without allowing *inappropriate* wheel-spin.

Excessive throttle. As with a car on ice, too much throttle will 'over-torque' the driving wheels and make them spin. With such low gearing in the low ratio gears, the same thing can happen with your Land Rover in slippery conditions. Drivers will quickly develop a delicate throttle foot and learn when the conditions are putting the vehicle on the verge of wheel-spin.

Spinning wheels dig. Spinning wheels represent loss of traction, often a loss of directional control as well and can also result in ground being scooped by the spinning tyres from under the wheel and the vehicle becoming stuck. In some cases (Section 4.7) this scooping will get through slippery mud onto drier ground – but not always. Alertness is the key-word. So there are many good reasons for acquiring a sensitive throttle foot and not choosing too low a gear. Both will avoid wheel-spin and help to maintain traction.

Electronic traction control, ETC. As already introduced in Section 2.1 under 'Traction controls', ETC, when fitted, will monitor, and inhibit, inadvertent wheel spin and considerably assist in maintaining traction under limiting conditions.

Ease off the throttle before you get sustained wheel-spin.

Wheel-spin and brake lock-up: two versions of the same thing – a discontinuity of rolling contact.

Slide, cadence braking, ABS

Excessive brake. Wheel-spin represents a discontinuity of rolling contact with the ground – the ground and the periphery of the wheel are not in stationary contact with one another. Exactly the same situation arises in the case of excessive braking on slippery ground. One or more wheels lock up and slide over the ground resulting in a discontinuity of rolling contact – the periphery of the wheel and the ground are not going the same speed. In one case the wheel is slipping past the stationary ground; in the other the ground is (relatively) slipping past the stationary wheel.

Cadence braking – same foot, same cure. And again the same cures may be

Continuous rolling contact. Using throttle or brake, avoid spin or slip. Think of your wheels and the ground as a rack and pinion like this.

Engine braking's progressive and controllable retardation is best for slopes like these (right) – and almost every other one too. But learn cadence braking for the times when you have got it wrong (above).

used. Lifting your right foot off the throttle will stop wheel-spin and lifting your right foot off the brake will stop wheel slide or skidding. In the case of braking, though, you applied the brakes because you wanted to stop. So re-apply them more gently and, best of all, employ 'cadence braking' technique – repeated jabbing of the brake pedal, quite gently, as fast as you can so that the wheel never gets a chance to lock. Though it takes will-power to take your foot off the brakes to do this when you are trying to slow down, cadence braking is remarkably effective.

ABS – automated finesse. It is thus no surprise to find out that the advanced anti-lock brakes (ABS) fitted to Land Rover vehicles operate on exactly the same principle. They employ a very fast

form of cadence braking to obtain the maximum retardation on the most difficult surfaces, *on or off road*, without locking up any of the wheels – you will hear and feel the brake relay working. So in the case of a vehicle fitted with this feature you will get maximum available braking and retain directional control – *for given ground conditions*. Beware, however; ABS will not reverse the laws of physics.

Engine braking – elegant, gentle. Engine braking, of course, is a very controlled and gentle way to achieve retardation as we shall see in the sections to follow. But even that should not be regarded as an infallible solution to every problem, especially when it is very slippery; you can still finish up with sliding wheels – see Section 6.4.

Wheel slide? Back off the brakes and re-apply with repeated gentle jabs.

Engine braking is best for steep down-slopes.

3.3. Geometric limitations

Clearance angles

Appreciating clearance. Common to negotiating all types of obstacle off-road is an appreciation of under-body clearance angles, clearance under the chassis and axle differentials and the amount by which the axles can articulate (move up on the near side and down on the off side – and vice versa – see next spread).

Ground clearances, under-chassis angles. It is soon obvious how well all Land Rover products perform cross country but a few moments to study the accompanying diagram will help to refine your judgement on the kind of thing that can and cannot be done without touching bodywork or chassis on the ground. Under-axle clearance is relevant to the size of a single isolated rock on the track between the wheels that can be driven over without fouling but under-belly clearance relates to the (bigger) size of ridge undulations that can be crossed.

Ramp angle – belly clearance. The angle measured from the chassis at the centre of the wheelbase down to the periphery of front and rear wheels is the ramp breakover angle, usually called the ramp angle. Its significance is self evident since it governs whether or not you will 'belly' the vehicle on a hump. Such a hump taken without thought of the ramp angle can result in getting bellied with the wheels grappling for traction and the vehicle's weight taken directly on the chassis on the top of the hump – see photos at Section 5.1.

Air suspension. A Range Rover fitted with electronic air suspension (EAS – see Glossary, Section 10.1) has the facility, with 'High profile' selected, to increase ride height by 40 mm over standard and, in the process, further improve ramp angle.

Be aware of under-axle clearance – and how it differs from belly clearance.

Low-set towing hitch can cause tail to dig in on steep ascents or crossing ditches.

Axle clearance. Under-axle clearance is a more obvious limitation. Whilst a Land Rover vehicle running out of axle clearance on soft going will sometimes plough out its own path, do not get into the habit of doing things this way. Deep ruts, rocks submerged in soft mud or encountering hard or rocky going will cause the vehicle to come to a sudden damaging stop when the axle differential housing hits the obstacle.

Approach and departure angles. Approach angles are large on all Land

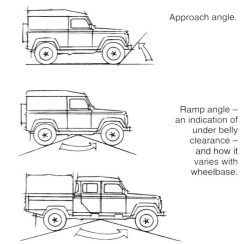

Approach angle.

Ramp angle – an indication of under belly clearance – and how it varies with wheelbase.

Departure angle – and how a towing hitch can affect it.

Under-axle clearance (top) – about 19-23 cm (about 7.5-8.5 in) – is less than under belly clearance. See Section 9 for exact model dimensions.

Try and develop an awareness, off-road, of where parts of the vehicle may touch the ground; the tow hitch (above) is the most commonly forgotten. Under-axle and under-belly clearances (diagrams) need remembering too.

Rover models but remember that tail overhang and departure angle is the one that will catch you out going up a very steep slope. Regarding the common problem of 'hitting the tail', the departure angle – already less than the approach angle – is further reduced when a low-set towing hitch is fitted and it is not uncommon for an inattentive driver to dig the tow hitch into the ground while going forward up a very steep incline and then find that he cannot reverse back because the tow hitch prevents him doing so.

Big wheels, short wheelbase. The biggest wheels and the shortest wheelbase will give best under-chassis clearance angles – a Defender 90 on 7.50 x 16 tyres takes the prize; its short rear overhang also yields the best departure angle. Details of all clearances and geometric limitations for all models and variants are shown at Section 9.

Long wheelbase and tail overhang call for more caution on rough ground.

The significance of – left to right – approach angle, departure angle and ramp angle.

...continued

3.3. Geometric limitations – contd

The short wheelbase
Defender 90 has a smaller
turning circle than a 130.

*A short wheelbase
vehicle will be more
agile than one with a
long wheelbase.*

Manoeuvrability

Axle movement. We have already
seen that articulation is the amount by
which one axle can move – left wheel up,
right wheel down or vice versa – in relation to the chassis and its fellow axle.
Clearly it represents the degree to which
your vehicle can keep its wheels on the
ground on undulating 'twisty' terrain and
thus retain traction under difficult conditions. All Land Rover products have very
good articulation due to having coil
springs and large wheel travel. But for a
given amount of articulation – say a 40
cm lift under one front wheel before the
other front wheel begins to lift – a shorter
wheelbase actually represents a greater
'twisty ground' capability than a long
wheelbase. So do not expect your
Defender 130, although it has about the
same axle articulation as a Defender 90
(assuming full wheel movement), to be
able to traverse equally tortuous ground
without lifting a wheel. See 'longitudinal
articulation angle', Glossary, Section 10.1
and suspension movement figures on the
tech data pages in Section 9.

*Axle articulation
permits the ultimate
'twisty ground' per-
formance; keeps
wheels on ground
and producing trac-
tion.*

Manoeuvrability, lateral lean. As the
diagram shows, the shorter the wheelbase
the tighter the turning circle. The angle to
which the vehicle can lean laterally without tipping is very similar on all models
with standard bodywork. As covered in
Section 4.6, 'Traversing slopes', this is a
static figure and should not be relied on
when driving. Local bumpiness and the
effect of even minor steering corrections
make a considerable difference and a
limit of half the figures shown is recommended.

Wading depth. Maximum wading
depth (see also Section 4.10, 'Wading') is
quoted as 0.5 metre but for special cir-

Land Rover products' long
wheel travel gives exceptional articulation, ensuring optimum off-road performance.

Land Rover do not quote exact lateral lean limits; exercise extreme caution at all times. See also Section 4.6. Do not wade without fitting wading plugs – see Section 4.10.

If you are close to the limits, get out and take a closer look – see next spread.

cumstances using diesel engines and a raised air intake this can be increased.

Inspection first. When close to any of the above limitations a preliminary survey on foot is what is required, preferably with someone to marshal you through or round the obstacle. Whilst all Land Rover products are tough and capable off-road vehicles, it is pointless to risk underbody damage or getting stuck for the want of properly surveying the obstacle first. This is fully dealt with in the next spread.

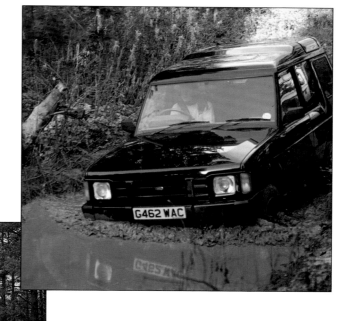

Photos show uses of articulation (left) in crossing ditch – see Section 4.3. Note gentle bow-wave when wading – see Section 4.10.. Side slopes always feel worse than they are – but don't press your luck!

3.4. Look before you leap

On-foot survey

Inspect before you drive. It is invariably beneficial to do an on-foot survey of difficult obstacles before committing the vehicle. The aim of the survey is to pick the best route and ensure there are no previously unnoticed hazards such as rocks to foul the axles, deep ruts hidden in undergrowth or the lie of firm ground under snow. A reconnaissance also gives you the chance to test the firmness of visible ground – soft mud or the strength of the sand crust on a dune.

Prod before you drive. An on-foot recce is especially important when fording streams and rivers where there is no established safe path. Nor will it be easy since you will have to establish not only the firmness of the river bed but also its evenness. Dropping into an underwater rock hole or suddenly descending to a depth that will drown the engine will require fundamental and major recovery procedures. Water deeper than about 35 cm demands that wading plugs be fitted to the clutch housing and cam-belt drive housing. (See 'Wading', Section 4.10.)

Always worth it. An on-foot survey will delay you and is usually mucky or wet. It is, however, far preferable to damaging the Land Rover or finding you have a major recovery problem on your hands.

Always make an on-foot inspection of difficult obstacles.

Use an external marshaller to direct you where clearances are tight.

Marshalling

External guidance – marshalling. If you are not alone, an invaluable adjunct to negotiating difficult ground with small clearances is to have your passenger marshal you through from outside the vehicle. Only someone outside the vehicle can properly see all four wheels and where they are going – and see the exact clearances under the axle casings (see photos Section 4.9).

Overall view, take it steady. A marshaller should stand 5 to 15 metres ahead of the vehicle – facing it – where all the wheels can easily be seen. Guidance by the marshaller should be given unam-

On-foot inspection especially important in rivers where hazards are hidden.

On-foot pre-inspection establishes feasibility. Then marshaller can see all four wheels, gives precision guidance and can avoid tyre damage on rocks.

biguously and entirely by hand and arm signals rather than by voice. At the risk of stating the obvious, be sure there is just one marshaller who is in total charge and make a conscious effort to take things one step at a time. Situations in which marshalling is required frequently spawn two or three people all shouting half-heard directions at one time; the general tension often generates a feeling that something decisive and effective must be done, immediately...! The calm and measured approach is to be preferred!

Marshaller in control. Obey the marshaller completely. Try not to take your eyes off him or her to make your own judgements on a situation you cannot assess as comprehensively as someone outside the vehicle. Stop if you are not happy but once moving, the marshaller is in control.

One marshaller only in control. Directions by signs, not voice.

Advance   Go back   Stop   Steer in this direction   Steer in this direction

Hand signals for marshalling are simple and unambiguous, given close-to or at a distance.

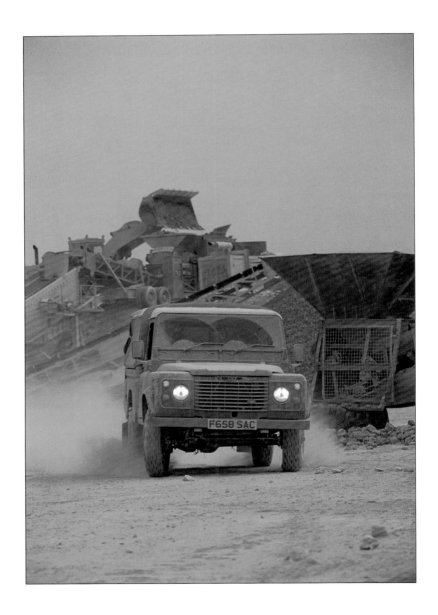

Section 4

Operating techniques

4.1. Towing – on-road

Preliminaries – the theory
Theory matters? There will be many who, faced with pulling *that* trailer (no choice) with *this* vehicle (no choice) are of a mind to doubt the value of theory and just get on with it. An understandable view from a busy operator but airline pilots, similarly limited in choice of type or design of the aircraft they fly, do benefit a great deal – and safety is immeasurably enhanced – by knowing what is going on aerodynamically. There is much folklore and many rules of thumb associated with towing and it is helpful and refreshing to know that what goes on really is quantifiable now and every parameter may be taken into account – from the spring rates of the towing vehicle (tug) to the types of bushes fitted to the suspension.

When trailer weight exceeds around 75% of tug weight, the laws of physics dictate you are entering a critical zone for stability. Be aware of the theory of trailer dynamics and know what is going on.

However hard-nosed and down to earth the job, knowing the theory will make operations safer.

Famine and feast. Land Rover's Design Analysis computer could produce enough information and study of variables to fill a book on this subject alone. The object of this section, in just eight pages, is to steer a middle course between the information famine of preceding years and the feast of data now available. The good news, for readers braced for another 'breakthrough' and overturning of received wisdom, is that virtually all the rules of thumb are valid. Knowing why, though – and their limitations – is absorbing and there are enough surprises to make it worthwhile reading further.

Trailer dynamics
Stability. Overriding priority will be given by all operators examining this subject to the question of stability and safety and brief treatment will be given therefore to:
- Straight line stability.
- Oscillation or weave.
- Steady turn stability.

Straight line stability. Consider a towing vehicle (tug) of infinite mass – the implication being that the towing pin moves in an undeviating straight line, uninfluenced by the trailer. The trailer behind it will tow straight for the same reason a dart or aircraft flies straight; as soon as the trailer deviates due to a gust or random side-load, the tyres will then be at an angle to the direction of motion

With imaginary non-deviating tug, trailer displacement gives rise to tyre slip angle which in turn generates restoring side-force to put trailer back on course in single or decaying series of swings. If trailer can influence tug (diagram opposite, far right) complex swings can be self-sustaining.

Slip angle

Yaw angle; here same as slip angle

'Non deviating' tug

and as a result a side-force will be generated by the tyres to push the trailer back in line behind the tug.

As the trailer approaches zero slip angle the side force also reduces until, when it is in line again, the side force has disappeared. Fairly obvious stuff but it is important to consider this – the concept of slip angle and tyre side force – before going on.

Oscillation, weave
Concept of decaying or increasing oscillation.
Few who have seen TV pictures of caravans 'mysteriously' turning over on motorways will need a definition of weave, yaw or snaking. However, distinguish between decaying (convergent) and increasing (divergent) oscillation; the difference between what is mildly alarming and peters out and the ever-increasing swing that can result in an accident. Take an ordinary school ruler (the type with a hole in one end) and let it swing on a pencil held in your hand – diagrams below.

The middle diagram (the hand remains perfectly still) corresponds exactly to the tug of infinite mass mentioned opposite where the tug continues undisturbed on a perfectly straight course. The swing of the ruler gradually decays to nothing. The third diagram corresponds

Right – an illustration not designed to scare but inserted (from a complete computer sequence) only to indicate that the result of a given combination of parameters and driving techniques can be predicted as a matter of routine. (50 mph, 2000 kg trailer, CG aft of axle, severe avoidance manoeuvre, .22 g braking.) How to avoid it in absence of precise data is less easily predicted; knowledge of general theory, care and caution are best ingredients. Diagrams below – dynamics of tug/trailer interface with decaying or increasing oscillation can be analogous to swinging a school ruler on a pencil. See text.

to a tug that can move. As you know, moving your hand in a particular way can make the ruler swing with increasing amplitude. In moving your hand (holding the pencil pivot) to make the ruler swing you are instinctively introducing an appropriate frequency and phasing of your movement to make the ruler swing as wide as possible. Try analysing *exactly* what you are doing and you will see how difficult it is to pinpoint the phase lead and frequency you are introducing. This is mentioned because although the computer, when given the tug/trailer dynamics to sort out, can apply the equations of motion and all the myriad modifying influences with tireless brilliance and accuracy, it reflects the number of variables and how critical they are when the overall stability result is considered.

Exact prediction of dynamics is possible.

But the myriad criteria and their varying influence make it impractical to attempt in every case.

Displace ruler   Static hand, decaying swing   Moving hand, increasing swing

...continued

4.1. Towing – on-road – contd

Whiplash effect. Let us therefore resort once more to an analogy, again using the school ruler. This time hold it in a horizontal plane, with your thumb and forefinger over the hole. Flick your wrist left and right and you will see as you do so that the ruler trails, moves and then over-shoots the action of your wrist – what may be termed a whiplash effect. Get the combina-tion of thumb-grip (damping) and wrist-speed wrong and nothing much happens; get it 'right' and a perfect 'whiplash' takes place; again you will note there is a par-ticular combination of parameters that 'excite' the system and these are related to the weight of ruler, speed of motion, etc.

The parallels between these three 'ruler cases' and a tug and trailer –

- The decaying oscillation
- The increasing oscillation due to hand movement and
- The 'whiplash' effect – closely related to the above.

– will be seen at once. With the ruler/pendulum the restoring 'side-force' is provided by gravity and inertia where in the case of the trailer the side force is provided by the tyres.

Applying the analogy. It is clear so far that lateral motion of the *tug* – at given phase differences and amplitudes – is a fundamental influencing factor in the generation, sustaining and 'amplification' of lateral oscillation. Because it will affect what we can do about it, it is worth now probing just a little deeper into the actual situation with a tug and trailer.

We have considered the ruler (trailer) swinging about the pivot point (tow hitch) for convenience because that is

Forward trailer CG benefits stability in weaves but too far forward will exacer-bate problems in sharp turn manoeu-vres.

Aim for trailer CG 10-20 cm ahead of axle. Knowing the length of your draw bar the equivalent nose load can be cal-culated. See Note in diagram, next spread.

what actually happens. But we must now grasp the fact that a trailer (or any other 'body'), given a turning motion, will *natu-rally* want to rotate about its own centre of gravity (CG). Spin a Coke bottle on the kitchen table and it will spin about its CG. If you constrain one end while it is revolving (trailer nose hitched to a tow-hook) it will turn about that point but is still trying to rotate about is own CG so will exert a reactive lateral force on the hitch.

Look now at where, in a typical tug/trailer combination, the tug and trail-er CGs are located and how this affects the influence of trailer on tug – diagrams opposite (upper)

In a swing, a forward trailer CG tends to reduce yaw angle Ø; in effect reducing the angle between the tug and trailer. This situation therefore permits the oscillation to decay. This gives a result like the mid-dle diagram (no hand movement) on the previous spread. The *aft* CG, on the other hand tends to increase Ø, tending there-fore, to encourage an increasing swing. Most readers will already know that a for-ward CG is best for trailers. When we look to the next sub-section, however, we will find that CG should not be *too* far for-ward

Steady-state cornering
Extreme forward trailer CG. Where you might perhaps have felt that the fur-ther forward the trailer CG the better would be its stability, the *destabilising* effect of the trailer on the tug actually increases with forward movement of trail-er CG in fast bends. The computer con-firms that moving the CG even 30 cm ahead of the axle in an accelerating steady turn can, in certain circumstances, cause breakaway of the tug towards the centre of the circle and subsequent roll-over. The lower diagram opposite makes clear what

Swing

Tyre side force

Swing

Swing

Trailer C of G forward of axle

Assume trailer displaced to right, so tyre side-force is from right. Tyre side-force tends to turn trailer about its own CG, imparting motion to tail of tug that is stabilising (forward CG – left) or destabilising (aft CG – below)

Tyre side force

Swing

Swing

Trailer CG aft of axle

is happening. Although it is tyre side force acting about the trailer CG, you may find it easier to think of it as 'centrifugal force' on the mass represented by the CG; either way, the trailer CG, being far forward, tends strongly to push the nose of the trailer (and tail of the tug) towards the outside of the circle. There comes a time when the rear tyres of the tug can no longer hold on and the tail of the tug breaks away and the trailer, in hot pursuit, can provoke a rollover.

The compromise

Moderation in all things. In concept, therefore, we have a conflict. The weave damping case demands a forward CG and the steady-state turn is sensitive to a too-far forward CG. Whilst *all stability problems are more critical with a high trailer weight*, your particular combination of variables and cornering methods will dictate your choice of CG position. On most of the initial computer runs a CG about 10-20 cm ahead of the axle gave the best margin for stability. There are also, as

we shall see, other factors that favour limiting the forward CG position such as keeping a moderate trailer nose load on the tug's towing hitch.

Evening–up the (side) loads. Clearly to minimise the effect of the trailer on the tug (where a trailer of comparative weight to the tug is used), we must aim to spread the cornering forces evenly between all the wheels involved. In an *ideal* world: same load, same tyres, same tyre pressures on all axles. The world is not ideal so we must instead be sure of the following:

- Do not overload the rear axle of the tug.
- Tyre pressures appropriate to axle load; if in doubt err high.
- Trailer CG forward but not too far.

High trailer weight makes things worse – everything! Drive with extra care.

Fast or tightening steady turn with far-forward CG on heavy trailer can eventually cause tug rear tyres to give up, permitting tail end to slide to outside of turn due to excess 'centrifugal force'. Long tug rear overhang makes things worse as trailer has more leverage.

Extreme forward trailer CG

Tyre side force required on each axle

...continued

The Land Rover Experience

4.1. Towing – on-road – contd

Practicalities

Safety first. No apology is made for the over-used cliché nor for the accent so far in this section on stability and safe operation. Provided the dozens of relevant parameters are known, the behavioural characteristics of any tug/trailer combination can be predicted but in the real world they are not known and awareness of the principles of what is going on is doubly important. In many parts of the world, and here the UK is included, legislation for trailer operational safety is skeletal and flimsy. Though complex, it extends to little more than construction and basic use and no regulations cover regular testing or functional checks to what are, in many cases, infrequently-used vehicles. Apart from catch-all 'roadworthy condition' regulations, no periodic tests for brake function etc are laid down.

Your responsibility. It thus behoves the user more than ever to ensure that trailers are in first-rate condition. Readers of this book will in many cases be those using heavy trailers up to and exceeding the weight of the towing vehicle. Be aware that, even using a Land Rover tug product, *once you are past a trailer weight of around 75% of the weight of the towing vehi-*

cle the simple laws of physics dictate you are entering a critical zone in regard to stability, steering and braking; unrelenting care in operation is your responsibility.

General towing considerations. The diagram opposite encapsulates all the criteria relevant to optimum load and stability in a trailer and should be studied care-

Surprisingly, trailer operation is under-legislated with no periodic or age-related tests.

Intermittently-used vehicles such as trailers are prone to rusting-up or jamming of brakes. Don't let it happen to you.

Heavy trailers are potentially dangerous. Loading, operating and driving requires unrelenting care.

From top: RTC9565 3500 kg limit ball – also with twin rear towing shackles. Combination 3500 kg tow ball/jaw RTC8159 with variable height hitch – essential for twin-axle trailers (see Item 6, opposite). Four-bolt-fixing hitch cleared for 3500 kg on ball, 5000 kg on pin. Bottom 'NATO' pintle.

Manufacturer's approved maximum gross trailer weight (subject to local regulations)						
Trailer/braking	On/off road	Defender with 2.5D kg	Defender, any other engine kg	Discovery kg	Range Rover kg	New Range Rover kg
1. Unbraked trailer	On road Off road	750 500	750 500*	750 500†	750 750	750 500
2. Trailer with overrun brakes	On road Off road	3500 1000	3500 1000	3500** 1000†	3500 1000	3500 1000
3. 4-wheel trailer with coupled brakes (see above).	On road Off road	3500 1000	4000 1000	4000† 1000†	4000 1000	3500 1000
* 750 kg for 110 with self-levelled suspension.		**Discovery Mpi 2750 kg		†Not Discovery Mpi		

The Land Rover Experience

General towing considerations

Centre of gravity (trailer plus load)

Go slowly through the variables:
1. A:E – minimise the ratio (small A, big E) when considering a towing vehicle.
2. A:B – minimise the ratio (small A, big B) when considering a trailer.
3. C:B – C not to exceed 40% of B, so keep CG low.
   C not to exceed 95% of trailer track (small C, wide track).
4. E:B – Small E, big B makes for easier reversing.
5. T – Tyre pressures – hard: use GVW settings (Sec 8.2) unless off road (Sec 6.4).
6. H – Same for trailer and towing vehicle. Specially important with twin-axle trailer.
7. **N** – Trailer nose weight. More nose weight equals more anti-weave stability but less cornering stability (lower diagram, previous spread and Note in Trouble Shooting table next spread) – 7% of trailer gross weight is a guide, BUT:
   1. Do not exceed limits of ball hitch or coupling head – usually 100–150 kg.
   2. Remove twice this amount from towing vehicle payload – ie if N = 75 kg, take 150 kg off listed max payload of vehicle when working out how much else you can carry in towing vehicle.
8. W – For a given nose weight, concentrate load close to trailer axle to reduce moment of inertia.

Note. CG position. To calculate CG position you need to know trailer gross weight (weighbridge), axle-to-hitch distance (drawbar length) and nose weight (bathroom scales or weighbridge). Then:
CG position (in cm, ahead of trailer axle) = Nose load in kg times drawbar length in cm divided by the trailer gross weight in kg.

fully in relation first to your particular requirements and then to the trailer/tug combination you have. Nose load is critically important to towing stability when setting up a given trailer.

Braking and weight. Braking method and capacity are especially important. Design and regulatory limitations applicable to all Land Rover products are shown opposite. Above 3500 kg trailer gross weight coupled brakes are mandatory but will be beneficial below this for their sensitivity. Single or twin line air or vacuum brakes with various reservoirs may be fitted. Fitment of such systems requires specialist knowledge and workmanship and should only be carried out by Special Vehicles department at Land Rover or their designated agents.

Tow hitch, coupling head strength. Remember that the widely used 50 mm ball hitch is limited to a 3500 kg trailer gross weight. Above this use one of the hitches shown opposite. Nose load must normally not exceed 150 kg.

Rear axle load. The effect of trailer download on the rear axle of the tug has already been shown to be very relevant to stability – some but not too much is required. The download on the towing hitch is also like having additional payload far aft of the centre of the vehicle load bed – check the diagram at Sec 8.1 (3rd spread) and you will see that 250 kg carried on the tailgate actually increases the rear axle load by 341 kg. The same applies to trailer nose load; see Note 2 under 'N' (Item 7) in diagram above.

Trailer nose load is critical to stability. Be sure too that you are within the strength limits of the tow hitch.

Nose-load is tug payload. Take double the nose-load off your residual tug payload.

...continued

The Land Rover Experience

4.1. Towing – on-road – contd

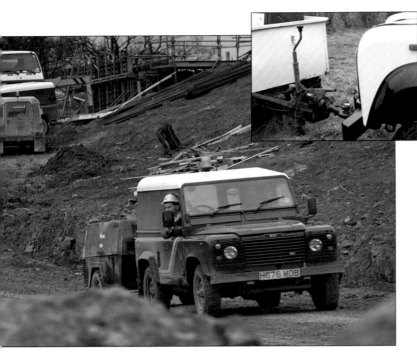

Where vehicles are in continuous heavy-duty industrial use it is especially important that tow hitches and brakes systems chosen are appropriate to the maximum loads towed and that fleet use is properly monitored. Front-mounted hitch can be invaluable for precise manoeuvring and positioning.

As soon as you are moving, check braking response and behaviour.

Braking aggravates any potential stability problem. Always keep maximum space between yourself and vehicle ahead.

Keep tug and trailer in line for braking. Always use a braked trailer if you can; it will be more stable.

Driving with a trailer

Always check brakes. Although light, unbraked trailers will seem not to affect the vehicle very much it is wise to check overall braking action as soon as possible after starting off. Trailers with overrun brakes – especially if they have not been used for some time – can suffer from grabby, non-progressive brakes due to rusty brake drums and a test on a clear piece of road is essential before setting off with a newly loaded trailer. Whilst coupled brakes should be more progressive, a test is still wise since the trailer may not be proportionally braked and still exert some residual push on the towing vehicle during braking.

Braking, general. Whatever the regulations, braked trailers are more stable than unbraked. That said, *any* braking situation will exacerbate a marginal stability or safety problem. Keep this always in your mind together with the need to avoid braking except when the trailer and tug are in line. These considerations should lead to a conscious and consistent effort to drive with as much space between you the vehicle ahead as possible so that you are never called upon to brake suddenly or fiercely. Often your cargo (horses, say) will dictate this anyway.

Reversing. Reversing with a trailer is a well known difficulty for drivers not used to it. In general, trailers which are long relative to the wheelbase of the towing vehicle (such as articulated trucks) are easier to reverse than those that are short. Those that are shorter than the wheelbase of the tug are all but impossible to reverse any distance. As with all aspects of operating your Land Rover, do not be afraid to admit you have got it wrong. If a trailer is that short, it will also be light and uncoupling to manoeuvre it by hand will save the difficulty of reversing it.

Auto-reverse brakes. Overrun trailer brakes work on the principle that a braking tug will cause the trailer to push against the hitch and in doing so apply its own brakes. Reversing such a trailer would ordinarily therefore cause the trailer brakes to come on and you must get out of the vehicle to apply an inhibiting catch before and after doing so.

Gross trailer weights above 3500 kgs demand a ring-hitch and coupled brakes – a special vehicle modification. Top and centre (left) show electrically driven compressor unit and associated couplings for air brakes (as opposed to vacuum brakes) – a Land Rover Special Vehicles fit; lower shot shows heavyweight turn-table trailer which is stable but brings its own reversing problems.

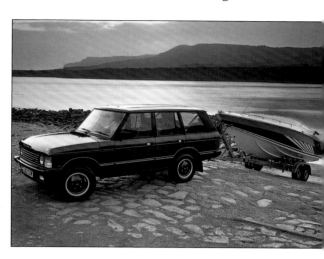

Currently, all new trailers with overrun brakes have an auto-reverse fitment that senses the difference between overrun and reversing and no driver action is required. Be sure you are aware of which brake type you have.

Excessive braking. Harsh braking when towing causes the trailer to increase down load on the towing vehicle

hitch (hence need for centre of gravity constraints, diagram previous spread). This produces a rotating moment about the rear axle and a resulting off-loading of the vehicle front wheels which can, in slippery conditions, produce front wheel lock-up. This will not happen with ABS brakes and the risk can be reduced by use of cadence braking (Sec 3.2).

Electrics. Lights, brake lights and direction indicators should be checked with the trailer and electrics connected.

Towing off-road – see Section 6.4.

Does your trailer have auto-reverse brakes? Or must you operate a catch before and after reversing?

Towing – trouble-shooting guide	
Symptom	*Things to do*
1. Weaving	Move trailer CG forward, reduce trailer weight, reduce moment of inertia (concentrate weight closer to axle), increase trailer and tug tyre pressures, fit a hitch yaw damper, increase trailer drawbar length, reduce speed.
2. 'Oversteer' cornering (tendency to 'tuck-in' when cornering)	Move trailer CG further *aft*, reduce speed, increase tug rear tyre pressures. small reduction in tug front tyre pressures, reduce trailer weight, increase trailer drawbar length.

Note. You will see that, from the point of view of trailer CG position, the two conditions above are (literally) 'swings and roundabouts': improve the weave (swing) stability by moving the trailer CG forward and you are in danger of encountering divergent oversteer on sharp/fast bends (such as roundabouts). Tendency to weave will in some cases be due to an inherent conditions (in relation to your load) you can do nothing about – such as tug rear overhang, for instance. You may be compelled here to move trailer CG further forward than you would wish in order to quench tendency to weave. In these circumstances it may be the right decision so long as you ensure your cornering speeds are reduced.

The knack of reversing is easier with a long trailer than a short one.

4.2. Driving on tracks

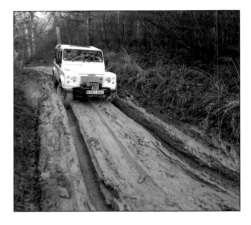

Deep ruts with slippery sides can mask normal steering feedback. You can be unaware your wheels are not pointing straight ahead and when grip is available, vehicle suddenly veers. See also Glossary, Section 10.1, 'Steering feel'.

Existing wheel tracks

Driving – smooth, calm. When a rough track is encountered your driving technique should aim to have the vehicle flow smoothly over it rather than jolt and jar. All current Land Rover products are coil or air sprung front and rear with progressive dampers so this will be easier basically to achieve than on most other makes of off-road vehicle. The application of the mechanical sympathy mentioned in Section 3.1 will do much to foster an appropriately smooth driving technique for these conditions. Taking a calm and unhurried approach will also help.

High gears, low range. As mentioned before (Section 2.4, 'Low range – when and how') the high gears in the low range are often very useful on rough tracks. Such tracks usually have short, difficult sections for which the steady control of the low range will be required without constant use of the brake and clutch pedals. Thus taking a track in, say, top gear low ratio will allow the driver to make a good pace yet change right down to 2nd or even 1st when the ultimate low speed control and torque is required – without the need to change transfer gear range. (High range, of course, is often quite adequate for track driving; to get a clear picture of the overlap between high and low range gears, see Section 6.1, 'High/low range overlap'.)

Railway line effect. Driving along a deeply rutted track where the ruts are cut into slippery ground can be like driving along railway lines; turning the steering wheel left or right does not have any effect since the tyres will not grip on the steep slippery sides of the ruts. The dan-

ger of this situation is that you can be driving along with some steering lock applied (which the vehicle is not responding to) and not know it. When the vehicle reaches level ground or a patch where traction permits it to respond to the steering lock applied, the vehicle will suddenly veer off the track with possibly dangerous consequences.

Wheels straight ahead? Since this condition is not met every day it is doubly important to have the possibility in the back of your mind that the prevailing conditions may be of this type when you are in ruts. The way to preclude the occurrence is to monitor the self-centring of the steering; periodically reduce your grip on the steering wheel by keeping just a frictional grip with the palms of your

Aim to flow smoothly over rough terrain – don't let the vehicle jolt and jar.

High gears in the low box very useful for rough tracks.

Let self-centring castor-action periodically align your wheels in deep ruts.

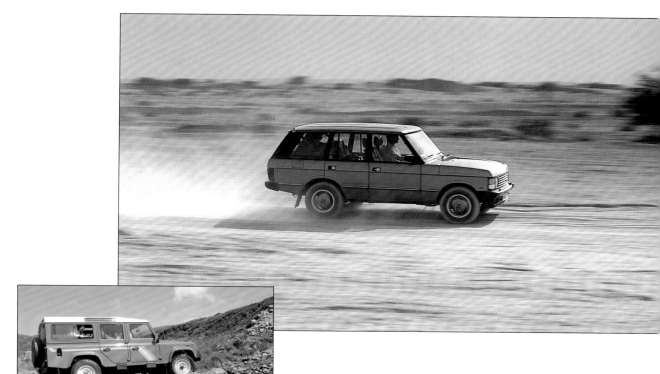

Typical rough tracks have moderately fast sections (above) for which 5th low ratio may be ideal. Low ratio enables you to change down to a cautious 2nd for the really rough bits (left).

hands, letting it regain, through castor action (see Glossary, Section 10.1), the straight ahead position. Also a visual check from the driver's window will establish which way the wheels are pointing. When using the window in this way beware of branches of shrubs or trees flicking in your face.

Existing wheel tracks – traction. If there are already wheel tracks along the unsurfaced road you are travelling, this can affect the traction of your vehicle – for better or for worse. On wet or muddy tracks or in snow it is best to follow in the tracks of a previous vehicle since, in gen-

eral terms, that vehicle will probably have cut through to the drier ground beneath and this will offer your vehicle more traction. See also Section 4.4, 'Climbing steep slopes', and Section 4.7, 'Soft ground' .

Desert and bush. On sandy tracks in desert or bush or on routes over desert plains avoid the tracks of previous vehicles since they will have broken the thin crust that normally forms on wind blown sand. Beneath this crust is soft sand offering less flotation; often this is badly churned which will make flotation and traction even worse. See 'Sand', Section 4.8.

Beware driving with non-gripping steering lock on.

Drive in previous wheel-tracks in mud and snow, but not in soft sand.

...continued

The Land Rover Experience

4.2. Driving on tracks – contd

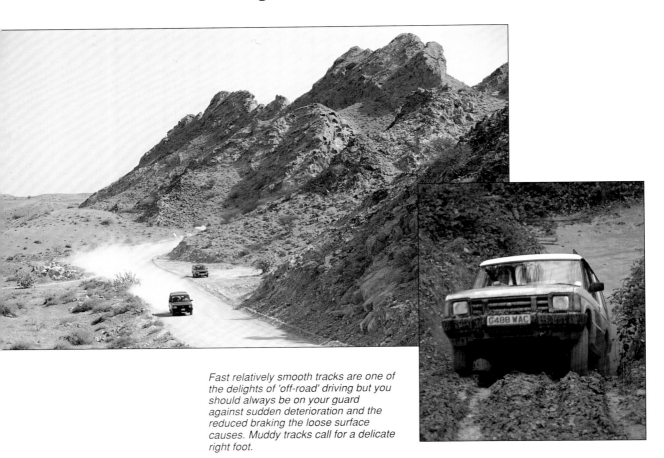

Fast relatively smooth tracks are one of the delights of 'off-road' driving but you should always be on your guard against sudden deterioration and the reduced braking the loose surface causes. Muddy tracks call for a delicate right foot.

Deep ruts, gullies

Under-axle clearance. Rough tracks will sometimes deteriorate into deep V-shaped gullies due to water erosion or extra deep ruts caused by the passage of trucks with big wheels. Keeping in such ruts will lead to grounding the chassis or axle case of your vehicle and anticipation is needed to take appropriate advance action. As the diagram shows, you should aim to get out of the ruts early so as to straddle the gully. Care will be necessary to avoid steering up one or other of the

Be on the lookout for ruts that have become gullies. They will run you out of under-axle clearance.

gully walls which could lead to the vehicle being trapped with its side against the gully.

Steering feel. As indicated in the previous spread, because of the depth or slipperiness of the rut or gully, you may well lose the natural feel of the steering and find it hard to know exactly which way your wheels are pointing. For this reason and to ensure front and back wheels are surveyed all the time when driving over gullies, use a marshaller ahead of the vehicle giving you precise directions. If

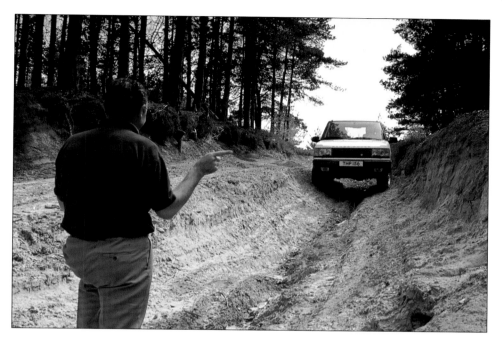

Rain or flood erosion can cause deep ruts to become gullies and there is the danger of the vehicle slipping down one side. Careful guidance by a marshaller who can see all wheels is the only way to negotiate this kind of obstacle.

Do not stay in badly eroded ruts (1). Get out of ruts and (2) straddle the gully. Vehicle must be carefully guided in gully to sit evenly across it. If necessary, cut steps with a shovel to give tyres a positive footing and use a marshaller.

1.

2.

You will lose steering feel driving gully sides. Get guidance and/or look out of the window.

you do not have a marshaller then lower the driver's window and observe the front wheel yourself, being careful, as already mentioned, of tree or bush branches flicking in your face.

The Land Rover Experience

4.3. Ridges and ditches

'Landscaping' – digging under the hung-up wheels – will lower the vehicle so that all four wheels are in contact with the ground and traction is regained.

Diagonal wheel-spin is the main hazard. Know your vehicle's articulation limits.

Diagonal suspension

Ridge – a mirror-image ditch. Ridges and ditches can be encountered both on tracks and across open country. Though one is a mirror image of the other, ridges and ditches can introduce the same problems for the vehicle – grounding the chassis or hanging diagonally-opposite wheels in the air and losing traction by reaching the limits of articulation. The method of crossing these obstacles will require judgement according to their size since the recommended method of crossing a small ridge will lead to trouble if it is applied to a big (or abrupt) one.

Methods of crossing ridges and ditches vary according to the size of the obstacle.

Size determines technique
Potential hazards. The diagram shows the potential hazards and the best *general* advice is to take ridges and ditches diagonally with as much momentum as you judge to be prudent. If that seems like the ultimate escape clause, remember that some obstacles are better taken at right angles (if you can) to avoid risk of diagonal hang-up; others are best taken diagonally (if you can) to avoid jarring or hitting the tail as you exit – check the table below. Consider these obstacles in three sizes:

1. Small ridges and ditches. These may be taken at right angles within the limits dictated by vehicle underbelly clearance and rear overhang (departure angle). However this does mean that the respective front and rear axles will hit the obstacle square-on and probably impart an undesirable jolt. By taking the obstacles diagonally the vehicle will flow over the obstacle with a rolling motion but without any shock loading. Indeed if, when driving quickly over a plain you encounter a shallow ditch which you had not seen earlier, alter direction immediately to take it diagonally.

2. Medium sized ridges and ditches. These may be classified as those that will give problems of underbelly or departure angle clearance and therefore cannot be taken at right angles. With these ones you thus have no option but to take them diagonally. The technique outlined above should be used.

3. Tall ridges and deep ditches. On-foot inspection and the assistance of a marshaller will almost certainly be neces-

Diagonal approach is always best – but beware severe ridges and ditches.

Ridges and ditches: diagonal approach vs right angles		
Approach	*Advantage*	*Disadvantage*
Right angles	Precludes diagonal hang-up	May jolt, belly vehicle or hit tail
Diagonal	Avoids jarring	May cause diagonal hang-up

*Photographs show close-to-limits artic-
ulation as vehicles cross ridges and
ditches. 'Hanging' wheels have little
load in this situation so could spin if
provoked. Aim for optimum balance of
momentum and throttle.*

sary. These are obstacles that definitely
cannot be taken at right angles and also, if
taken slowly diagonally, will result in
diagonally-opposite wheels lifting to
allow wheel spin and loss of traction. In
these cases you have two options:

a. *Provided the going is smooth enough*
take the obstacle diagonally but fast
enough for momentum to carry the vehicle past the momentary lifting of corner
wheels.

b. *Provided it is permitted,* 'landscape'
the ground with a shovel to remove the
top of the ridge or edge of the ditch that
will cause grounding of the chassis or tail

end or suspension of the wheels and then
proceed as at 1 above.

Learning gently. As with so many
skills it takes longer to write and read this
advice than to apply it. You will quickly
learn to judge which situation you are in.
So long as you do not jolt the vehicle
badly or ground the chassis it does not
matter if you do not get this right first
time – at least on small and medium
obstacles. As ever, do not be afraid to take
it gently at first or admit you got it
wrong; back off and try again – no damage has been done. (See also 'Self recovery', Section 5.1.)

*Judgement required:
speed and diagonal
approach can help.
Digging under
hung-up wheels may
be needed.*

4.4. Climbing steep slopes

Grip, gradient, momentum

Grip and gradient. The twin problems with steep slopes – gradient and grip – usually reduce themselves to one in most cases with a Land Rover since all Land Rover products have the power and appropriate gearing to climb a continuous slope of nearly 1-in-1 or 45° if the grip is there. Grip is far more likely to be the limiting factor and we have seen in Section 3.2, 'Gentle right foot', how use of the right gear (not necessarily the lowest one) allied to a sensitive right foot can eliminate the wheel-spin that can result from insufficient grip. Climbing steep slopes is the classic application of sensing grip and being gentle with the throttle – and, see below, admitting defeat early in cases of wheel spin. Don't floor the throttle when you get wheel-spin in the vain hope of getting up the slope; the vehicle could slide sideways off course and may tip – see diagram, right.

Grip invariably the limiting factor on steep slopes. The right gear (usually 2nd or 3rd low) and a sensitive throttle foot is the answer.

Go straight at the slope. Whilst a walker would take diagonal tacks up a steep hill to reduce the gradient, you should take the fall line direct in a vehicle, ie take the slope at right angles, head-on. This is to ensure the vehicle is laterally level – your walker can stand up straight when traversing a steep hill; a vehicle leans over (see 'Traversing slopes', Section 4.6) and is in danger of tipping down the slope in extreme cases.

Momentum, traction, throttle control. Commonsense steep slopes need no more than commonsense tactics: if it is reasonably smooth and not excessively steep take a bit of a run at it in the right gear and do not over-torque the wheels to provoke wheel spin. Select the right gear before the slope and stay in it; only an automatic will do a smooth enough

Keep at right angles to the slope – going up or when reversing back down – see next spread.

Going up a slope at right angles to the lip of the ridge is safe; a diagonal approach can provoke a roll-over down the slope. The risk is made worse by any wheel-spin.

change if one is needed. But on really difficult slopes, as ever, an on-foot survey will help. Such slopes are unlikely to be smooth and tramping out the chosen route to locate any local bumps, tree stumps or rabbit holes that might cause a wheel to lift will be useful.

Extra grip – from the steering wheel. If the track is rutted – and this can apply on level ground too – limiting grip can be enhanced by moving the steering wheel from side to side (11 o'clock to 1 o'clock) and cause the tyre sidewalls to contribute grip.

Higher gear – with lift-off. Unless you are tackling an unusual and excep-

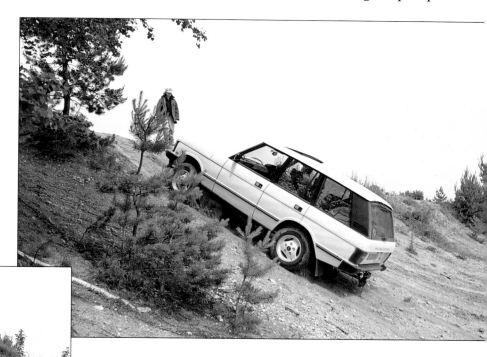

Classic example (above) of a 2nd gear low range slope needing a bit of momentum at the bottom and a readiness to lift off the throttle towards the top. One of the rare 1st gear low range slopes (left) where grip permits full use of vehicle's ultimate climbing ability.

tional climb such as 40° on rough dry concrete, 1st gear low box will be too low and will provoke wheel-spin. Most 'normal severe' climbs will be best tackled in 2nd gear low box, or, if there is any amount of run-up available, 3rd. Use the most run-up momentum you can, having established the ground is smooth enough to permit it, since the more you can utilise this, the less will be the demand for grip from the ground actually on the slope. As you near the top of the slope your momentum may be running out and the vehicle will become more reliant on grip and traction. This is the point (quite near to the top) where the wheels are most

likely to start slipping or spinning – and it is thus, paradoxically, the point where you may find that lifting off the throttle helps put that final bit of power on the ground without spinning the wheels.

Automatic applications. The equivalent of lift-off to de-stress the ground where traction is marginal will occur on an auto transmission vehicle if 3rd is selected before a steep climb. The gearbox will change to 3rd as the throttle is lifted and reduce the risk of wheel-spin. Note that the new (1994/95) Range Rover automatic used in low range 'Manual' mode will behave like a manual gearbox – see Section 2.3.

Be prepared to lift off near the top to preclude wheel-spin.

...continued

4.4. Climbing steep slopes – contd

Nothing to fear getting it wrong even on slopes like this (left). But remember to keep both hands on the steering wheel and back STRAIGHT down the hill.

Just as you would always go up a slope at right angles to the maximum gradient, do the same coming back down.

Remember that in reverse, steering castor action is also reversed. Grip the wheel firmly to prevent 'runaway'.

Engage reverse with the engine dead. Then foot off clutch, touch the starter.

Failed climb, recovery

First-time scare. If you are losing grip on a steep climb don't boot the throttle and accentuate the wheel-spin; de-clutch and apply the footbrake. Your first failure on a very steep climb – nose of the vehicle pointing at the sky, brake leg trembling, maybe a dead engine and a plan view of the world in your rear view mirror – can be mildly scaring; it can sometimes also be mechanically traumatic for the vehicle if a driver tries to bluff it out or attempt impossibly quick sequences of control selections during the 'recovery' descent.

Slowing the adrenaline. Observing – and practising – the following procedures makes a fail-and try-again climb so matter-of fact that both driver and vehicle have a far easier time. Knowing this means you do not cane the vehicle unnecessarily hard in a white-knuckle attempt to get up first time. Climbs can fail with or without a dead engine:

1. Forward motion ceases, engine running, wheels spinning – grip problem.

2. Forward motion ceases, engine stalled – gradient problem.

Using the following procedures you will come back down the hill with both hands on the steering wheel (important, that), feet off the pedals – ie not on clutch, or footbrake but covering the throttle. Engine braking controls your speed of descent and no frantic use of gear lever or handbrake is needed. (Procedure for manual transmission shown; Auto procedure is shown in brackets)

Failed climb, engine running. If you have failed the climb through loss of grip and wheel-spin:

1. Clutch pedal down, hold the vehicle firmly on the footbrake, engine idling. (**Auto:** allow engine revs to die, brake, engage **'R'** low box, gently release brake, jump to step 4.)

2. Engage reverse gear low range.

3. With *both hands* on the steering wheel and leading with the clutch, release the clutch and footbrake. The vehicle (engine still idling) will start back down the slope fully controlled by engine braking. At this stage your feet can be off all three pedals – ie you are in reverse, clutch fully engaged and engine idling. Remember that *in reverse, steering castor action is also reversed and there is a tendency for the steering wheel to 'run-away' to full lock* if you do not hold it firmly.

4. Keeping both hands on the steering wheel, go straight back down, at right angles to the slope, to less steep ground.

5. Note. The admit-defeat-early credo is very important in a traction failure on a hill – ie with spinning wheels. If you do not quit the moment it is clear you are not going to make it, it is very likely the vehicle, wheels spinning on a slippery surface, will slew sideways-on to the slope and there is a risk of it capsizing down the hill. Even if it does not do this, the spinning wheels – usually one front wheel with its diagonally opposite back wheel – will scoop depressions in the ground to make your next attempt more difficult.

Failed climb, stalled engine. If you have failed the climb and stalled the engine in the process (see also diagram sequence right):

1. Engine is dead. Hold the vehicle on the footbrake, clutch position immaterial. (**Auto**: go to step 5.)

2. Engage reverse gear low range and remove left foot from clutch.

3. With both hands on the steering wheel, slowly lessen the pressure on the footbrake until your foot is off it. The vehicle is now held by the engine.

4. The vehicle may begin to move backwards on its own and in so doing 'bump'-start the engine. In which case let it continue, under full control of engine braking, keeping both hands firmly on the steering wheel.

5. If the engine has not started under gravity, take one hand off the wheel to operate the starter motor briefly – with the vehicle still in reverse gear and clutch fully engaged. This will invariably kick the engine into life and you are, as in 4. above, slowly descending back down the slope in full control, in gear, clutch fully engaged, left foot on the floor, both hands on steering wheel to resist any steering 'run-away', right foot hovering over throttle. (**Auto**: foot still on brake, select **'N'** or **'P'**, start engine, engage **'R'**, both hands on wheel, slowly release footbrake.)

6. Just as you would climb the slope at right angles to the gradient, make sure you go straight back down the slope – still at right angles to the gradient. When you reach less steep ground, use the controls in the normal way.

Dead-engine failed-climb – so straightforward and calm it is worth shutting off the engine to use this procedure even if it has not stalled. Stalling engine puts very high stresses on it. Feet off all the pedals (but throttle-ready), touch starter.

1, 2.

These procedures take far longer to read about than to do. They are really very simple. Practice on gentle slopes, then steeper ones.

3, 4.

5.

Aim after a failed climb is to come straight back down the slope, both hands on the wheel, feet off pedals.

Recovery sequence, stalled engine – list, adjacent column. 1, 2. Clutch, footbrake, into reverse. 3, 4. Feet off all pedals – but throttle foot ready. 5. Touch the starter briefly; both hands on steering wheel. 6. Preferably reverse back on mirrors.

4.5. Descending steep slopes

Stop 2m from the edge (engine off, 1st gear, handbrake) and inspect on foot. Plan to use engine braking.

Gear to use

Remove the drama. Land Rover vehicles' extraordinary agility may make your first really steep descent an intimidating experience. A 45° down-slope itself is unusual enough but to this angle you add the fact that you are looking even further downward over the bonnet; the result can seem vertical, especially when you are hanging forward in your seat harness. But this is an experience that you will very quickly get used to – usually after just one steep descent. As with climbs, the aim is to take the drama out of the situation and utilise the vehicle's facility for keeping you in control.

Get out and look. A 45° slope is extreme but there are many lesser slopes that can still seem very steep and, as with the climb, an on-foot inspection is advisable to ensure that your planned route is safe. This is doubly important since when you come to the edge of a steep descent you can sometimes see nothing over the nose of the vehicle except the other side of the dip; only when you are actually pointing down the slope can you see the ground immediately in front of you. (For this reason, among others, stop the vehicle for the on-foot inspection at least two metres before the edge of the slope – engine off, in gear, handbrake on. This will give you time, when you do start the descent, to get the vehicle fully in gear and with your foot off the clutch for the descent.)

Gear – rule of thumb, 1st gear low range. Using 1st gear low range will in nearly every case result in a perfectly controlled, feet-off-all-pedals descent. Actual retardation will depend on whether you have a diesel or petrol engine, whether or not it has a manual transmission and the condition of the slope but the rule is a good one and a safe one. It is important to

The view over the nose comes only when you are committed to the slope; so recce on foot first. At the point of commitment you can often only see sky or the far side of the dip.

Use 1st gear, low range, foot off the throttle to brake you down 99% of all steep slopes – see Section 6.4 for the other 1%.

remember that due to their higher gearing and the way they function, *automatic transmission offers poorer engine braking* down steep slopes

The rationale. Your aim is to obtain maximum retardation without resorting to the brakes which despite the sensitivity and feel of the disc brakes on Land Rover vehicles, can result in wheel locking and sliding. As always your aim is to preclude any possibility of discontinuity of rolling contact (see Section 3.2, 'Gentle right foot') – ie no wheel-spinning or, more likely in this case, sliding.

Ready for throttle. If the ground is too slippery to provide the grip for the retardation of the throttle-off engine and you begin to slide, be ready to use the accelerator to help the wheels 'catch up' with the vehicle and eliminate any wheel slide.

Ready for exceptions. There may be occasions – typically long descents of loose ground or extremely slippery clay,

Retardation will will be greater with diesels and manual transmissions.

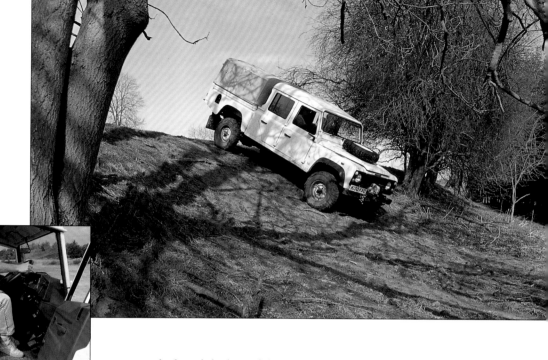

The ideal descent is with both feet on the floor and the engine doing the braking. Be ready to use throttle if the retardation is too strong and the wheels begin to slide.

steep initially – where low range 2nd gear will be better in order to preclude an initial sliding-wheel glissade. One or two exceptions are covered at Section 6.4. Some descents – see photo Section 6.4 – will actually demand 3rd low range and considerable throttle to prevent nosing-in on a soft surface. As before, it is best to select the gear for the whole descent and stay in it.

Brakes

Brakes? Never... An easy generalisation - and for good reasons – is to counsel against ever using brakes on a steep slippery descent. Braking on wet, muddy or loose-surface slopes – even with the excellent sensitivity of the Land Rover's discs – can easily cause one or more wheels to

lock and the loss of directional control in the resulting slide could be dangerous. The use of engine braking down steep slopes makes, in general, for a very safe, controlled way of keeping the vehicle from gaining speed and there is no danger of overheating the brakes. Often you are able to take both feet off the pedals and rest them flat on the floor while the vehicle trundles gently down the slope with the engine idling.

But... But there are times when engine braking is not the infallible solution (see Section 6.4) and the sensitive use of brakes or, preferably, cadence braking as described in Section 3.2 can help. If your Range Rover or Discovery is fitted with ABS brakes - Land Rover's Wabco systems is one of the few that can cope on- and off-road – then brakes may be used on a slippery down-slope. There is a very good case, however, for getting into the habit of using engine braking first.

Rule of thumb – 1st low and do not use the brakes. But... see Section 3.2 for cadence braking and ABS is magic in reserve. Accelerate if necessary.

4.6. Traversing slopes

A static rig-test tip angle is around 40° but the dynamics of real driving make this dangerous to approach. Escape manoeuvre (below) applies if you feel you are getting close to tipping.

Assessing the ground

Side slopes are different. From the last two sections – 'Climbing steep slopes' and 'Descending steep slopes' – the doctrine of always taking such obstacles at right angles to the slopes implies that traversing a slope is dangerous. And so it can be when the angle of gradient is severe. There will be times, however, when, on less severe slopes, you do need to traverse the slope laterally. Like your first steep climb and descent, your first traverse will be unnerving. Unlike climbs and descents, however, you will not quickly get used to it. And that is a good thing since the consequences of getting it wrong on a traverse are a great deal more serious than getting it wrong on a climb or descent.

Trust your instincts. There appears to be a built-in safety feature of human perception that makes a traverse feel a lot more dangerous than it is. Your vehicle will actually tilt to quite high angles on perfectly smooth ground without rolling over but to the driver, a traverse along a slope even one third of the maximum per-

Side-slopes don't feel right. Trust your unease and treat them with great caution.

As ever, inspect on foot looking for bumps or hollows that can affect vehicle's lateral stance.

missible can feel alarming. Follow your instinct and do not traverse slopes that feel dangerous. As ever, carry out an on-foot reconnaissance first:

1. Slippery surface. Assess the surface to be sure it is not so slippery that the vehicle will slide sideways down the slope.

2. Bumps and dips. Look out for dips that the down-hill wheels may encounter and bumps that the up-hill wheels may roll over – rabbit holes and sawn-off tree stumps in particular. Both will increase

The on-foot inspection is especially important. Look for bumps or dips that affect lateral lean. Every inch of ground irregularity makes approximately 1° difference to lateral lean – a 4" bump equals 4°. Digging away the hillside ahead of the up-slope wheels can lower the actual tilt angle. Lateral slopes that are also slippery (right) demand special caution.

the tilt of the vehicle and increase the risk of it tipping over.

3. Secure load. Any load in the back of your vehicle should be secure and as low as possible. Be particularly wary of roof-rack loads. Passengers should sit on the up-hill side – or dismount.

4. Marshalling. If there are any doubts about the effect of the terrain or if there are obstacles to avoid, then use a marshaller (see Section 3.4) to see you forward and make sure he or she keeps an eye on all four wheels.

Escape manoeuvre

Be ready. Steer down the hill if the vehicle slips or seems too close to the maximum tip angle. As with normal steep descents, the nearer you can get the vehicle pointing directly down the slope the less the danger of lateral tipping. If you feel the machine getting laterally unstable turn down the hill quickly and give a little burst of throttle. The centrifugal force of the quick turn, further enhanced by the blip of throttle, will help keep the vehicle upright.

'Escape' by steering down the hill, with a touch of throttle.

The Land Rover Experience

4.7. Weak ground

'Green lanes' are classic examples of low vertical and low horizontal ground strength combined – a mixture of the soft and slippery. If a vehicle is used continuously on unstable ground, snow-chains can be useful traction aid.

A 4x4 under power generates, on the ground, horizontal thrust (top) and vertical thrust (centre) to produce a resultant diagonal (bottom). Decreasing weight or tyre pressure (weight per unit area) and exercising care with throttle and brakes reduces both components of ground stress.

Ground stress – horizontal, vertical
Reading the ground. Soft ground is weak ground – vertically and laterally as well. The vertical context is well known – the tendency for a vehicle to sink in it – and the lateral connotations mean it will not take much thrust (or braking) from wheels without degenerating into slippery wheel-spin (or slide); the gentle right foot on brakes and throttle (Section 3.2) comes into its own. Read the surface and adjust your throttle foot accordingly: getting the traction where you can, backing off where you can afford to do so in order not to lose the traction you do have – and occasionally (on the right tyres) applying a carefully judged burst of wheel-spin to get through slime onto drier grippy ground; reading the ground.

'Fifth-wheel' traction. On the limits in rutted ground, turning the steering wheel from side to side, 11 o'clock to 1 o'clock, is effective in getting that little extra traction from the tyre sidewalls – especially with bold-tread mud tyres.

Soft ground is weak laterally as well as vertically – so it's that gentle right foot again.

Lock the centre diff, read the ground, judge what it will take without spinning the wheels.

Horizontal load – throttle, brakes. The most immediate control you have when encountering weak ground is from within the vehicle. You should be in four wheel drive – which you are in all current Land Rover products – and the centre differential should be locked so as to preclude the possibility of one axle spinning any faster than the other. No hard and

The Land Rover Experience

Examples of ground that is vertically weak (soft, left), horizontally weak (slippery, below left) and close to the limit on both (right).

fast rule can be laid down as to the 'best' action then to take. Some situations will demand you accelerate on the good going to take you through the soft and slippery patch using momentum, others will demand you slow down to take it gently because it is uneven or of extended length. The only invariable rule is to heighten your awareness of the risk of wheel-spin and to take appropriate action with the controls. Choose the highest gear you judge will get you through without either wheel-spin or over-stressing the engine – this will often be 2nd or 3rd low range. As for brakes, remember they stress the ground in the same way as driving torque at the wheels and insensitivity will result in sliding.

Low range 2nd or 3rd will usually be the gears for soft ground.

...continued

The Land Rover Experience

4.7. Weak ground – contd

Tyres and tyre pressures

Tyres. Section 8.2 deals with tyres in more detail but the subject is inseparable from weak ground operation so some coverage is given here. Differentiating between vertical and horizontal weakness in soft ground is important. As already mentioned, some weak ground needs cutting into to get to the firmer ground beneath: an aggressive, probably quite narrow, very open tyre tread for mud – mud is slippery, fairly shallow and thus horizontally weak. Other types of soft ground need the 'soft-shoe' approach – more tyre width to give flotation on bog or peat or moorland where the surface is fragile and damage has to be minimised; this ground is notable for being vertically weak. Sand is a special case (Section 4.8) but is also classifiable as vertically weak and thus needing maximum flotation; for special reasons it also requires a very mild and particular tread pattern. As Section 8.2 makes clear, tyres can only be 'best' in one set of conditions and 'compromise' or all-purpose tyres are exactly that – a compromise. Nor is it true, as you see above, that the fattest tyres are the 'best'.

Vertical load – per square inch. Once you have your chosen tyres and are on your 'chosen' terrain, vertical load per unit area – the tyre pressures, rather than total vertical load – is what you will have easiest control of. You may not think tyre pressures would make much difference since the total weight of the vehicle will usually remain the same, sitting on the same four tyres. But bear in mind that 'emergency flotation' pressures (Section 8.2) can be two thirds of road pressures or less. This means the tyre footprint size increases (see diagrams Section 8.2) and the weight of the vehicle is spread over a correspondingly larger area so that – as in recognising the benefits of 4x4 which spreads the thrust over four instead of two wheels – you are asking less of the ground that is already having difficulty in supporting the vehicle's weight.

Reduced tyre pressures – when and how much. Reduce pressures only when

Weak-ground tyres for 'cutting' and 'floating'. Michelin XCL (left), class-leader in mud/clay – open, bold, self-cleaning tread but noisy, L-rated (75 mph max, see Section 8.2) and less than ideal on road. High flotation version (265/75 x 16) of Goodrich Mud-Terrain (right) is S-rated, quieter and grippier on-road but tread pattern (even on narrower variants – 235/85 and 225/75) not as ultimately effective as XCL on mud/clay, No one tyre can be good at everything.

Weak-ground tyres can effect a 'cutting' or 'floating' role. And inevitably, for different terrain, well-judged mixtures of both.

Reduced tyre pressures increase flotation and ride comfort but MUST be accompanied by reduced speed.

Horizontally weak (slippery – left) and vertically weak (soft – below) ground need appropriate tyres and techniques. Note (left) how narrow a good mud tyre really is – here being used with controlled wheel-spin to cut through to better traction. Flotation (below) absolutely on the limits; left tyre has broken crust, right tyre just holding on. See next Section.

needed – then re-inflate (see Section 4.9, 'Rock, stones, corrugations). The golden rule is not to run with low tyre pressures without reducing your speed. With inappropriately low tyre pressures the steering and handling of the vehicle will be adversely affected. Moreover, if you don't slow down serious overheating of the tyre will occur which could lead to tyre damage and loss of control of the vehicle. Tyre pressures for particular conditions will vary according to the vehicle, the axle load and the manufacturer of the tyres. Typical axle loads and off-road tyre pressures for Land Rover vehicles are given in Section 8.2, 'Tyres'. Rule-of-thumb guidance figures are shown below:

1. Tracks and poor roads – 80% of road pressures, maximum speed 65 kph (40 mph).

2. Emergency flotation pressures – about 60% of road pressures, maximum speed 20 kph (12 mph).

Vertical load – reducing the total. It is commonsense that reducing the overall load will give the vehicle a better chance

in soft going also enabling reduction in tyre pressures to be used. In practical terms few users will be able to dispose of payload to suit the going but the principle is worth remembering for the case of recovering a bogged vehicle - see Section 5.1, 'Self-Recovery'.

Previous wheel tracks. As already mentioned (Section 4.2, 'Driving on tracks'), if the weak ground is wet or muddy, it will usually pay to follow the wheel tracks of a previous vehicle since that vehicle will have cut through to firmer ground and you will be able to take advantage of that. If the weak ground is sandy see next section.

Tyres MUST be re-inflated before exceeding the low pressure speed limits.

Choice of tyres is important for frequent soft-ground operation – see Section 8.2.

4.8. Sand

Innocuous-looking sebkha (above) can be extremely treacherous. Tracks (far right) can be difficult when previously traversed by large trucks; there is then a case for getting onto untrodden sand – rarely quite as firm as this example (near right).

Initial rules
Different types. Wet sand, damp sand and a dozen types and conditions of dry sand each lead to different expectations of vertical and horizontal strength (flotation and surface shear strength) as well as behaving differently as far as compaction strength is concerned. Each thus demands different driving techniques. Avoiding wheel-spin, a golden rule of most off-road driving, is nowhere more important than in sand. All, where there is doubt, demand on-foot inspection and 'stamping out' to ascertain firmness and, when close to the limits, the vehicle will have a far better chance if tyre pressures are reduced – see diagrams and tyre pressure/speed limit tables Section 8.2, 'Tyres'.

Initial rule-of-thumb. Initial guide rules are therefore in order if you are to get through the sand rather than trying to learn all the different varieties of problem at once.

1. Dry sand. If you are running out of traction or flotation, keep off previously churned or broken sand. Make your own new tracks.

2. Damp sand. Follow previous tracks which will have compacted the sand and made it firmer.

3. Wet sand. Keep off altogether. It can contain areas of 'floating' sand, or quicksand – bottomless with virtually no vertical strength.

4. Sebkha (salt flat). Very dangerous – unpredictably soft and bottomless. If a well-used track goes over a sebkha it will have compacted the surface (seemingly from beneath) into a smooth, relatively strong route. Do not stray off the hardened track by even a tyre's width.

Sand types - the detail
Dry sand. Being an aggregate of small grains and large grains, nature's wind-blown sand, helped by night dews and diurnal heating and contracting, forms a surface crust which has more strength than the sand beneath; it is stronger in the cool of the morning than in the heat of the day. Use these characteristics to your advantage and be very careful not to break through into the soft sand beneath; think of the analogy of driving on a pie crust.

1. Sandy tracks. Sandy tracks, by reason of the previous passage of vehicles, have no pie crust. Difficulty is likely where there has been a lot of previous truck traffic. Three things will happen here – the ruts will get deeper, the depth of churned sand will increase and the width between the ruts will increase. This is simply a function of the size of the previous vehicles – their wheel diameter and the width of their axles. As ever, be ready to admit defeat early – before getting into real trouble – and steer out of the track onto virgin ground if you can. The higher gears – 3rd, 4th and 5th – in the low range (centre diff locked) will probably be best for tracks of this kind. The advantage of being in low range is that it will enable you to accelerate through suddenly worsening conditions without the risk of being unable to restart, having stopped to change from high to low box. For this reason do not stop except on firm going – or if you do have to stop be gentle with the brakes. As the going gets heavier and more demanding you will find you have to be firm with the throttle and use a lot of the torque at your disposal; this is different from the technique used on virgin sand.

2. Virgin sand. Some desert sand is remarkably firm and strong. But if you are close to the limits of flotation when on virgin, unbroken sand in the open desert (or once out of the ruts on the track) you have to be more delicate with the throttle in order not to break the crust of clean sand supporting you. The same goes for the brakes and steering. On some dune surfaces there is a good case for letting the vehicle come to a rolling stop without brakes at all. Similarly, when stopping your vehicle on sand remember that restarting when facing up a slope is almost impossible and you should therefore stop on level ground, or, if possible, with the vehicle facing downhill.

Previously unbroken sand, particularly, has a 'pie crust' that can be surprisingly strong. But be careful with throttle and brakes.

...continued

4.8. Sand – contd

Sand types , dry sand – contd

3. Sand dunes. Small, closely packed dunes (randomly oriented, up to four metres high) are better driven round rather than attempting to drive over them. When dunes are that small the sand is invariably loose and weak. Dunes larger than 4–5 metres are usually sufficiently spaced-out to permit driving between them and taking advantage of the firm areas. The variation of flotation over a dune structure is soon learned – the hard way. Whilst no two dune chains are the same, the diagram shows the general principles of where to expect the firm bits. Avoid the sand-falls completely. No vehicle will ever get up one but most are so soft that the vehicle will sink and lose steering-way even trying to descend one – but see photo at Section 6.4. Also in this context, see Section 10.1, 'Glossary', Caster angle and Steering feel.

4. Fesh-fesh. Fesh-fesh is a thin crust of fine gravel or sand over powder-fine dust with very little surface strength. Maximum flotation and instant application of power will be required to avoid getting stuck.

In general, going is firmer where the up-wind side of the dunes meet the valley floor.

Damp sand. Sand that is damp – such as it might be after a rain shower or even morning dew – just makes driving easier. The water binds it together, strengthens it, gives more flotation and on tracks actually makes it compact to yield considerably more strength than the dry, churned-up sand had before the rain.

Wet sand. It becomes a matter of judgement and definition to say when damp sand gets to be wet sand. Beach sand will frequently behave as dry, cut-up, churned sand where it is dry and become considerably firmer where it is washed by the tide – though this is not an invariable rule. The warning sounded earlier refers to really wet sand of the kind encountered where a river or stream meets the sea and where a kind of 'floating' sand is encountered. This is akin to a quicksand where motion by the person or vehicle on it just causes further sinkage.

Sebkha (salt flat). Sometimes also marked on maps as 'chott', a sebkha forms where lakes used to be and consists of a crust of dried salt-mud covering soft, bottomless salt-mud underneath. The crust is of variable and unpredictable strength but appears to have the curious characteristic of consolidating from underneath when progressively heavier vehicles run over it. Thus a track over a sebkha usually consists of wheel marks indented probably no more than a few centimetres into the surface – implying that the surrounding ground is firm. Yet as the stern warning above indicates, this is not the case and straying off the track even a tyre width or a metre can sometimes result in disastrous sinkage. A vehicle stuck in sebkha will quickly sink to the chassis and sometimes go on sinking. It is usually impossible to effect self-recovery and even assisting vehicles should have very long tow ropes or winches in order that they too do not sink.

Sand tyres. As already indicated, each kind of terrain demands its own specialist tyre. This is particularly important in the

The classic desert tyre of all time, the Michelin XS – worn example at reduced pressure shown left – with a tread optimised to get the most traction out of all types of sand. Diagrams Section 8.2 show increase in footprint area of XS deflated to emergency soft. Certain parts of dunes can be surprisingly firm but (above left) even with the best tyres, the limits can be found.

case of sand. Even here the carefully named 'desert' tyre has to accommodate the different requirements of travel on rock and sand. In general, however, the greatest design conflict would be between a mud tyre and a sand tyre – the one requiring a bold angular tread and the sand tyre needing a far gentler, more subtle tread design. And whilst the sidewall of a desert tyre must be strong to resist rock damage it must also be flexible to accommodate the greatly reduced tyre pressures used in the worst sand condi-

tions. If contemplating desert operations, your vehicle's performance will be considerably enhanced if desert tyres are fitted. Section 8.2 shows tyre types, axle loads and tyre pressures for typical conditions. See also 'Sand tyres', Section 10.1, 'Glossary'.

Getting stuck, recovery. Self-recovery and assisted recovery is covered in this Section 5. Inevitably, sand is a little different. Just as inevitably, the recovery methods are commonsense honed with pragmatism and experience.

Fitting specialist desert tyres is particularly important in achieving optimum performance in sand.

4.9. Rocks, stones, corrugations

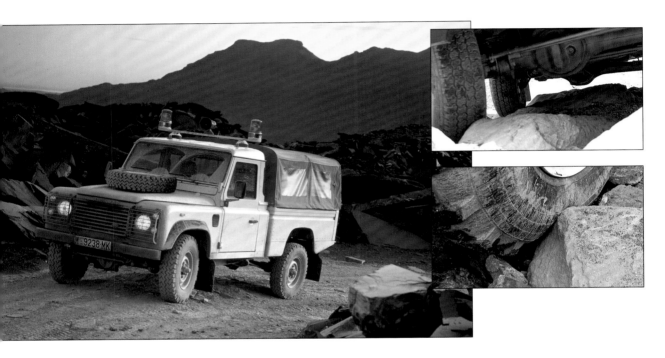

Regular operation in rocky conditions demands extra awareness of under-axle clearance and of tyre sidewall vulnerability.

Under-axle and under body clearances dictate 20–30 cm rocks as about the maximum size to drive over.

Take every precaution against grounding the vehicle on rock. As usual, use a marshaller when clearances are tight.

Risks – chassis, tyres

Rocks – 30 cm high. The sections dealing with use of the low transfer box and the methods of driving on rough tracks (Sections 2.4 and 4.2) will prepare you for the techniques best suited for driving over rocks and stone. The rough definition applicable here to 'rocks and stone' is that stones are taken to be anything from gravel up to fist-sized stones and rocks are taken to be over fist sized and up to about 20–30 cm high – the maximum permitted by the under-body and under-axle dimensions of Land Rover products.

Clearances. What you have read about clearance angles and under-axle clearances at Section 3.3, 'Geometric limitations', is doubly important in the context of driving over rocks and stones. Getting it slightly wrong on clearances when traversing mud will probably scrape earth from the obstacle and take paint off the underside of the vehicle. Making the same mistake over rocks will likely bring the vehicle to a very abrupt halt and be likely to damage components as well. Land Rover products' robustness and resistance to 'battle damage' should be regarded as accident insurance, not

When forced onto limiting rocks for short distances use a marshaller and 1st gear low range. See also photo at Section 2.4.

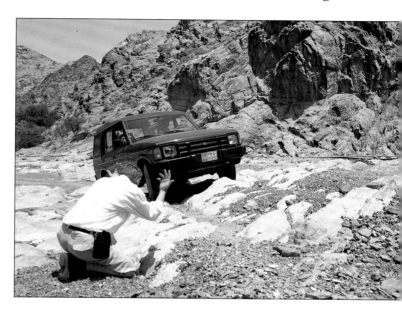

part of deliberate everyday driving. Take every precaution to ensure you do not run the vehicle into contact with heavy stones or rocks.

Tyres. Tyres too are potentially very vulnerable to damage on rocky ground – especially the sidewalls of radial-ply tyres – but this and overall operating costs can be reduced by attention to:

1. Inflation. Be sure the tyres are fully inflated to road pressures before traversing rocky going – even if this means re-inflation after deflating for previous soft ground.

2. Sidewall awareness. The most vulnerable parts of a tyre on rocks are the sidewalls. The best on/off-road tyres are radials but these, with their thinner, flexible sidewalls, are particularly prone to 'bacon-slicer' damage – so-called because the action of the tyre sidewall against an intrusive sharp rock. Develop 'sidewall awareness' when driving over rocks.

3. Cross-ply tyres. Where operations are almost exclusively off-road on rock or stone – such as fleet operations in quarries – the more damage-resistant qualities (at full inflation pressures) of cross-ply tyres could help keep operating costs down. It is essential, however, to consider and accommodate the following criteria:

a. Virtually all 7.50 x 16 cross-plies are 'L' speed rated (see table Section 8.2), ie limited to 125 kph (75 mph), so should not be fitted to high powered vehicles operating on-road.

b. Cross-ply tyres have higher rolling resistance so will slightly reduce fuel economy.

c. Cross-ply tyres have marginally less grip than radials so handling on-road would be affected.

Stony tracks and plains. Not all your rock/stone traverses will be over on-the-

limits boulders. Stony tracks or vast stony plains in the desert will be very much less hazardous. Well inflated tyres and an alertness for potential further hazards, however, will be important. As with corrugations (next spread) braking will be much less efficient on loose stones.

On-foot survey, marshalling. All the points mentioned so far point to the need for looking at a difficult rocky stretch or obstacle on foot and then being marshalled across by a helper. This will ensure – since the marshaller can see all eight sidewalls and the under-side of the vehicle and axles – that no damage is done.

Low range control. The relevance of low range and its ability to control the vehicle's forward motion steadily (rather than just make considerable power available) is nowhere more applicable than in traversing large rocks. First gear, low range, clutch fully-in, low engine speed will enable the vehicle to crawl steadily – without heaving, jerking or lurching – over the very worst rocky terrain.

Cross-ply tyres could lower costs in continuous rock/stone operations. BUT, note speed limitations.

Braking is far less effective on stony going.

On-the-limit rocky going demands 1st gear low range for control.

...continued

4.9. Rocks, stones, corrugations – contd

Palliative effect of the 'harmonic' speed applies <u>only</u> to transverse corrugations of the type shown opposite. Irregular obstacles like the boulders shown left can only be taken at a crawl – 1st gear low range – with the foot fully off the clutch and the centre diff lock disengaged. Steering feedback can be sharp, even with power assistance, so thumbs must be kept on and parallel to the rim of the steering wheel. With great care and the use of a marshaller, no damage should result.

Transverse corrugations on track demand a 'harmonic' speed to reduce the vibration on the vehicle.

Corrugations

'Harmonic' speed. A special manifestation of something between stony going and rough or unsurfaced tracks is the phenomenon of transverse corrugations across graded earth, sand or gravel tracks – regular, wave-form undulations that can stretch for tens of kilometres in front of you on remote area routes. The corrugations, also called 'washboard' in America, have a peak-to-peak distance of 0.5 to 1 metre and can be as much as 20 cm deep. They are formed by the action (and harmonics) of the suspension and tyres of the track's major-user vehicles on the soil. This latter is an important point since the technique to adopt when driving over them involves using the natural harmonics of your own vehicle's suspension to minimise the apparent roughness of the ride. There will be a speed of driving – usually between about 40 and 60 kph (25–35 mph) in Land Rover products –

where the effect of the corrugations *on the vehicle body* will be minimised. The italics are used as a reminder that the suspension and un-sprung parts such as the axles are undergoing a rare form of torture over such ground, even though the body and passengers may be (relatively) more comfortable.

Reduced brake effectiveness. An indication of the ordeal of the unsprung components will be clear when enduring the acceleration to these speeds and when decelerating from them. (If you still have

The 'harmonic' speed reduces body shake to just-bearable limits but still tortures unsprung components like axles.

Range Rover travelling at 'harmonic' speed on moderate corrugations (below) reduces jarring on body though suspension still suffers. Remember dramatically reduced steering and brake effectiveness. Travel on such tracks is invariably accompanied by thick dust clouds (below left).

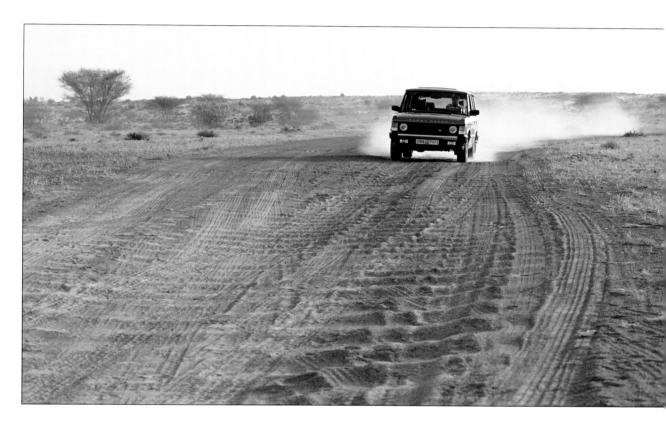

any doubts about what the suspension is going through, look out of the driver's window at the front axle.) It is vital to remember also that, since the wheels are virtually jumping from the crest of one corrugation to the next, they are in touch with the ground for a fraction of the time they would normally be. *Steering and particularly braking effectiveness will be dramatically reduced* when going rapidly on corrugated tracks. Driving a Land Rover on a track where the corrugations were formed by, say, a four-ton truck will be especially unpleasant since the suspension harmonics of the truck will not match those of your Land Rover and there will be no 'magic speed' where the ride appears to smooth out.

Dramatic reductions in braking and steering effectiveness take place when driving on corrugated tracks.

4.10. Wading

Preparations

Think ahead. Think of wading as a wet, blind and usually cold manifestation of every other type of obstacle and hazard you may come across. This is not meant as an unduly gloomy warning so much as a reminder that the same kind of potential problems can lurk beneath the water as you may see on dry land and that advance knowledge of them is no less important.

The same obstacles can lurk – unseen – under the water as on dry land. Plan, and recce, ahead.

Wading plugs. Other advance knowledge it will pay to acquire well before you get anywhere near a wading situation is the location of the vehicle's wading plugs and how to put them in. All Land Rover products are provided with drain holes in the clutch housing between the engine and gearbox and also (where such a belt is fitted) at the bottom of the camshaft belt drive housing at the front of the engine beneath the fan. These holes are a safety feature to ensure that, in the event of an oil leak in these regions, the oil can drain away and not get onto the clutch or

Always fit the wading plugs. Make the plugs, a 13 mm spanner and a groundsheet part of your standard kit.

cam drive belt. In case of deep wading, however, these holes must first be blocked off by the insertion of screw-in wading plugs. It is convenient to keep these plugs (available from Land Rover dealers) and the appropriate 13 mm (or 1/2" AF) spanner handy within the vehicle. It is important that the plugs be removed after wading – not necessarily at once but within a few days. If a vehicle is used for regular wading the plugs should be removed, checked for oil leakage and replaced every week or two. The new

Always walk the stream before commit-ting the vehicle – above, and Section 3.4.Wading plugs (left) are fitted in clutch housing (photo opposite, right – location above and ahead of chassis cross member) and, if applicable, in the bottom of the cam drive-belt housing (opposite, left – location ahead of the sump; above, and slightly aft of front axle casing).

R380 manual gearbox leaves the factory with wading plug already fitted; it should be removed periodically to check for pos-sible oil leakage or it may be removed and refitted only for wading as above.

Walking the course. Water obstacles, large or small, should always (as men-tioned at Section 3.4, 'Look before you leap') be examined first. Rubber boots and a long stick are the extras required for an on-foot survey before committing a vehi-cle. Generally, stagnant water is more likely to be a hazard than a river or a stream as flowing water tends to prevent a build-up of silt. The silt in a stagnant pool or mud hollow can be several feet deep and very soft. Ensuring that the bot-tom of the pool or stream is firm enough along all of your proposed traverse is essential and it will inevitably take some time to do thoroughly. Markers may be necessary (such as sticks) to be sure the vehicle follows the route you have proved on foot.

Always walk through first with a stick. Better to get wet legs than have your vehicle stuck in an underwater hol-low.

...continued

The Land Rover Experience

4.10. Wading – contd

Limitations
Wading limitations, how to proceed.

The maximum advisable wading depth for Land Rover products is 0.5 metre – about 5-6 cm (a thumb length) below the top of the wheel rim or, perhaps more memorably, 5-6 cm higher than the top of the average rubber boot. Note the implications of this – your brakes will be completely immersed in water but the radiator cooling fan will be clear and so will the exhaust pipe exit – just. Land Rover customers all over the world frequently travel through water where the depth exceeds 0.5 metres. In these conditions the following precautions are advisable:

1. Gear and speed. Low range with a gear appropriate to the amount of power and control over rocks required. Keep enough rpm to preclude water entering the exhaust pipe if it is submerged. Speed in general should be low but fast enough to keep a small bow-wave ahead of the bumper and thus reduce the height of the water behind the bumper, so keeping water away from the fan. In practice, low range 2nd gear is usually about right.

2. Keeping the ignition dry. If you are using a petrol engine equipped vehicle it is important to keep the ignition dry. The right bow-wave will help. A sheet of plastic lowered in front of the radiator will stop water cascading straight through and onto the fan, reducing the chance of spray over the electrics; it will also prevent liquid mud from blocking the radiator matrix. Additionally an old coat, blanket, sack or other heavy fabric can be draped over the engine behind the fan to keep the harness dry; remember, however, this can be a fire hazard so keep it well clear of the exhaust manifold. *Do not remove the fan belt* as this will stop the water pump and damage the engine.

Normal wading depth limit 0.5 m – just below the top of the wheel rim.

Not too fast, not too slow – fast enough for a small constant-height bow wave. Probably 2nd low.

It is VITAL not to let water near the engine air intake – through splash or any other cause.

The normal wading depth limit of 0.5 m runs just beneath the top of the wheel rim, just above the door shut line and about equal to exhaust height.

3. Essential – keep engine air intake clear of water. Major damage to engines can result if even small amounts of water get past the air filter and into the cylinders. Never risk this happening. Choose another route where the water depth is less. You may have seen pictures of Land Rover vehicles taking part in the Camel Trophy almost submerged in water but these vehicles will have been specially modified with raised, roof-level air intakes for the engine.

After wading. It is essential to dry your brakes after wading, especially if your vehicle has drum brakes. Whilst still in low range, drive a short distance applying the brakes lightly; this will squeegee the discs or linings dry. Remove any plastic sheeting or other engine protection used for the operation. The wading plugs need not be removed immediately if further wading is envisaged – but see previous spread about regular use. Remember the handbrake too will be wet.

Oil contamination. If you regularly undertake wading be aware of the risk of water contamination in the vehicle lubricating oil. This will manifest itself as emulsified oil, easily identified because of its milky appearance. A hot axle case or

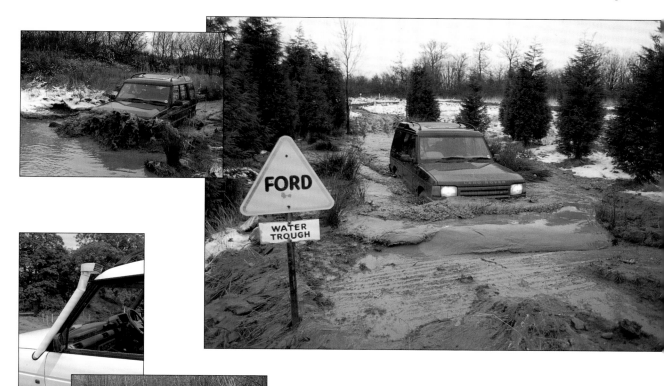

Bow-wave – too much upper left, optimum above – produces dip aft of bumper, keeps water away from fan. Raised air intake permits deeper wading for diesels. Pre-attached tow rope useful precaution. Select air suspension on Range Rovers to high profile.

gearbox plunged into a cold stream for any time will cool suddenly, tending to suck water in through oil seals or breathers. All Land Rover vehicles now have carefully designed remote breathers (long black nylon pipes that vent the transmission casings high in the engine compartment) but periodic checks are still advisable.

Getting stuck, recovery and precautions. Covered fully under Section 5, recovery principles remain the same but are complicated by the lower part of the vehicle being under water. Anticipation is the key – such as pre-attachment of a tow rope (or pre-extension of the winch line) so that you do not have to grope with the problem under water.

Squeegee the brakes dry after wading – 20 m or so, low range, against light brake.

Pre-attach tow rope and coil it on bonnet if there is a risk of needing a tow.

4.11. Ice and snow

More traction, same brakes

4x4, 4x2 differences. Most readers of this book will have experience of driving on snow and ice in ordinary cars. Indeed many will have bought a Land Rover product partly because it will give them more reliable transport in wintry conditions. Though traction in snow is best in temperatures below -20° to -30°C and less good between -20°C and freezing point, the basic principles of being very gentle

4x4s are better than 4x2s on snow and ice for traction – but remember your braking is very similar.

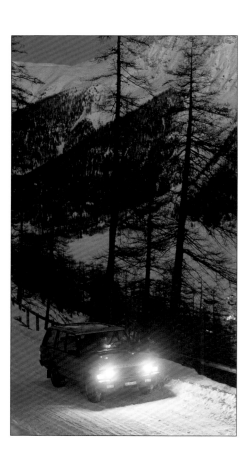

ABS will give the best possible braking under the prevailing conditions – but cannot change packed snow into dry tarmac.

with both the throttle and the brakes will apply in just the same way on a 4x4 so it is well to establish first just what the differences are between the two types of vehicle:

1. Double the traction.... As we have seen, the 4x4 has double the traction. In snow and ice conditions this should be regarded not as a means of putting twice as much power on the road but as a means of putting the same power on the road spread between twice as many wheels. This asks less of the surface in terms of grip and so you are less likely to get spinning wheels.

2. ...but the same braking. What is often forgotten in the feeling of confidence that a 4x4's tractive performance in snow generates is that the method of stopping is the same as that of any normal car – four wheels on the ground, each one's rotation retarded by brakes. Indeed, 4x4s are generally a lot heavier than normal cars and have a correspondingly increased amount of kinetic energy to arrest. Beware, therefore, of letting your feeling of invincibility extend to the braking department when you are on snow or ice.

3. ABS – very good, but not magic. ABS anti-lock braking will give you *the best braking possible under the circumstances* but will not reverse the laws of physics. Land Rover's ABS system is one of the best and most versatile there is and it will eliminate the human error of locking the wheels; it will yield the maximum retardation possible from given surface conditions – as well as enormously improving directional control – but it will not turn ice into dry tarmac. The surface conditions are still the limiting factor.

Gentle right foot – again

Driving technique. The driving techniques employed for snow and ice are generally similar to those used for mud or wet grass.

1. High gear. Select the highest gear possible for the conditions. ('D' in Auto.)

2. Diff lock. Engage the centre differential lock (if manually selected) – and disengage it as soon as non-icy ground is reached.

3. Throttle, brake, steering. Use minimum throttle opening when driving away and accelerating, even if electronic traction control (ETC) is fitted; avoid violent movements of the steering wheel. Drive slowly and brake with great caution to avoid locking the wheels. Cadence braking will help (see Sections 3.2 and Glossary at Section 10.1).

....contd

The same principles apply as for slippery slopes – highest gear possible, gentle and sensitive use of brakes, throttle and steering.

When you have to get through – or even when it would just be convenient – a good 4x4 is only half the battle; the other half is a sensitive driver.

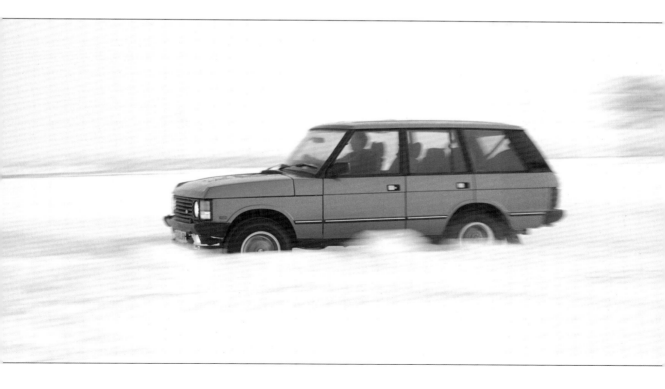

4.11. Ice and snow – contd

What lies under the snow? If you are the first out, it will just be road.

Snowfall on top of compressed snow will be very slippery. A classic case for diff lock in high box.

As a 'first on the road' vehicle hub-high snow is no problem. Deeper than that and with small drifts, use momentum laced with discretion.

Carry a long tow-rope, shovels, gum boots to low-box others out of ditches and be on your way.

Gentle right foot – contd
What lies beneath. As with sand, there are, of course, a dozen combinations of criteria affecting snow and ice – mainly concerned with what lies beneath the present surface of the snow. These will extend or reduce the limits of traction of your vehicle; they cannot be quantified in any book but acquire new relevance in the light of a large-wheeled 4x4:

1. First on the road? If, as if often the case, you and your Land Rover are first on the road after the first snow on untreated roads, this is the best traction you will get in snow. Bold and/or sharp treaded M+S tyres will cut through the soft snow either to the ground beneath or will make the first compressed snow 'rails' for you to travel on. These are as grippy as they will ever be. Conditions get worse from now on.

2. Second or later? When others have been on the roads first, their compressed tracks will make slippery going and, as you will have done many times, driving out of the previous tracks will get fractionally more traction. As before, 4x4 will give more traction but no improvement, *per se*, in braking. On long descents or hairpin bends stay in a low gear.

3. Subsequent snowfalls. Snowfall on top of previous compressed tracks which may in places have slicked-over into streaks of pure ice is another well enough known phenomenon in which a large-wheeled and heavy 4x4, delicately driven, will prove its worth in obtaining traction. Braking will be fractionally better than a car by reason of the tyre treads but only as long as it is done gently. Again, if you have no ABS, cadence braking (see Section 3.2 and Glossary) will pay dividends and the big wheels' ability to steer

through and towards snow having no underlying ice will prove an advantage.

Auto transmission, traction control. Land Rover vehicles fitted with automatic transmission, electronic traction control (ETC) and ABS will be at an advantage in wintry conditions but these aids to gentler traction enhance the 'gentle right foot' driving philosophy; the don't replace it.

Snowdrifts. A Land Rover's big wheels, locked centre diff and appropriate tyres driven on all four wheels are ingredients for charging snowdrifts and getting through. Or they can be ingredients for getting it wrong and finishing up sitting on top of a vehicle's length of compressed snow and having to dig the snow out from under the vehicle. Do not be too ambitious with what you attempt to barge through. Anything above hub depth is starting to get marginal for sustained travel; individual small drifts deeper than this can often be successfully tackled. As ever, the low box, probably in 2nd or 3rd (with diff lock), will be the appropriate weapon.

Helping yourself and others. Other traffic and those inappropriately equipped having got into trouble will all too frequently be the cause, in winter conditions, of your not getting through to your destination despite your having, without them, the capability to do so. To free them and yourself from delays, carrying a long tow rope, shovels, gumboots, gloves and some kind of under-wheel

Off-road snow demands careful sounding – on foot with a stick. On road, with the right tyres, hub-high snow will present little difficulty. On front wheels use only Land Rover approved snow chains.

traction aid (Section 5.1, 'Self-recovery') will help reduce everyone's problems. Pulling a car from a ditch with this equipment and careful use of the low range and throttle takes only minutes – see Section 5.2, 'Recovery – towing out'.

Tyres and tyre pressures. As mentioned already, each type of terrain has an optimum tyre type and whilst your Land Rover can cover a wide variety of terrain, a single set of tyres for such a spread will limit your capability in one or more medium. In general, a mud or M+S (mud and snow) kind of tyre – they will have quite a bold, sharp-edged tread – will be best for use in snow. Use normal road tyre pressures. Details: Section 8.2 – 'Tyres'.

Snow chains. If you do not have a full set of four snow chains fit the first pair to the front wheels since this will give you grip as well as steering in slippery conditions. To some extent it will also prepare a path for the back wheels. Since a 4x4 has four driven wheels a second set of chains will be beneficial. If using front snow

chains off road there is a danger, with certain types of chain, that full axle articulation and full steering lock at the same time could enable the chains to damage the front brake pipes. A new type of chain, more easy to attach, is now available as an approved Land Rover accessory which obviates this danger (Land Rover part numbers RTC9590 for 7.50 x 16 tyres and RTC9589 for 205 x 16 and 6.50 x 16 tyres). Check with your dealer 235/70 x 16 tyres. Also Section 5.1, 'Self-recovery'.

Snow off-road. As there is not a smooth potentially slippery surface beneath it, snow off-road is easier to cope with than snow on tarmac carriageways. A moment's thought, however, highlights the dangers of minor drifting of the snow covering potentially destructive obstacles such as small rock outcrops or gullies on hillsides. The situation is similar to fording streams in that the dangers are hidden; the solution is the same – an on-foot inspection and prodding with a stick in doubtful areas.

Tyres with bold sharp tread patterns are best. Fit only the latest Land Rover approved snow chains.

Off-road snow is generally easier - but probe for hidden obstacles like rocks or ditches.

Section 5

Recovery

5.1. Self-recovery

Traction aids

The calm approach. Having got 'stuck', self-recovery is the art of remedying the situation without the need to call upon outside assistance. The brutal truth is that in most cases getting stuck is a function of driver error – misreading the ground or the obstacle, or not accurately knowing the limitations of your vehicle. Whilst we all try our best with these things and all gradually get better, equally certain is the fact that we all occasionally make mistakes. Admitting this is at least half the battle for it enables you to go about the remedial action in the right spirit – philosophically cheerful acceptance of a minor challenge rather than agitation, embarrassment, bluster or the suspicion that life has just dealt you the ultimate humiliation!

Everyone gets bogged occasionally. Do not take it as a personal slight!

Knowing the problems. It helps to know what problems may be ahead. The categories in which you may find yourself stuck are shown below. Knowing this helps you see the problems coming and avoid them.

Wheels spinning – two causes.. A given amount of power plus a combination of not enough grip and not enough weight on a wheel can cause it to spin. In these circumstances ETC (Electronic Traction Control – see Section 10.1, Glossary), if fitted, will brake the spinning rear wheel automatically. Without ETC, in the case of not enough weight on the wheel (the axle may be at an angle to the chassis and the lower wheel is spinning) see under Articulation on the next spread. If grip is the problem in a static re-start case, first try a higher gear and a very gentle throttle.

If you've missed the chance to reverse out, admit it, smile and go on to the next stage ....

More grip. If that fails, inserting some gripping medium between the wheel and the ground is the solution – stones, brushwood, mats, baulks of timber or items designed especially for the purpose: sand ladders, metal planking and recovery channels. Beware (see sub para 2 below) of anything that can flick up beneath the vehicle and cause damage.

1. Sand ladders can of course be used in any medium – sand, mud, snow – and are specially made aluminium ladders about 1.5 metres long, 35 cm wide and with rungs about 15 cm apart (gripping edges outermost). They are thrust under the front – or rear – of the wheels (if necessary scooping out earth or sand to get them farther in) and the vehicle will find grip on the ladders and haul itself out. If necessary, the ladders are moved round to the front (or rear) of the vehicle a second, third or fourth time to provide further traction in the direction of travel. Sand ladders of the right type – side members 6-7 cm deep – can be used for minor bridging of ditches.

2. Steel planking (PSP – the perforated lengths of interlocking steel planking originally made for WW2 bush airfields) is used in the same way as sand ladders. PSP is heavier and more difficult to use than aluminium sand ladders; it is too flexible to be used for bridging (and can bend upward to snag the underside of the vehicle) but is excellent for laying over logs or branches to provide a vehicle trackway. Despite the contradiction in terms, PSP is sometimes available in aluminium.

3. Recovery channels. These combine the best aspects of sand ladders with a third of the bulk. They are in effect a pair of purpose-built aluminium alloy grip panels 1.5 metres by 35 cm, each cut into three equal lengths and joined with nylon rope – large photo opposite. The articulation afforded by the rope links makes them easier to push in front of the wheels without – as is the case with ladders or PSP – the danger of the remainder of the unit fouling the vehicle chassis. Best of all, when you have finished with them, the

...the next stage is digging and the use of something to put under the wheels.

The same principles apply to use of traction aids in mud or dry sand. Use them before the situation gets too bad and dig sufficient space for them to work first time.

three sections can be folded up, bagged and stowed within the vehicle. (At present these items are only made and available from Barong, F.92370 Chaville, France.)

Flotation – sinking in soft ground. Although technically there is a difference between a lack of traction and a lack of flotation, in practice the two usually strike together and a joint solution – use of reduced tyre pressures (see Section 8.2, 'Tyres') and/or load spreaders such as sand ladders etc mentioned above – will be the answer. If no load spreaders are carried, branches or brushwood should be used. If sinkage is considerable so that the vehicle is hung up (see next page) digging to remove the obstacle or jacking to permit the channels to be put under the wheels will be necessary.

Use shovels early to save a wheel-spinning bogging getting worse. Invest an extra few minutes' digging and get out first time.

Always dig away in front of a wheel before inserting the sand tracks. This helps ensure first-time extraction.

...continued

5.1. Self-recovery – contd

Use a marshaller to prevent this. Digging the ground away from under a vehicle hung-up on the chassis provides good motivation for not letting it happen again.

Avoid under belly hang-up on ridges and rocks – can be damaging. Recovery awkward, time consuming.

Digging, recovery tools
Under-vehicle obstacles – hung-up on ridges or rocks. Least forgivable of driver-inflicted situations (especially if you have a passenger with you who could have got out and marshalled you over the obstacle), getting the chassis hung up on ridges or rocks is also potentially the most damaging. The price will be paid, however, since the only way out of this predicament unless you have a high-lift bumper jack (see 'Recovery tools' below and diagram/photo opposite), is actually to dig the obstacle away from under the vehicle with a shovel. It will be difficult using the shovel at full arm's length under the vehicle and in addition the vehicle will be tending initially to collapse down onto the shovel as it is used. Knowing what is involved and having the patience to do it slowly but surely will unfailingly get you out of this situation. If it is immovable rock and you are hung up with the centre of the chassis on it the situation is more serious but jacking front or rear to put packing under the wheels will achieve a recovery just as reliably.

Exceeding articulation limits is a common way of becoming immobilised. Dig under the 'high' wheels or pack under the 'low' ones.

Articulation – diagonal wheels in the air. As we have seen (Section 4.3, 'Ridges and ditches') it is possible to get a vehicle immobilised by misjudging the amount of axle articulation involved in crossing a ridge or ditch diagonally. (An axle is on full articulation when one wheel is pushed up into the wheel arch as far as it will go and the other wheel is hanging down as far as it will go.) A very common manifestation is 'the diagonal tightrope' in which, say, the rear offside wheel and front nearside wheel are both on full bump and the complementary wheels are hanging down – with the axle differentials permitting the hanging-down wheels to spin when you apply power (see photos Sec 4.3). This situation will stop you

For planned off-roading, carry a full self-recovery kit.

but has a very straightforward solution – either pack up beneath the spinning wheels or dig away beneath the full bump wheels. It is difficult to get earth packed in tightly enough under the hanging wheels (though inserting a sand ladder, levering up and packing with rocks can work) so almost invariably digging under the hung-up wheels is the solution. As with the case above, the vehicle is trying to collapse on your shovel as you dig but, again, patience will invariably win the day.

Recovery tools. If you are planning a journey in which off-roading and the risk of getting stuck exists (see also Sec 7.4), the following equipment is worth taking:
Rubber boots, gloves, overalls.
Electric tyre pump for re-inflation of tyres.
Two shovels (pointed blades, not square ends like spades).
Two tow ropes (totalling 25 metres) and appropriate end fittings.
Articulated sand channels or sand ladders – see previous page.
Hi-lift jack – if appropriate to the vehicle (see below).
Wood block about 30 x 20 x 5 cm to prevent jack sinkage.

Hi-lift jack is a valuable recovery tool but must be used with strict adherence to safety instructions – including use of diff lock. Bottle-jack with shovel and timber baulks can be used in similar fashion on wheel or hub. Use wood 'cushion' on alloy wheel rims.

Hi-lift jack can be used to raise a vehicle out of deep ruts and 'lateral pole-vault' it onto easier ground.

Hi-lift jack. As the sketch shows, the hi-lift jack is a mechanical bumper jack capable of a lift of a metre or more. A Defender, for instance, that has been run into deep ruts and is unable to get out could have the front end physically lifted out of the ruts and, by then pushing the jack over sideways, could be 'pole-vaulted' onto more suitable ground. Equally, the front end could also be lifted to insert ladders or branches under the wheels. Hi-lift jacks are very effective in operation – one can also be converted into a hand winch – but are very heavy and awkward to carry; additionally, as bumper jacks they require the square section of the Defender bumper and are not suitable to use on a Range Rover or Discovery – unless special bumper modifications are done. If you have an operating spectrum in which a hi-lift jack would be a useful recovery tool, it would be worth making modifications to enable it to be carried in a rack and used on appropriate sockets on the vehicle.

Hi-lift jack – safety. Pay special attention to safety when using a hi-lift jack. As a 'mono-pod' it is inherently unstable and hand-brake, diff-lock and wheel chocks should be used to prevent the vehicle rolling forward or back. *Do not leave the jack unless the operating handle is in the vertical position.*

Winch. Unless required for operating in particular conditions, a winch is expensive and heavy to have as a 'just-in-case' recovery aid. When trying to co-ordinate it with power from driven wheels it is slow in operation, but provided there is something to winch onto – it can work wonders in certain self-recovery situations. See Section 5.4.

Hi-lift jack versatile, effective, needs care in use – plus brake, diff-lock, chocks.

5.2. Towing-out

Ropes and attachments
Second-vehicle safety; long ropes.
Where conditions are likely to be close to the limits of your Land Rover's capabilities, you are strongly advised not to go off-roading without a second vehicle. As this and the next spread will show, the potential for recovery where one vehicle is able to help another is a considerable improvement on the situation of a solo vehicle trying self-recovery. Firstly, always use a long towing rope – better still a combination of two that make up a long rope. That way the towing vehicle will not be in the same bog or soft sand that has stopped the first one. As with any rope, do not let it tangle round axles.

Tow rope attachment – vehicle. Tow rope attachment to the towing vehicle should naturally be at the towing hitch if one is fitted. This uses the longitudinal chassis members and the rear cross member to provide a load-spreading attachment point. At the front and rear of all Land Rover vehicles, beneath the chassis, lashing points are fitted (two front and two rear), principally for securing vehicles on trailers. If a tow hitch is not fitted these can be used (as pairs, not singly) for towing. Better still, and designed to cope with far higher loads, extra-strong lashing/towing rings (Land Rover part no RRC3237) can be fitted in lieu of the normal lashing rings at the same chassis points (lower left photo opposite).

Bridle and two attachment points.
The standard lashing points are designed for loads less than maximum towing loads but can be used for normal recovery towing (not snatch towing – see next section) if *both* eyes are used with a long bridle – a rope attached to both lashing eyes and joined to the main tow rope two or

Attached at mid point, tow rope will bend a weak bumper, drawing chassis members together. Move rope close to bumper attachment points.

Too short a towing bridle will have same effect – also putting extreme strain on bridle rope.

Make towing bridle about 2 m long – spreads load without any 'pinching' component.

three metres away of the vehicle. (Do not make this bridle less than two metres in length and do make it of a rope to each lashing ring rather than a single loop through both rings. This way you will minimise rope tension and also eliminate any tendency to draw the chassis members together – see diagram.) Never put a tow rope round a bumper since this will lead to the rope being cut by the bumper's sharp edge. Nor should a rope be put

U-bolt and pin is reliable, repeatable way of attaching ropes (top). Standard tow hitch cleared for 3500 kg (upper right). If not fitted, use long bridle on lashing eyes or RRC3237 shackles (above and right).

round an axle since this involves the virtual certainty of damaging brake pipes.

Tow rope ends. Ensuring that your tow ropes have properly prepared ends is a very worthwhile precaution. Few things can add so effectively to the problems of having to extract a bogged vehicle than finding that tow ropes have to be knotted round tow points and then need a marlin spike in order to undo the knot afterwards. Spliced-in metal eyes and the use of U-bolts and shackle pins on properly prepared ropes makes the exercise extremely simple and quick. If you do not have a tow hitch at both ends of the vehicle, prepare a suitable length of rope with U-bolts at each end to pick up on the chassis lashing eyes and act as a two metre bridle onto which the main tow-rope can be attached. The main tow rope should be similarly prepared for your particular vehicle.

Ideally don't use bumpers for towing; most bumpers cut tow ropes. In emergency pad with sacking, move rope close to attachment bolts.

...continued

The Land Rover Experience

5.2. Towing-out – contd

Co-ordinated recovery

Meaning, procedure. A co-ordinated recovery is one in which the power and traction of both vehicles – even though one of them, being stuck, has a limited capability – are used together at the moment when the tow is undertaken. This is a commonsense point but all too often, in the stress of a vehicle becoming bogged, the point is forgotten and spinning wheels and slack, then jerking tow-ropes become the ingredients of minor confusion. A helpful sequence aide-memoir for a normal assisted recovery would be as follows:

1. Marshaller, co-ordinator. Ingredients of a co-ordinated recovery: one stuck vehicle, one recovery (towing) vehicle, appropriate – long – tow ropes, two drivers and a third person to act as marshaller and co-ordinator.

2. Take your time. If the stuck vehicle is hung up on an obstacle invest ten minutes spade work to ensure the first extraction attempt is the one that works. Even if there is no digging, still take your time.

3. Backwards best? Towing out backwards is sometimes a more reliable option. At least the stuck vehicle has wheel tracks leading to its present position. In this case, with the vehicles back-to-back during recovery, a second marshaller standing in 'front' of the stuck vehicle is useful to keep that driver in the picture by relaying the hand signals of the principal marshaller ahead of the tug. As with reversing back down a hill (Section 4.4), the driver of the stuck vehicle should keep both hands on the steering wheel to preclude steering 'runaway' in reverse.

4. Towing vehicle clear. Position the towing vehicle so that it is well clear of the conditions that bogged the first vehicle (a long rope is almost invariably more use than a short one for this reason), attach the rope to both vehicles, position the third person so that both drivers can easily see him and have him marshal the tug forward until the rope is tight.

5. Visual signals, simultaneous clutches. Decide on the gear to be used – not necessarily 1st low range; 2nd could well be better – have both vehicles start engines, engage gear and wait for the signal from the marshaller for both drivers to engage the clutch. As with all marshalling, (Section 3.4 'Marshalling') this should be a visual not a spoken signal: a raised arm to instruct both drivers to be ready and in gear, raised arm describing small circles to instruct them to rev the engines, then drop the raised arm to instruct them to engage the clutches.

6. Marshaller in control. The marshaller should move backwards as the vehicles move towards him, still controlling the operation and being ready to give an immediate STOP signal if he sees any problems. He is the only one who can properly judge how the recovery is going. He too can judge when it is done; he can signal the lead vehicle to stop and the now mobile towed one to come forward slightly to slacken off the rope before disconnecting.

Safety – the danger of breaking ropes. A tow rope breaking whilst under

Use a long tow rope and a marshaller to control the operation. Take your time.

Marshaller should use only visual signals, not voice, to co-ordinate both vehicles' power.

WARNING. When tow starts, NO-ONE should be anywhere near the tow rope.

If stuck vehicle is heavy or badly mired a tandem-tow, carefully co-ordinated, will usually achieve first-time results.

A third-man marshaller is invaluable (right) to ensure clutches of both vehicles are engaged at the same time. A fourth, 'relay', marshaller (left) is useful in a reverse tow.

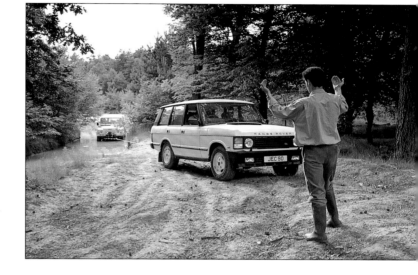

strain can be lethal or inflict serious injury. No bystanders or crew should be allowed near a tow rope during the actual tow. Four to five metres is usually a safe distance but the danger area varies with the length of rope and the techniques used – see next spread, 'Snatch towing'. A breaking rope recoils with whiplash violence. Adequately strong tow ropes are essential as well as rigidly enforced safety procedures in their use.

Pull required. As a guide, the pull required to move a vehicle (as a proportion of its total weight – ie including payload) assuming level ground, is given below:

Hard metalled road – about 5% of total vehicle weight.

Grass – about 15%.

Hard wet sand, gravel, soft wet sand – about 15-20%.

Sand – soft, dry, loose – about 25-30%.

Shallow mud – about 33%.

Bog, marsh, clinging clay – about 50%.

Rule-of-thumb. It makes sense that the rope to keep in the back of your Land Rover is the worst-case rope – the one for marsh/bog/clay. Allowing a safety margin to account for unseen damage to the rope and other exigencies it should have a quoted breaking strain about equal to the laden weight of your vehicle. For example, a 14 mm 3-strand polypropylene rope has a breaking strain – when new and undamaged – of 2.79 tonnes (quoted breaking strains are governed by British Standards in the UK) which would be an appropriate minimum for all except a laden Defender 110 or 130. For details of laden weights of all Land Rover products see Section 9, 'Technical Data'.

Use a tow rope with a breaking strain about equal to the weight of the vehicle.

WARNING. Breaking tow ropes can be lethal. Regularly inspect for damage. Keep bystanders away.

The Land Rover Experience

5.3. Snatch towing

WARNING. Snatch towing can involve very high forces and is a potentially dangerous procedure. Use only the fixtures and ropes of the kind specified below with methods to ensure loads in the rope and towing fixtures do not exceed 3.4 tonnes – a figure allowing essential safety factors. Ropes, towing fixtures and their attachment areas on the vehicles must be in sound mechanical condition without rust or physical damage. Only the procedure outlined on these pages can be recommended; use it only for vehicle recovery, not on static objects such as tree stumps.

Small, strictly limited, amount of momentum can help recover stuck vehicle.

Vital criteria

Using 'stretch' energy and momentum. Stretching an elastic rope is a means of storing energy. Using vehicle acceleration and then momentum – two different entities here – to effect that stretch is a means of achieving a higher towing pull to recover a bogged-down vehicle than would be achieved by traction alone. The momentum (or more accurately the Kinetic Energy or KE) is stored in the rope and added to the vehicle's tractive effort.

Two types of force. Total pull on the rope derives from:

1. Traction. Traction between the ground and the wheels of the towing vehicle - theoretical maximum around 1.73 tonnes on dry concrete (Defender 90, Tdi, 205 x 16 tyres, 2nd gear low ratio).

2. Kinetic energy. Any KE the towing vehicle has at the time the rope goes taut.

The concept of operation outlined here is that *the sum of 1. and 2. above must never exceed 3.4 tonnes.* If traction is good, KE must be limited; if the towing vehicle is on mud, KE can be allowed to rise to keep the sum at 3.4 tonnes.

Why 3.4 tonnes? This is the factored maximum load, in snatch towing conditions, to be applied to a pair 'JATE rings' part no RRC3237 (see below).

NEVER exceed permitted 'step-back'. Table shows examples. Towing attachments MUST be in first class condition.

Main picture shows correct 'JATE-ring' attachment and safety lanyard. Far right, result of towing fixture tearing out of rusted chassis. Complete tow hook and pintle recoiled through front and rear windscreens of the stuck vehicle. Miraculously there were no injuries.

Special ropes only. ONLY nylon ropes or straps specifically designed for this procedure should be used – with the manufacturer's recommendations. Snatch towing with chain, steel or other inextensible rope will result in major structural damage to both vehicles involved due to shock loading.

Inherent danger. The potential dangers of snatch towing cannot be over-emphasised. Although widely practiced on an ad hoc basis, few operators are aware of just how high are the forces involved. Some currently practiced procedures incur tensions in excess of 13 tonnes – enough to tear out towing attachments with explosive force and lethal potential – see photo opposite. This, not rope breakage, is the main hazard.

Essential criteria. Consider:
Specification of rope used.
Weight of towing vehicle.
Speed of towing vehicle.
Strength of towing attachments.
Note that the weight of the vehicle being towed is immaterial. Whatever is stuck may be stuck fast – whatever its weight – so the rope and procedure has to cope with an 'immovable' load.

Twin rope attachment points. Use a bridle on both vehicles plus safety lanyards (from the eye of the rope) attached respectively to the front and rear trailer hitches – see photo. The safety lanyard will restrain any hardware coming lose.

Attachment points. These should only be military specification Land Rover towing shackles ('JATE rings': part number RRC3237) – on both vehicles.

Rope specification. Use only ropes developed specifically for snatch or kinetic energy recovery. The table below refers to a one-off test on a rope of the following specification:

Identification: Yellow colour (polyurethane coating) with marker yarn.

Construction: 24 mm diameter, multiplait nylon.

<u>Ultimate</u> *breaking strain* : 12 tonnes.

Length: 8 metres with formed, sheathed end eyes and 20 mm safety lanyards.

Attachment bridles: 6 metre yellow 18 tonne roundslings supplied.

Weight and speed of towing vehicle. The particular rope above would be suitable for all Land Rover products from an unladen Defender 90 (1645 kg) to a laden Defender 130 acting as towing vehicle but speed at the point of snatch – here catered for by the amount of 'step-back' from the taut rope condition – must be lower for the heavier vehicle.

Procedure – keep people clear

1. Attach ropes and safety lanyards as above. Drive towing vehicle (tug) slowly forward until rope is taut. As with normal towing, keep people clear of rope.

2. 'Step back'. Reverse tug an appropriate distance to avoid exceeding 3.4 tonnes load – see examples below.

3. Using (only) 2nd gear, low range, accelerate hard to extract stuck vehicle.

4. If stuck vehicle does not move, do not exceed a rope stretch beyond normal length (on the rope specified here) of 22% - about two paces on the ground with this rope. This stretch represents 3.4 tonnes pull – a useful cross-check.

Life of the rope, storage, care. A nylon KE rope has a finite fatigue life depending on the load to which it is subjected. It must be kept clean, free from grit and sand or other sources of abrasion and must not be stored in direct sunlight. Store dry, in a breathable canvas bag.

ONLY specifically designed snatch-tow ropes should be used for this purpose - using manufacturer's load criteria. These ropes are not widely available. Do not be tempted to improvise.

Keep nylon snatch-tow ropes clean, dry, out of sunlight. They have a fatigue life dependent on load.

Maximum 'step-back' from taut 8 metre rope (specified above) to not exceed 3.4 tonnes pull Assumes 2nd gear, low ratio, strong acceleration			
Vehicle type and load	Dry concrete	Dry grass	Wet grass/mud
1. Defender 90, unladen	<u>Zero</u> step-back. Rope sags 100 mm*	1.5 metres	2 metres
2. Defender 130, laden	Do not attempt. Will cause overload	1.8 metres	2.3 metres

Note: The tension achieved in the rope is extremely sensitive to the amount of 'step-back' combined with the type of traction surface you are operating on. It is essential that the safety limits inherent with the 3.4 tonne maximum pull are not infringed. Interpolate between values shown above both for vehicle weight and traction conditions.
* Only unladen Defender 90 (ie low mass vehicle) suited to dry concrete, strong acceleration case with this rope.

5.4. Winching

Capstan winch (above). Mechanical drive direct from crankshaft or power take-off shaft. Low geared, operates from idling engine. 20 mm Terylene or Polyester rope.
Drum winch (left). Electrical (or mechanical/hydraulic). Geared, HD electric motor, uses around 350 amps. 8–9.5 mm wire rope.

Concepts, winch types
Weighty decision; safety vital. The subject of winching cannot be covered fully in this section but a broad overview can be provided which will enable you to make your choice and get a feel for some of the principles of operation. Winching is comprehensively covered in a Land Rover Directory publication, 'Winching in Safety'. You are advised to read this book in detail before purchasing or operating a winch. Give careful thought to the implications of a winch before buying – it is more than an add-on accessory. In general winches are expensive and heavy, sometimes requiring special front springs for the vehicle. Depending on the type of winch, mechanical and electrical additions will have to made to the vehicle – power-take-off shaft drives, hydraulic pumps or fitment of an up-rated alternator or second battery where an electric winch is involved – further increasing weight. Winches require special care in operation since enormous mechanical forces are involved; children, animals – and under-informed adults – should be kept well away, and that includes spectators in the vicinity of cables under tension.

Be sure a winch is what you need before fitting one.

Electric drum winches not well suited to continuous use. Capstan or mechanical drum winches best for continuous heavy duty work.

Fit only Land Rover approved winches and installations.

Slow operation. Winches are slow - but immensely powerful and capable of precise control in most cases. This will be what you want a winch for: there are many applications for this low speed alone – the slow controlled pull of a boat from the water or of heavy tree trunks. But for recovering other vehicles you will find many occasions are better catered for by towing with a rope (see Section 5.2); using a winch to recover a stuck vehicle makes it hard to coordinate the slow speed of the winch with power from the stuck vehicle's own engine (though this 'drive and winch' technique can be beneficial provided care is taken not to over-run the cable when traction does become available.) On the other hand, extreme boggings where a towed extraction can be difficult can be handled with ease by a winch and if your business includes recovering passenger cars from ditches or the like, the slow speed and precise controllability of a winch will be exactly what you need.

Approved winches. You are most strongly advised to consult your Land Rover supplier when buying a winch and to buy only winches supplied through Land Rover Parts. These will have been approved for your vehicle and the accessories kit will have been specifically engineered for it with safety in mind and so as not to overload the vehicle. Winches may be ordered factory-fitted. Additionally there will be a small Handbook of Winching Techniques issued with the winch which will summarise how to prepare and operate the unit. The following few pages cannot deal with the subject comprehensively.

Winch types. There are two generic classifications of winch:

1. *Drum winches* comprise a drum rotating about a horizontal axis parallel to the bumper and use 8–9.5 mm wire rope stored on, and spooled onto, the drum. They can be driven electrically or there can be mechanical or hydraulic drive for continuous heavy duty operation.

2. *Capstan winches* consist of a bollard – like a giant cotton reel – rotating about a vertical axis. Such winches do not store any rope; they function by moving appropriate ropes – usually 20 mm Terylene/polyester or polypropylene – which have been wound two or three times round the bollard and tensioned on the out-feed side. Capstan winches are mechanically or hydraulically driven and are suitable for continuous heavy duty work.

Pros and cons. Relative advantages and disadvantages of the different types and drive methods are dealt with in the table on the next spread.

Know your proposed needs for a winch, study the concepts on this page plus the tables on the next spread. Then go firm on what you will buy.

Of prime concern is whether your work is intermittent – 'casual' – or continuous heavy duty winching. See next spread.

Capstan winch (above) powers rope – of any length – looped round capstan. 10000 lb Superwinch E10 (above right) is among most powerful electrically powered winches and designed for intermittent heavy duty use; stores cable on drum. Mechanical H14(right) is designed for continuous heavy duty work.

...continued

The Land Rover Experience

5.4. Winching – contd

heat is generated and very high charge rates from the alternator are required. A mechanically driven capstan or drum winch is an altogether more relaxed concept which operates directly from the engine at tick-over; it can thus be used all day without mechanical stress.

Be aware of the different generic types of winch and the very broad spectrum of applications.

Casual or heavy duty. Winching can be 'casual' – towing a boat out of the water or the occasional use for self recovery – or 'heavy duty' which implies regular *continuous* use, usually for professional purposes such as logging or cable laying. Electric winches are not normally suitable for continuous heavy duty use; very high amperages are involved, considerable

Assess your requirement. Assess your needs very carefully and accept the fact that installation of a heavy duty winch will be necessary for where use is continuous and that such an installation will be heavy and relatively expensive since either mechanical shafting from a power take-off (PTO) or else installation of a PTO-mounted hydraulic pump will be required.

Span of applications is so wide that a winch ideal for one kind of usage can be quite unsuitable for another.

Table 1. Winch types and general characteristics			
Type	*Applications*	*For*	*Against*
Electric drum	Intermittent light, medium or heavy duty use according to specification.	Low cost, simple installation, relatively low weight 54-87 kg. Wide range from light to medium/heavy duty. Easy to use. Minimal maintenance. Wire stored on drum.	Electric motor will overheat if used for long periods. Very high amperage draw from battery necessitates high engine rpm and alternator output to recharge. Installation may need second battery.
Hydraulic drum	Continuous heavy duty industrial use.	Can operate for long continuous periods of industrial use with engine at low output or tick-over. Automatic rpm control. Vehicle has capability for other hydraulic tools/applications.	High initial cost for winch and PTO hydraulic pump installation. Needs specialised maintenance for precision components. Engine must be running. Heavy – up to around 115 kg.
Mechanical drum	Continuous heavy duty industrial use.	Can operate for long continuous periods of industrial use with engine at low output or tick-over.	High initial cost for PTO gear and drive shafts to winch position. Two-man operation – one controls engine, one controls winch. Engine must be running. Heavy – up to around 112 kg.
Mechanical or hydraulic capstan	Continuous heavy duty industrial use.	Can operate for long continuous periods of industrial use with engine at low output or tick-over. Constant pulling power due to rope being constant distance from drum axis all the time. Easy to operate. No limit to length of rope used. Around 63 kg.	High cost plus specialist maintenance if hydraulic drive. No room for mechanical drive on current Tdi Defender. Rope not contained on winch. Engine must be running.

Type	Name	Max line pull	Gearbox type	Brake type	Free spool	Elec/hydraulic power requirements
Table 2. Data on some Land Rover approved winch types (Superwinch)						
Electric drum	1. X6 2. X9 3. Husky 4. E10	6000 lb 9000 lb 8500 lb 10000 lb	Planetary Planetary Worm/wheel Planetary	Dynamic In drum Irreversible Disc, wet	Lever Lever Lever Plunger	12v, 390 amps 12v, 435 amps 12v, 360 amps 12v, 360 amps
Hydraulic drum	1. H8 2. H14W	8000 lb 8000 lb	Planetary Worm/wheel	Disc, wet Irreversible	Plunger Plunger	32 litre pump, 2500 psi 32 litre pump, 2500 psi
Mechanical drum	1. H14W	8000 lb	Worm/wheel	Irreversible	Plunger	Power take-off shafts
Mechanical or hydraulic capstan		4000 lb	Worm/wheel	Irreversible	N/A	Power take-off shafts or PTO hydraulic pump

Terminology

1. Gearbox type. This is an indication of the kind of reduction gear used in the winch. Worm and wheel can be arranged (and is here) to be irreversible hence there is no need for a brake.

2. Free-spool. Free spooling is the process of disengaging the winch in order to reel out the cable to the item being winched. 'Lever' or 'plunger' indicates the method of activating winch cable release.

3. Brake. Braking is provided for the mid-pull power failure case. Knowledge of brake principle is needed. 'Dynamic' brake is only the running of the winch motor in high-geared reverse as a generator so is a retarder rather than a stop brake. (X6CD has centre drum brake.) Drum and disc brakes activate automatically via one-way clutch in the event of power being lost in mid pull. Worm and wheel gearing is itself irreversible so runaway after power failure is just not possible.

In considering choice of winch, relate your proposed work to existence/type of brake, power requirements and amount of use at a given session.

...continued

Discovery with Superwinch X6 winch in a low-profile fitting. Protrusions under driving lights indicate 'crush cans' fitted from '95 model year; these establish set deformation rate in collision for air-bag deployment. Only approved and compatible winch fitments should be used on these vehicles.

Air bag equipped vehicles. In choosing your winch it is essential to remember that ONLY Land Rover approved winches are fitted to vehicles fitted with air bags. Being front-mounted, the mountings of these winches will have been engineered to exhibit the correct crush-rates compatible with the triggering devices for the air bag Secondary Restrain System (SRS).

The Land Rover Experience

5.4. Winching – contd

Protect living things – trees, by using a strap; people by observing safety rules and keeping clear of ropes and cables.

Unless self-recovering, anchor winch vehicle with ground anchors or ropes to other trees.

Always use thick leather gloves when handling winch cables.

Techniques overview

Accessories. Paradoxically, it is wise to consider the accessories you will need before going firm on your choice of winch since you must envisage the entire operating regime and method of use before you have a clear picture of what is involved. Number of operating crew is a fundamental first consideration since if you are always going to be solo then a mechanical drum winch will not be suitable. Length of cable is a consideration. Most drum winches are supplied with 30 metres (100 feet) of cable and, whilst this can be attached to extensions, there may be times when a continuous long pull is required and thus a capstan winch would be the best equipment. If this is the case then thought must be given to storage of the rope – which will be bulky and must be kept in good condition – within the vehicle. For any winch you are going to need some or all of the following additional ancillary equipment:

• **D-shackles** – see Section 5.2. For winching, where line pulls will be higher than for normal vehicle-to-vehicle tow-outs, stronger D-shackles will be needed. A 3/4-inch pin diameter is a good guide.

• **Tree strap.** Usually available from the winch manufacturer, an 8-foot by 4-inch tree strap should be acquired to put round trees to protect them from bark damage that would occur when using a tree as a winching anchor with a bare cable. Always use a tree strap – and as low as possible on the tree.

• **Split pulley block**. Where direction of pull is likely to be off vehicle axis or where a double-line pull is needed (or possible) to increase the line pull, a pulley block (see photo) will be needed – see diagrams next spread.

• **Ground anchors.** Where high line pulls are envisaged, possibly on slippery ground, a pair of ground anchors will be necessary to prevent forward movement of the vehicle during the pull. The right ones will be heavy and cumbersome and take up space and payload in the vehicle.

• **Back-anchor rope.** Where ground anchors are not available or where additional security is required, winching vehicle can be anchored with rope and tree strap to a tree behind it.

• **Gloves.** Steel cables can have small broken strands along their length; use thick winching gloves to protect your hands. Do not let a steel winch cable slip through your hands even when using gloves. Always pay it in or out hand-over hand. The same gloves will be useful for the handling of capstan winch ropes too.

The extent of your proposed winching activity will dictate how much of the above you need – it will vary from very little if you are going only to pull a boat out of the water once per week end to virtually the whole kit if you are going to be a recovery marshal on an off-road trial or are carrying out logging operations in a forest area. It will all figure in and be part of your eventual choice of winch.

Slope and line pull. Knowledge of your required line pull in various conditions is necessary as the final consideration before choosing a winch.

1. Level ground. For recovering vehicles – or any wheeled object with reasonably large wheels – the pull required to move it varies according to the surface on which it is standing. The pull, as an approximate proportion of its weight, is:

Hard road – 5%
Grass – 15%
Hard/soft wet sand, gravel – 15-20%
Soft dry sand – 25-30%
Shallow mud – 33%
Bog, marsh, clay – 50%.

Thus if the vehicle to be winched is a part-laden Discovery with a total weight of 2300 kg (5060 lb), the line pull to get it out of shallow mud will be just under 1700 lb.

2. Sloping ground. If the ground you are winching up is sloping you must *add* an increment to account for this. This is very simply calculated as the slope in degrees, divided by 60, times the total load of the vehicle being towed. Thus going up a 15° slope with the Discovery above would add 15/60 = 1/4 of its 5060 lb total weight to the line pull. So in this example we have:

Terrain component = 1700 lb
Slope – 1/4 of 5060 = 1265 lb
So total pull needed is 2965 lb.

Note that the slope component is surprisingly high – and this is assuming an even slope. In real life, of course, ground is uneven and a small local obstacle like a boulder or a tree root can put the immediate local slope up to 30 or 40°. Note also that it is the heaviest ground, eg clay, that is likely to get you stuck and in this case the terrain component goes up to 2530 lb and the whole total to 3795 lb.

Margins. Comfortable margins and, probably even more important, a knowledge of how the winch works and whether your usage is to be intermittent or continuous should then be applied in establishing your choice of equipment. Electric winches being hard-working, high revving, hot-running devices that also require the vehicle engine to be running fast are obviously less suited to continuous work than, say a capstan winch running at engine idle speed. Their relative lightness and cheapness, however, would win the day where the occasional winching of a boat or caravan is concerned.

Simple approximations enable required pull to be calculated.

Pulley is invaluable 'carry always' accessory to double or direct pull.

Ground anchors (opposite) prevent winching vehicle sliding forward when hauling heavy loads (diagram next page). Winch cable looped through split pulley block (right) and back to vehicle bumper doubles effective pull of winch – 8500 lb Husky shown in this mode above (see diagram next spread). Pulley can also be used for indirect pull – photo next page.

...continued

5.4. Winching – contd

Safety first. Whilst a clichéd paragraph heading like this will not always do its job, the reminder is nonetheless very necessary since winching is laden with the possibility of accidents if real care is not taken. The good news, however, is that you, as operator, are in charge and there is seldom if ever any rush. Rest

Photo shows indirect pull electrical winching with cable through pulley block – see facing page. Although itself winch-equipped, stuck vehicle (left) is being winched up slippery slope by recovery vehicle (right). Note use of strap to preclude damage to tree bark and that the winching vehicle is square-on to the direction of initial pull.

assured that thinking ahead, thinking things through, keeping people away from tow ropes and winch ropes, observing the few rules outlined here and *reading the instruction book thoroughly* WILL result in safe winching.

Breaking cables. Breaking cables and ropes are extremely hazardous. Never step over a cable under tension and ensure no-one is close to it when winching is in progress. Wire cables as used on drum winches flail laterally when they break so are particularly dangerous.

Control cable safety. Be particularly careful that electrical winch control cables are kept well clear of the winch wire. Caught up in the winch, a short circuit could make the winch unstoppable without disconnecting the control wire.

Directing – or doubling – the pull. Unlike the bulk and weight of ground anchors, split pulley blocks (previous

Pulley doubles winch maximum 'power' for moving obstacles

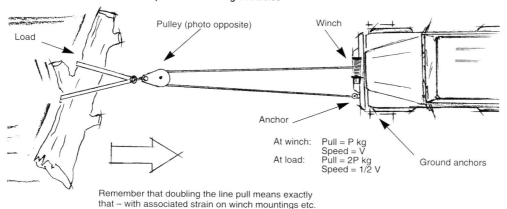

At winch: Pull = P kg
Speed = V
At load: Pull = 2P kg
Speed = 1/2 V

Remember that doubling the line pull means exactly
that – with associated strain on winch mountings etc.
Never try shifting the immovable with a double pulley.

*Pulley is invaluable
'carry always' acces-
sory to double or
direct pull.*

Pulley reduces line strain in self-recovery

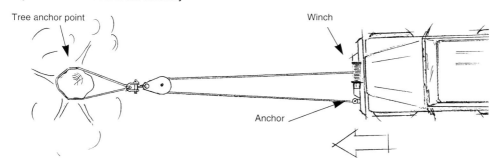

spread) are light and small and worth
carrying at all times with extra straps and
ropes. Be sure its rating is compatible
with your winch. They are invaluable as a
means of producing an indirect pull (facing photo) and for producing a given pull
with half the strain on the winch at half
speed.

**Maintenance, care of cables and
ropes.** Drum winch cables should spool
onto the drum evenly and will do so if the
pull is at the correct angle. If there are
signs of it not doing so, stop the winching, pay out the cable and spool back onto
the drum guiding it by (gloved) hands.
Inspect and clean cables and ropes regularly; excessive mud will get into the

strands or fibres and cause damage.
Extend the cable to full length and check
in detail for damage. Check gearbox oil
levels and for the presence of hydraulic
leaks regularly.

**Towing attachments – vehicle recov-
ery.** As with towed and snatch recovery,
the towing attachments on vehicles being
recovered must be sound and purpose-
built. Attach cables using D-shackles
tightened and then backed-off half a turn.
NEVER attach cables to axles or steering
components.

Training and practice. Fully absorb
the winch instructions, be familiar with
the equipment and take time to train and
practice before real-life use.

*Practice to gain com-
plete familiarity with
your equipment
before using it on real
situations.*

The Land Rover Experience

Section 6

Advanced driving

6.1. High/low range overlap

Each bar represents the speed you can do in that gear between max torque (about 1800 rpm) and max power (about 4000 rpm). Diagram drawn for Tdi diesel engine but values for other Land Rover engines are reasonably similar. Optimum change point for low box to high on the move is clear.

Speeds in the gears

High/low range overlap – your choice. You will see if you study the gear ratios data – and the diagram above – that there is some overlap between low range and high range – for example 4th gear low is roughly equivalent to 2nd gear high so that a given piece of ground could be covered equally well in either. You will frequently find, however, that being in low range rather than the high will give you the ability to tackle sudden track deteriorations such as road washouts or obstacles, without having to carry out a range change. (See also 'Low range – when and how', Section 2.4.)

Low to high change – when you need it. As already shown there are times when it is very useful to be able to start your Land Rover in low range and, once you are moving, continue in high. Typical examples of this are towing a heavy trailer on hard roads (Section 4.1), towing a trailer off-road (Section 6.4) or just starting the vehicle in marginal trac-

tion conditions such as soft sand or mud where it would be risky, once moving, to stop in order to re-select high range.

On-the-move range change - manual Low/high change – what gear, what speed. We have seen there is an overlap between low range and high range so a change across from low to high from 3rd, 4th or 5th could be useful – and is possible on vehicles having a lever range change (ie, not electric range change). In practice it is best to get the vehicle properly moving – say 20-25 mph – before doing a range change; that way, momentum will keep you going when you execute the change. The diagram also shows that the speed/rpm band between max torque and max power nicely suits a 3rd low to 2nd high change. Naturally before contemplating a change from low range to high you should also be sure that conditions are suitable for sustained travel in high range since to change back again you will have to stop.

Low range is not just extra-low gearing. It overlaps high range to let you choose best overall gearbox span.

Changing from low to high on the move – without clunks – is well worth learning.

3rd low to 2nd high on the move – procedure. As the diagram opposite shows, 3rd low is roughly equivalent to 2nd high in terms of road and engine speed. Given the max torque and max power rpm vs speed in the two gears, the range change will have to be made fairly briskly but need not be hurried.

1. Start off in 1st or 2nd low range, accelerate through the gears until you are doing 20-25 mph in 3rd gear, low range.

2. With the main gear lever still in 3rd, double-de-clutch the transfer lever towards you from low to high range, ie depress the clutch and move the transfer lever into neutral; clutch up. (Note, this will need a short, sharp action with a definite halt at the mid-point of the lever's range of movement.) Clutch down again and transfer lever all the way into HIGH .

3. With clutch still depressed, main gear lever 3rd into 2nd gear – towards you again, and across. As the engine was losing rpm whilst you moved the transfer lever, you will find you will need a blip of throttle to raise engine revs to the right level for 2nd gear, high range at 20 mph. Continue in high 2nd on up through the gears. Retain or de-select centre diff-lock as required (Defender and Discovery).

Electric range change. Low to high mobile range change on manual transmission new Range Rover is possible only up to 10 mph. At this speed in low 2nd, select gear lever neutral, press range change button; when Message Centre registers 'H', select 1st high and procede.

High to low on the move? No. This can be done under certain conditions to demonstrate driving skill but there is little practical application. Deteriorating heavy going is when you might need this change and here the time taken to execute it will be enough for the speed to have decayed to nothing. Make life easy; always change to low range when stationary, or easier still, just before the vehicle comes to a halt and with the main gear lever still in a gear.

1.

Low 2nd /3rd to 20-25 mph

2.

3rd

Double de-clutch – L-N-H

3.

With clutch still down, 3rd to 2nd

Low to high – do it from 25 mph in 3rd low. Seems complex to read but is simple to do.

Practise it first on hard roads, then off-road. Momentum decay will be different.

Classic situation for low-to-high change on the move – softish sand, hard to start in but which, moving, you can take in high range. More usual example, nearer home, is trailer towing – hill starts or moving off from traffic lights.

Do not bother trying high to low on the move. Stop to make the change.

6.2. Automatic transmission

*To tow a dead-engine automatic with all four wheels on the ground, unlock steering and put **both** gear levers into '**N**' – see Section 2.4 for selection of transfer neutral with electric range change. (See driver's manual for details of lifted tow and prop-shaft disconnect). Tow-starting is not possible.*

Low to high range on the move is easier to do well on an auto than on a manual.

Low to high – moving (auto). As in the manual transmission case (Section 6.1) there are many occasions when it is very useful to start in low range, attain a speed and positive momentum where high range can take over – probably 20-25 mph – and then effect a change of transfer ratios without stopping. Using the procedures shown here, this is possible where range change is by manual lever. (With electric range change and automatic transmission, as explained at Section 2.3, speed sensors will prevent range change above 5 mph. In this case, and to eliminate any consequent clunk, it is arguably better to execute the change with the vehicle stationary.)

With electric range change an electronic speed sensor prevents range change on automatics above 5 mph.

Low/high change – what gear, what speed. The diagram of speed in the gears at Section 6.1, although drawn for the Tdi engine and five-speed manual transmission, reflects a state of affairs similar to that of the four-speed ZF automatic fitted to Discovery and Range Rover. The prin-

It is worth learning to obviate the excess torque converter slip that would result from a high load start in high box.

ciple of change-over points remains the same – getting to a high part of the power curve in low range at a speed that will not decay through ground rolling resistance too much to enable transfer to a suitable gear and part of the power curve in the high range.

Low-to-high change – procedure. Since the auto transmission will take care of selecting the appropriate main gearbox ratio, it is only necessary (unlike manual Section 6.1) for the driver to attend to the moving of the transfer lever (*diagram facing page*):

1. Start off in low range with '**3**' selected. Accelerate to 3000 rpm once the gearbox has changed up to 3rd ratio.

2. When at 3000 rpm, simultaneously lift off the throttle and, as the transmission goes from drive to over-run, move the transfer lever aft into neutral.

3. When the rpm have dropped to 1500, ease the transfer lever further aft into the HIGH range position.

1.

Auto – 3rd-hold; stay in it

2.

L
↓
N

Low to high, mobile. Snick transfer lever into N – remember detent is very small so make a sharp, positive stop with your hand when moving the lever from L to N – allow revs to drop, then pull back from N into H. See text and diagram left.

Low to high range on the move – where range change is by manual lever. Diagram shows sequence corresponding to text on facing page.

3.

N
↓
H

High to low, moving? Sometimes.
Unlike the firm 'No' given at Section 6.1 in the manual case, following the Driver Manual procedure of changing down to low transfer on the move can be done if forward speed is at or under 8 kph (5 mph). Whilst rate of speed decay in worsening conditions will be the same as in the manual case, the auto transmission's ability to re-select the main gear ratio virtually instantaneously will make this a practical manipulation in cases where speed decay is not too rapid:

1. Slow to 8 kph (5 mph) in HIGH.
2. Lift off accelerator, move main selector to 'N' and transfer lever to LOW.
3. Re-select 'D' and drive on.

Unlike manual transmission, high to low with auto can be a useful technique in certain cases.

Although this is a very simple operation, it will pay to practise it on road and in undemanding conditions before using it in earnest. As with the manual transmission case, it its important to judge movement of the transfer lever into neutral properly.

6.3. Engine braking

Steep initial section, you find you have too low a gear; wheels are sliding.

Engine braking in general is a safe, eco- nomic way of reduc- ing speed.

Slippery slopes
Engine braking recommended...but.
Read this section after reading Section 4.5. Engine braking is the safe way to reduce speed. On long hills use engine braking to keep your speed from building up because that way you are not overheating the brakes – important, since even today's disc brakes can suffer from a degree of 'fade' (reduced efficiency) when they get very hot. All this is a well accepted part of our armoury of safe driving techniques.

Sensitive, delicate braking. But think first of a two-wheel drive car on an icy road. Engine braking derives retardation through one pair of wheels on the driven axle whilst sensitive and delicate use of the foot brake uses all four. The same retardation spread between four wheels instead of two reduces the risk of wheel locking. The relevance of this example is to make the point that there is a place for sensitive and delicate braking in many sit- uations in which we have 'learned' to leave the brakes alone. ABS and cadence braking (see Section 3.2, 'Gentle right foot') are especially relevant here.

Just as excessive braking can cause wheel slide, so can excessive engine braking – 1st gear low range on a very steep, long, slippery slope.

Beware sliding wheels. In the case of a 4x4 the situation is improved since both engine braking and slowing with the brakes is achieved using all four wheels. But just as excessive use of the brakes can cause lock-up and discontinuity of rolling contact between the wheels and the ground, so excessive engine braking can cause exactly the same thing – sliding wheels. So tackling a really steep slippery slope using 1st gear low box can amount, in special circumstances, to excessive engine braking and result in wheel slide. Be ready to use the accelerator. Or it will likely be better to use a higher gear such as 2nd – even 3rd sometimes. (See Section 4.5 and photo top right opposite.)

Be ready to use the accelerator – and keep cadence braking in the back of your mind all the time.

Emergency procedures
Discs for delicacy. The brakes on all current Land Rover models are power assisted discs, light and sensitively pro- gressive. Delicacy of control is easy to achieve and there are some extreme down-slopes where, if you are not equipped with ABS, this delicacy com- bined with cadence braking (see Section 3.2) will give more controllable retarda- tion than engine braking alone. There are two classic cases to consider:

1. Almost the right gear, brake assis- tance. Take the case of an initially steep, long slippery down-slope with a loose surface. You judge that 2nd low is appro- priate and begin your descent. But the ini- tial section is so steep that the vehicle gains speed faster than you anticipated. Clearly it is inadvisable to attempt to change down at this critical stage (even an automatic will not always change down to 1st in these conditions – see Section 2.2) so a gentle and intermittent use of the brake pedal – gentle cadence braking – can be used to slow the vehicle within the limits of the available grip for the initial steep part of the descent. Don't let the wheels lock; and if they do, release the brakes altogether, immediately.

2. Wrong gear, cadence braking take- over. Take the same steep, long, slippery down-slope. Starting down it in 1st gear low box may result in wheel slide because in such a low gear – even with the engine revving hard – the wheels will not be able

Id throttle. Delicate application of brake;
it at the first suspicion of lock-up.

If, in gear, wheels just cannot keep
up with speed increase, de-clutch
and use cadence braking. Keep front
wheels pointing straight down slope.

Select a higher gear once the problem
is over, boost the revs as you engage
clutch and resume engine braking.

*A matter of judgement (above). If it is
this steep you want retardation but too
low a gear when it is slippery or loose
will give you slide. 2nd low, rather than
1st, would be best if it were muddy
earth. In the special case of this giant
sand dune you need to go higher still –
3rd or 4th low or even 1st high range –
to prevent the vehicle nosing into the
sand. (In this context see also Glossary
'Castor angle', and 'Steering feel',
Section 10.1.) With ABS (left) the
brakes are always a reliable fall-back.*

to turn fast enough to maintain rolling contact with the ground. You realise too late that you have got the wrong gear so, after using all the throttle you can, you must undertake a rescue operation. De-clutch so that the wheels can regain rolling contact with the ground, then with great sensitivity carry out cadence brak-ing – *rapid gentle jabs at the brake pedal that never permit the wheels to lock* but which give you the best retardation the circum-stances allow. The Range Rover and

Discovery's ABS brakes, of course, being anti-lock will carry this operation out for you if you just keep your foot on the clutch and brake pedals; it will signal the fact that ABS is operating by the audible pulses of the brake relay. (While you have the clutch down put the gear lever into 2nd or 3rd ready for when you wish to engage the engine again.) This is a rare scenario but keep it in the back of your mind rather than slide out of control, throttle wide, in 1st.

*Emergency proce-
dure: really sensitive
use of the brakes,
releasing them the
instant they lock the
wheels – or cadence
braking.*

6.4. Towing off-road

High-density industrial plant trailers (right) need treating with more than expected care off-road – mainly due to inertia and limitations of trailer suspension. Treatment of horse-boxes, boats and the like is more self evident (below).

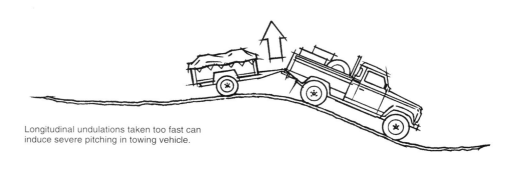

Longitudinal undulations taken too fast can induce severe pitching in towing vehicle.

Heavy trailer off-road – or light trailer driven briskly – will feed back considerable inertia loads to tug.

Potential problems
Greater trailer feedback. (Read Section 4.1, 'Towing – on-road', first, noting maximum off-road towing weights shown in the table.) Using trailers off road requires even greater anticipation and care. Feedback effect to the towing vehicle is much more noticeable than on hard road. For example, traversing undulations too fast can cause interactive responses between vehicle and trailer.

Specifically, the trailer can cause considerable pitch in the towing vehicle as it swoops into and out of a dip. This can be bad enough in extreme cases to lift the rear end of the vehicle momentarily off the ground.

Drag, push and lateral roll. Trailer drag over uneven ground and 'trailer-push' down steep slopes will be more pronounced – with braking correspondingly more difficult and liable, in extreme cases, to provoke the trailer to try and overtake the vehicle in a form of jack-knifing. Off-road there is also a surprising susceptibility to lateral roll. Trailer suspension is seldom damped sufficiently in the laden condition compared to that of the towing vehicle, often compounded by a degree of roll-steer due to crude axle location geometry on the trailer. Lateral roll over an uneven track which the Land Rover suspension will cope with easily can result in alarming roll angles on the trailer – sometimes resulting in capsizing. (See next spread, revolving tow-hooks.)

Centre of gravity position vital. This background and the aspects of trailer dynamics covered at Section 4.1 emphasise the vital importance of low, and forward centre of gravity (giving appropriate nose-weight) when off-road towing. Take twice the nose-weight out of the available vehicle payload.

Beware especially of under-damped lateral roll of trailer on poor tracks.

Trailer influence especially noticeable on steep slippery down-slopes – adversely affected rear wheel adhesion and tendency to jack-knife. Accelerate out of it.

... continued

The Land Rover Experience

6.4. Towing off-road – contd

Keep trailer payload as low as possible to permit low tyre pressures and give combination the best chance off-road.

Checks and procedures
Overload solution: provisos. For overlanding expeditions, use of a really robust trailer can be quite an elegant solution to the problem of having a payload requirement in excess of that shown as the maximum for your vehicle on its own. Spreading the load over six wheels is better than the unacceptable alternative of overloading the vehicle's four. The prolonged stress of an overland trip is perhaps an extreme case but it encapsulates the potential problems of all off-road tow-

Trailers can avoid an overload situation in expeditions – but tyres must be large and there must be manpower to man-handle the trailer when stuck.

ing so is worth examining. Four provisos should be remembered for sustained off-road trailer operation:

1. Weight. Minimise the weight of the trailer and load to give the vehicle the best working conditions off-road. An ex-military 750 kg trailer with overrun brakes, loaded to no more than 500 kg gross provides a sensible margin of strength and is in roughly the right category for a Land Rover towing vehicle.

2. Tyres. The same rationale mentioned earlier (see Section 1) about big wheels applies to trailers and is arguably even more important since the trailer wheels are following in ground already cut up by the towing vehicle. Trailer axle loads of the order indicated above will enable trailer tyre pressures to be lower (see Section 8.2) than those of the tug, enhancing flotation in the wake of the towing vehicle. Note that off-road a trailer needs the best combination of low rolling resistance and flotation (mainly the latter), not traction, so in absolute terms tyre requirements will be unique. However, in practice it is sensible to use the same wheels and tyres on the trailer as you have fitted to the towing vehicle; this is right functionally and has the additional advantage that the same spare wheel will fit trailer and towing vehicle. As noted, flotation can be optimised by the use of lower pressures.

3. Personnel. There will be times, off-road and overlanding, when the trailer has to be detached and man-handled. It will be necessary to have at least two people to do this; three or four will be better still.

4. Towing hitch. The standard 50 mm ball hitch is widely used in the UK and Europe but it should be remembered it is suitable for a maximum gross trailer weight of 1000 kg off-road on all Land

Rover products. The European specification ball hitch (Part no RTC9565) is stronger than the standard UK item. Note also the ratings of the 2-bolt and 4-bolt Land Rover Parts combined ball/pin hitches shown at Section 4.1. Because of problems of trailer lateral stability in extreme off-road conditions as noted on the previous spread, be sure your trailer has an EC-standard hitch that can rotate at the trailer since a tipped trailer would not then affect the towing vehicle.

Low range start. As with heavy trailers on hard roads (see Section 4.1) there will be many occasions off-road when it will make for a smoother start to move off in low range 2nd gear, continue up the low ratio gears and change into high range on the move using the techniques outlined in Sections 6.1 and 6.2 . For off-road towing, low range is sometimes the better choice to stay in.

Pay meticulous attention to condition of towing hitch, bolts and attachment areas.

Classic demonstration (below) of the benefits of trailer tyres being larger than those of towing vehicle and thus able to run on lower pressures; better flotation, less drag. Beware, however, since low trailer tyre pressures can cause weaving at speed. Fore and aft motion of loose fitting towing eye over long off-road distance caused considerable wear (left).

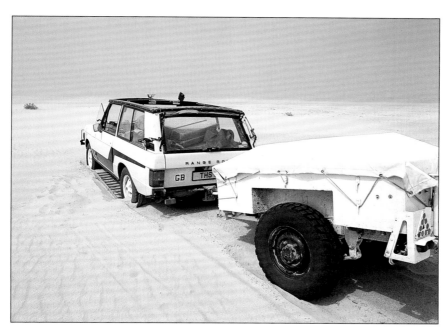

Starting in low range with an on-the-move change to high ratio is particularly useful with trailers off-road.

Section 7

Expedition basics

7.1. The call of the wild

Freeing the spirit

The pace of everyday life often constrains us to under-utilise what we have – be it our own skills, the potential of our hobbies or the potential of our four-wheel drive vehicle. Our early plans, made at the time of purchase, may not have been realised and we may be left with a gnawing urge to utilise more of the latent capability of our 4x4, to use it for some of the more adventurous projects for which we bought it. With a machine of such potential in your possession it would perhaps be the more unusual *not* to want to stretch its operating envelope. Without any doubt at all, there is little to compare with the feeling of being in the world's wilder places with a well-equipped and well trained expedition savouring the space, the beauty, the feeling of being self-sufficient.

Whilst this Section is inevitably aimed, primarily, at private recreational use it is hoped that it will also be of interest to commercial operators, perhaps in tourist-related or leisure pursuits, where operation of a vehicle in complete safety away from its home territory may form part of a package or proposal.

Basics only. Note, right from the start, however, that the whole of Section 7 is entitled 'Expedition basics' and it claims to be no more than that. An 'expedition' can be a half-day trip to the hills or a major three-month overseas project. They will have in common the importance of infallible preparation – an examination of all the 'what-if?' situations – but there will be in the major projects less margin for error and the need for very precise logistic control. This Section is an introduction to the subject and aims to help you prepare to broaden your enjoyment of your Land Rover product in relatively short trips. More demanding projects including the planning of overseas expeditions that may include a scientific project are covered in the book EXPEDITIONS, shortly to be published by Land Rover. The book also contains considerable extra detail on vehicle preparation, modifications, navigation, photography and emergency procedures.

'Expeditions' – be it half a day in the hills or a major overseas project – hugely enhance enjoyment of your vehicle. But you have just stepped into careful-planning territory.

Day trip or major expedition?

We are not all able to respond unquestioningly to the call of the wild since time, cost and other responsibilities will influence where we are able to go. What is certain, however, is the importance of how we tackle what we propose to do, however 'big' or 'small' it may be. As has been observed about that most unforgiving of all environments, the Sahara desert, you can die pinned under a capsized motorcycle behind a knoll a kilometre from the track just as easily as if you did the same thing 500 kilometres farther out in the desert. A sombre example that nevertheless makes the point admirably regarding the differences between everyday on-road operations where the swish of passing traffic is your assurance of some help, and being a few miles up a mountain track with what is becoming more than a minor problem on your hands.

Although a gentle progression up the scale of challenge is the natural way to do things, the importance of taking things a step at a time cannot too strongly be emphasised. Going hand in hand with this – importantly and almost inevitably – will be the growth in your confidence. Confidence begets early recognition of, thus avoidance of and measured response to problems. Confidence (well-founded confidence, not over-confidence or cockiness) further begets the ability, comfortably, to say 'no' and turn back before getting into trouble.

Savour but beware the feeling of amazement and invincibility you may

Safely operated, a 4x4 epitomises – and realises – the need to seek the earth's wild places.

have experienced on your first competent off-road demonstration of your (or your dealer's) Land Rover. The feeling of unstoppability is very strong but, as has been emphasised throughout this book, all vehicles, even Land Rovers, have their limitations and in a *competent* demonstration you will have been shown what *can* be done, not what happens when you get it wrong.

So, assuming you are just making a start, the answer to the 'day-trip-or-major-expedition' question is clearly 'day-trip' – and then only after planning and training. If you are already thinking that actually it was release you were after and not another career development project, be of good cheer; the training and practice is great fun – putting into practice what you have read in the other Sections of this book. And during training there is someone to help when you get into trouble; there is also a hot shower to go home to afterwards.

Planning

The aim. Paradoxically, despite the emphasis on planning, it will not be easy to plan in a 'capability vacuum'. In other words, until you know a little of what you individually can do with your vehicle it will be hard to make a realistic plan for an expedition. It is likely, however, that

Take your projects a step at a time. Confidence and competence will then build on a sound foundation.

...continued

7.1. The call of the wild – contd

Fundamental navigation is about maps, headings, distances – wherever you are. GPS devices (opposite) give pin-point fixes in desert, mountain, plain.

To establish an aim, know first what you and your vehicle can do – train; see Section 7.2.

you may want to explore some unsur-faced tracks you have seen on the map as part of a week-end break you may be tak-ing in the mountains. The aim can be as general as this for the time being.

Maps, research. Small, 'white-roads' trailing off into areas of close contours or wide-open space on the map, together with a ford or two and linking up with another 'white' or 'yellow' road away from all the traffic can have an irresistible appeal. It is worth, at this stage, re-read-ing the Foreword to this book to remind yourself that ownership of a 4x4 brings considerable responsibilities in regard to environmental care, the obligation to set an example and acceptance of the often complex matter of rights of access. This latter will be different in every country and must be individually checked. The rising general population of 4x4 vehicles has regrettably brought with it a small element of irresponsible users and a cor-responding tightening of access rules.

Be certain about rights of land access for off-road vehicles – an increasingly sen-sitive subject in developed countries.

Awareness of these rules is therefore essential. Quoting a summary of the UK will give an idea of what to expect in 'developed' countries – countries with rel-atively high populations and a legislature steeped in historical evolution. The UK situation is at once knocked slightly off-balance by the fact that a new system of classification in *being* introduced and is not yet reflected on all maps. The maps to use are the excellent 1:50,000 Ordnance Survey Land Ranger maps, backed, where possible, by the 1:25,000 series. On these maps there are:

- Public footpaths – vehicles not allowed.
- Public bridleways – vehicles not allowed.
- RUPPs (Road Used as a Public Path) – being re-categorised on most maps as BOATs (see below) and in many *but not all* cases, implies that vehicles may be used on them. Local Authorities do have an obligation under the Wildlife and Countryside Act 1981 to reclassify all RUPPs as byway, bridleway or footpath (see below, The Definitive Map).
- BOATs (Byway Open to All Traffic) – this is what it sounds like, vehicles are permitted.
- UCRs (Unclassified County Roads) – these are minor roads or lanes, many with a sealed surface, others comprising only rough stone. These may be driven by vehicles.

Some confusion may be added to complexity by the fact that, to quote the Foreword, the indication of a road on a map does not automatically confer a right of way. Worth the trouble, and in any more ambitious expedition essential, is a visit to the County Council offices where may be inspected the Definitive Map which will indicate the current legal access status of every road in the County. Since all of this is aimed at keeping within

Ascertaining compass heading in a vehicle is almost a contradiction in terms since the internal magnetic field is strong, variable and virtually uncorrectable for a normally mounted magnetic compass. Use the compass outside the vehicle and about five metres away from it.

GPS navigation. If your long-term aims include a demanding overseas trip and you have already obtained a GPS (Global Positioning System) navigator – which may be hand-held for use on the hills or vehicle-installed – then you will have satellite-derived speed, heading and position (accurate to 100 metres) at the touch of a button. Such equipment, especially after the labours and uncertainties of manual navigation in bad weather, is a boon and a minor miracle. With costs driven steadily downward by competition, most units can be removed from the vehicle installation, a vehicle position waypoint registered and the GPS taken with you when walking on the hills; in the event of sudden bad weather overtaking you, the unit can give you a bearing and distance back to the vehicle from your current position.

Second vehicle, safety message. Two vehicles driven in sensibly-spaced convoy is a wise precaution on most routes off-road. If one vehicle gets stuck in mud the other will be able to tow it free, or go for help if mechanical damage has occurred through sliding off the track. It is well appreciated, however, that the whole point of some trips will be to 'get away' in a single vehicle and it behoves you for such excursions to pick routes which you know will be safe and from which, even in bad weather, you will be confident to walk for help should the occasion arise. Training trips (see next spread) with schools organising safaris will give you a feel for the conditions and safety requirements. As with some hill-walking and mountain routes on foot, it is wise, wherever possible, to inform someone of your route and expected return time.

As with expedition projects, develop your navigation skills a step at a time. Map, compass, distance travelled, cross bearings.

the law and not upsetting people on whose property you may find you have inadvertently trespassed, asking permission from the local landowner, if you can ascertain who it is, will always be a safe alternative. Other local people will also usually know the status of tracks and interesting trails. A catch-all and usually temporary TRO (Traffic Regulation Order) can, however, be issued at the discretion of the Highway Authority on given routes in relation to given types of vehicles (to cover the case, for example, of local over-use causing damage – a reasonable enough concept despite the further confusion factor).

Navigation. It goes without saying that close attention must be paid to map-reading and navigation in order that you may, at any time, be able to pin-point your position on the map and know where the next track-junction or other waypoint may be. Accept that this will take time and that you will probably have to stop the vehicle frequently to check it all out. Heading-and-distance navigation will seldom be appropriate to back-lanes trips in countries such as the United Kingdom but it is a principle that must always be in the back of your mind.

Take a second vehicle for safety unless you are certain about a particular route.

7.2. Training for the trip

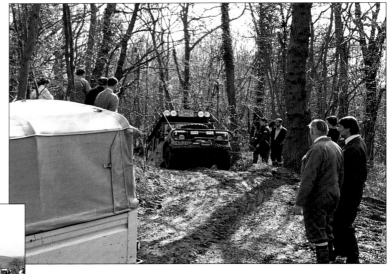

Before planning your own expedition, establish and hone your driving skills – first with professional tuition such as The Land Rover Experience, then with an off-road site day-pass, then within the safety of group safaris.

Learn the full spectrum of your vehicle's and your own capabilities before planning a trip.

Developing the skills. 'Training for the trip' may initially sound a forbidding concept when many 'expeditions' are no more than recreational excursions. But you would not go rock climbing without knowing how to do it and having the equipment and you would not go canoeing without being instructed on how to control the canoe and observe the correct safety precautions. To do any of these things without proper preparation would be foolhardy; and that applies to vehicle-based expeditions as well.

Off-road training. Use one of the many off-road driving schools to become familiar with your vehicle away from tarmac and in the low-range transfer gears. If you have read this book you will have the enormous advantage of having absorbed the theory – and the written-down practice – but it is essential that you try it yourself and become completely comfortable with your own and your vehicle's behaviour in demanding conditions before going out on an expedition, however 'small'. If you are in the UK and within range, clearly the best starting point is Land Rover's own LAND ROVER EXPERIENCE driving school at Solihull. You will not find that is enough on its own; you cannot become an expert in a single day. Taking on board their message, however, will be a very significant first step.

Practice on your own. You will have experienced the dynamics of off-road driving and the significance of the gentle right foot but you will need a lot more practice and for this you should go to a local school for consolidating tuition and, most important of all, a day-pass access to their off-road site which will enable you to 'play' in your own time and practice the techniques you have been taught. Take your time, read this book, know and analyse what you are doing. Being on a driving school site you will do so in the knowledge that should you get stuck, help will be on hand to tow you free. Such sites, additionally, are designated for off-road practice and you will not have the worry of seeking special permission for where you go. A considerable number of such schools advertise in the off-road magazines; go for the ones that emphasise thorough briefing and care for the vehicle. Do not be rushed into precipi-

tate driving methods; you are paying the bill and it is your vehicle.

Safari. A number of schools also organise 'safaris' lasting one to three days in which a small group of owner-driven-vehicles is led along pre-chosen routes which incorporate a variety of demanding driving conditions – and usually some exhilarating scenery. The experience is enjoyable in itself and valuable in a hundred ways for learning driving techniques. Choose a safari school that operates under similar terrain conditions to those you wish to travel later.

Fitness. Your off-road driver training and the physical effort required to push, jack, lay sand channels or dig out a stuck vehicle will be a reminder that your own fitness is no less important than that of your vehicle. In a perfect world your training will have conferred such skill and judgement that you never get your vehicle into a condition warranting the undignified description of 'being stuck'. Few will need reminding of the world's imperfections and from the fitness point of view it is wise to be prepared...!

Initial impressions of your vehicle's off-road performance will be dazzling; but learn the demarcation between what it can and cannot do.

After tuition, consolidate your abilities and confidence with practice on your own – with help at hand if required.

7.3. Vehicle preparation

Schedule service must be right up to date. But re-familiarise yourself with routine owner maintenance tasks. Jacking the rear is a long reach; groundsheet, overalls, wood block help.

Initial preparation will be mundane – simple things like knowing the driver's manual, jacking (and reading this book!)

What preparation? Rest assured that buying a Land Rover product will enable you to drive the vehicle from the showroom and turn in a best-in-class off-road performance without further preparation. Having said that, your attention will have been drawn already, in this book, to the fine-tuning that may be appropriate to given sets of conditions. Tyres in particular (where the point has already been made that particular tyres perform best in one set of conditions only), weights, wading plugs, loading, recovery equipment, towing hooks, underslung fog lights and spoilers are some of the items that spring to mind. And of course you must ensure that your vehicle has been properly maintained to Land Rover servicing schedules and is thus on the top line mechanically.

Vehicle knowledge. Your training sessions should have refreshed your knowledge of the traction enhancement facilities such as low range and the

Tyres, their fitness for the job you have in mind, condition, and pressure are fundamental to defining your expedition capability.

applicability for your vehicle of centre differential lock or viscous coupling, ABS brakes, Electronic Traction Control and the extra under-belly clearance available where Electronic Air Suspension has been specified. You should know and apply, for the tyres you have *and the weight of the vehicle as you will operate it*, the correct road pressures; be aware of what pressures you can reduce to for tracks (max speed 40 mph) and in the event of encountering exceptionally soft conditions (not above 12 mph).

Jacking. Tyre reliability these days is such that few of us get experience in fitting the spare wheel; an off-road expedition may result in sidewall damage and a flat if you are not sufficiently vigilant – see Section 3.4, Marshalling. Check the handbook procedures; practice choc-ing the wheels, positioning and operating the jack (take the main tightness off the wheel nuts with the wheel still in contact with the ground). You will find it quite a stretch positioning the jack under the rear axle; keep a set of overalls in the car for this job. Be sure you can undo and properly tighten the wheel nuts. If you have to jack on soft ground you will need a small wood baulk as a load spreader – about 45-50 mm thick and the size of this book; keep it in the vehicle. A second jack and wood block is useful where the ground is really soft and you may have to jack up a stage at a time.

Tyres. As indicated above, tyres can only be optimised for one set of conditions; other conditions, for those tyres, will involve a degree of performance compromise. Study the detail on tyre types, axle loads and pressures in Section 8.2. You will probably find your vehicle fitted with road-oriented or M+S tyres when you buy it and you would probably be wise to adjust the demands of your first expedition to be within the still considerable capabilities of these tyres before going to the expense of buying others. In temperate zones such as Europe you will find the main compromise with these tyres is reduced performance in mud/clay mixtures; this should not strike alarm since all Land Rover off-road press demonstration vehicles are fitted with these production-line tyres. Nevertheless where the best performance in mud is required, the Michelin XCL will provide it. (Be aware that only Defender will accommodate 7.50 x 16 tyres without modification. Range Rover and Discovery will take 7.00 x 16 with minor modifications at your dealer's discretion.) Remember that one aspect of a mud tyre's effectiveness derives from a carefully judged width – or narrowness – that enables it, together with an equally deliberate tread design, to cut through slippery upper layers of soft mud and into the grippier ground beneath. Thus the extra-wide after-market tyres frequently seen on recreational vehicles will usually yield poorer traction on wet grass and mud than will standard items; certainly they will be less effective than the mud tyres mentioned above. If fitting non-standard tyres outside those listed in Section 8.2 do check the Load Index and Speed Symbol (especially the latter) also listed in that section.

Ground clearance. Depending on type, specification and fitments to your vehicle, there may be alterations you wish to make to enhance ground clearance. For example, many Range Rover models are equipped with a front spoiler as standard and this may be removed (together with the associated driving lights) to improve approach angle and clearance at the front of the vehicle. If side steps have been specified on Discovery these too can be removed if you envisage there being a problem with lateral under belly clearance. Tow hooks too, especially those with an extra low mounting, can be temporarily removed if (see Section 3.3) you will need extra departure angle for tackling steep up-slopes. In extreme conditions where the rear wheels run up

Wide tyres, per se, are not always 'best'. These Goodrich Mud-Terrains shine where a combination of flotation and traction is needed (peat, marsh) but are outperformed on pure mud by Michelin XCL. Match to conditions.

against obstacles aft, mud flaps can get torn off by being trapped between the rear wheel and the obstacle. If this is a risk, the mud-flap can be rolled up on itself and tied in this position with cord or a small strap until resuming travel on road.

Tie-downs, internal stowage. As mentioned in Section 8.1, there is much to recommend the fitting of tie-downs in your vehicle if it is to operate over rough ground. Used in conjunction with modular containers such as lidded plastic storage boxes of the kind available in DIY stores, equipment such as wet-weather gear, camping equipment, recovery items, spare jack, and refreshments can be strapped-down so that they do not slide around the vehicle on uneven tracks or off-road. Some form of secure mounting will be essential for really heavy items such as a high-lift jack or even a spare hydraulic jack and shovels. This is part of the basic philosophy of eliminating loose articles so that not only does equipment avoid damage but the vehicle itself, as a result, is free from rattles and other internal noise. You will find that vehicles in this condition, tight and rattle-free, are driven better and more sympathetically than those full of nerve-jangling equipment avalanches.

Think ground clearance. Does spoiler or tow-hook have to be removed to enhance approach and departure angle?

Plan, containerise and secure the load. Read that bit again!

7.4 Equipment

A second vehicle and a long tow rope are two of the most comforting items of equipment to take when venturing far from the beaten track. An inadvertent bogging of a single vehicle need be no more than a brief incident when a safety vehicle is with you.

Simple problems can develop into emergencies when no help is at hand. Don't be self-conscious about taking sensible safety measures.

Influencing criteria. Television news bulletins continually remind us of how easily a short recreational excursion can turn into a life-threatening drama. Common to many of these news items is how simple were the precautions that could have avoided trouble. Occasionally, this is proven when someone, well prepared, has survived cheerfully by building a snow-hole or taking appropriate action that has enabled them to ride out the storm or assist rescue teams to find them when things have gone wrong. European weather systems, especially in the regions attractive to outdoor or adventurous people are notorious for their changeability and the suddenness with which conditions can become threat-

ening. Some of the 'what-if' questions that must be asked in deciding what equipment to take on an expedition are:

• **Weather.** If the weather turns from to-day's fine sunny conditions to 'snow-on-high-ground' or a downpour, am I appropriately equipped?

• **Track condition.** Can I self-recover a vehicle brought to a wheel-spinning halt in mud?

• **Off-road.** If my vehicle bellies-out on a bank can I recover it?

• **Overnighting.** If my recovery problems take so long that we are overtaken by darkness or sudden bad weather, have we food and warmth enough to overnight in the vehicle and resume operations in the morning?

• **Going for help.** If I get myself into such deep trouble off-road that I am unable to recover, how far is it to help and can I walk it with the equipment I have?

• **Emergency equipment.** Do I have any means of attracting attention?

(These are questions that will also influence your taking along a second vehicle)

Protective clothing

Plan for the worst. Usually you will be protecting against cold and wet. On any expedition, even a short drive on mountain tracks, you will not wish to – and certainly not be able to – remain in the vehicle with the heater on all the time. Assume, as a matter of course and whatever the weather at the start of your trip, that it will rain, get cold and blow a gale. Assume also that you will find it necessary to wade up to your knees in mud or water and/or walk a number of kilometres on rough ground. Equip yourself with appropriate clothing and add overalls and a groundsheet to lie on when you have to insert wading plugs or change a wheel. If you have not got recent (or any) experience of hill walking or similar outdoor pursuits, consult one of the many

Gumboots (note grip tread), light walking boots, extra socks, keep feet dry, warm and effective. Typical layers over day clothes: Helly Hansen fibrepile inner, Goretex trousers and outer (note drawstrings at waist _and_ hem, hood with drawstring). Woolly hat, scarf and, shown here, thin motorcycle gloves.

outdoor centres or camping gear shops for advice on the latest clothing. Some (for example Field and Trek in the UK) issue comprehensive catalogues containing invaluable advice on the pros and cons of different equipment. Standards of design and materials technology have never been higher – Goretex breathable water/windproof membrane and Thinsulate insulation being two developments that have made considerable impact on the design and effectiveness of outdoor clothing. Do your own study, adopt the layering principle – several layers of garments rather than a single very thick/warm one. The following will act as a guide:

• **Footwear.** Take two sets, knee-length rubber boots and hill-walking boots, each to be used with an extra pair of thick socks over your normal-wear socks. (You would not wish to walk far in gumboots nor carry out a reconnaissance wade-through of a stream in walking boots.) Keep them in a boot-bag or plastic sack to keep the inside of the vehicle clean.

• **Outer layer.** Fabric and Goretex overtrousers, roomy-fit hooded anorak of similar material with draw-cords at hood, waist and hem (preferable to waxed cotton which holds dirt, spoils seats, cannot be machine-washed, does not breath and needs regular re-proofing). Woolly hat or

Most common cause of problems is climatic – too cold or too hot. Be properly equipped.

Breakdown or bad bogging will involve prolonged work or walking outside the vehicle. Assume the worst weather and plan for it.

...continued

7.4 Equipment – contd

Don't let your enjoyment of scenery like this be marred by the consequences of cutting down on proper safety equipment. The same philosophy applies in 'green and pleasant lands' as in harsher climates elsewhere.

The satisfaction of being properly clad against the elements is complementary to that of being the master of difficult terrain in a 4x4.

similar to prevent heat-loss from the head. Two pairs of gloves – thin leather for driving, another set for mucky outside work.

•**Inner layers.** As experience demands. Fibre-pile jackets such as Helly-Hansen are excellent for warmth and wicking of perspiration; use as an either/or (or additional to) a Thinsulate zip-in liner to your anorak. Often a boiler-suit or overalls of generous cut can make a very practical inner layer over your day clothes when not wearing the wind/water proof out layers.

• **Other.** Groundsheet, as mentioned above.

• **Emergency.** Take a sleeping bag for emergency use in case you are overtaken by night or storm when stuck. It seems to be a rule of nature that all serious boggings take place just as the sun is going down.

• **Vehicle heater.** Remember, if you run the engine to keep the vehicle heater effective in snow, to be sure the exhaust pipe is clear of drifting snow that could prevent escape of poisonous exhaust fumes.

Recovery gear

Causes. Getting stuck with a greater or lesser degree of permanence will the be result of a temporary mis-match of your driving skills, assessment of the ground, capability of the vehicle and what the ground is actually like. More direct and

Goretex bivvy-bag and light sleeping bag (above) for emergencies. Below a selection of recovery gear – winch (with tree straps), load spreaders, <u>long</u> tow rope, shovels, fire extinguisher (cooking stoves?) and first aid kit.

specific causes will be:
- Soft ground.
- Slippery ground.
- Some manifestation of articulation limit.

Commonly a combination of all three is what will halt you. Note the exclusion of gradient as a cause of getting stuck. A vehicle capable of a nearly one-in-one climb on dry concrete is unlikely to be halted by any sensible gradient.

What to take, what to do. Getting close to the specifics like this will again emphasise the value of a second vehicle in the convoy. Re-read Section 5 and take:
- Two shovels (pointed ends, not spades); fold-away type will do.
- Long tow-rope, 7-tonne breaking strain minimum, not less than 25 metres long, with soft spliced-in eyes and U-bolt shackles.
- Standard hydraulic axle jack as supplied, wood baulk load spreader as above, plus second jack and baulk.
- Aluminium sand ladder. PSP or Barong grip/load spreaders.

Sound recovery gear need not be complex. Shovels, long tow ropes with shackles, jacks and load spreaders – re-read Section 5.

Section 8

Pressing down, pushing up

8.1. Loading

Capacity – weight and bulk

Never overload. This is probably the prime rule in operating any vehicle and, despite their reputation for strength, it applies to Land Rover products as well. Every engineered object has strength criteria to which it is designed – with margins that are adequate or generous according to design philosophy. To overload is to eat into strength and durability margins and, in the case of cargo in vehicles, will adversely affect handling and performance as well. Payloads for your particular vehicle appear in the Technical Data section – Section 9.1-9.6.

Margins of durability, strength, handling and braking will be eroded if you overload.

Minimise off-road weights. For a given duty load choose a vehicle specification which will comfortably cope with the weight involved rather than be on the limits. Do not exceed specification payload and gross vehicle weights (GVW).

Load density – weight vs bulk. A cubic foot of lead vs a cubic foot of compressed straw is an analogy of weight vs bulk that would immediately catch our attention. But in the rough and tumble of day to day fleet operation with loads of less obvious density variation it can be forgotten. This is particularly the case with high density loads where the availability of space can often obscure the fact that the payload limit has been reached. Operators should be especially alert to this and – following pages – pay attention to load distribution as well.

Bulk capacity – biggest single slide-in box (15 mm finger clearance sides/top)

Defender 90

Hard top

1030 (40.6)

1050 (41.3)

755 (29.7)

Pick-up, soft top

Spare wheel

830/1060 (32.7/41.7)

1160 (45.7)

800 (31.5)

Station wagon

1005 (39.6)

1050 (41.3)

660 (26.0)

Defender 110

Hard top

1750 (68.9)

1050 (41.3)

755 (29.7)

Pick-up, soft top

Spare wheel

1570/1780 (61.8/70.1)

1160 (45.7)

800 (31.5)

Station wagon

1100/1470 (43.3/57.9)

1050 (41.4)

660 (26.0)

Seats rolled forward

Discovery

3-door, 5-door
Rear seats up

Range Rover

100, 108 inch wheelbase
Rear seats up

1020 (40.2) 520 (20.5)

1080 (42.5)

1020 (40.2)

Rear seats rolled forward

1220 (48.0) 1080 (42.5)

820 (32.3) 530 (20.9)

800 (31.5) 1000 (39.4)

Rear seats rolled forward

1175 (46.23)
LSE: 1275 (50.2)

820 (32.8) 1000 (39.4)

1415 (55.7)
LSE:1515 (59.6)

Exact length depends on position of front seats

Defender 110/130 Hi Cap

Defender 110 HCPU

1060 (41.7) 1980 (78.0)

1160 (45.7)

Defender 130 HCPU

1060 (41.7) 1640 (64.6)

1160 (45.7)

New Range Rover

930 (36.6) 250 (9.8)

1000
(39.4)

1045 (41.1)

775 (30.5)

Rear seats
rolled forward

855 (33.7)

930 (36.6)

1365 (53.7) 1045 (41.1)

Exact length depends on position of front seats

Remember load den-
sity. Just because
there is room in the
vehicle does not
mean you have the
spare payload.

...continued

The Land Rover Experience

8.1. Loading – contd

Generic payload span*	
Defender 90	654–923 kg
Defender 110	1020–1245 kg
Defender 130	1400 kg +
Discovery	667–830 kg
Range Rover	400-440 kg

*Depending on engine, body type, suspension and transmission. See Section 9 for precise payloads for your vehicle.

Typical unit weights	
205 litre (45 Imp gal) barrel, empty	20 kg
205 litre barrel full of petrol, kerosene	185 kg
" " diesel, lube oil	200 kg
" " water	225 kg
20 litre (4.5 Imp gal) steel jerry can, empty	4 kg
20 litre steel jerry can full of petrol, kerosene	20 kg
" " diesel, lube oil	22 kg
" " water	24 kg

Tables show payload span of Land Rover product range and can be used with unit weights and diagrams opposite to get a feel for bulk/weight of typical standard-unit loads. Oil drums can be rolled into Hi Cap through its wider tailgate (below, left); they will fit, lying down, between standard Defender wheelboxes but cannot be rolled through tailgate (lower right).

**Standard 205 litre (45 Imp gal) barrel, jerry can
mm, (inches)**

Bulk and weight – common loads compared

Defender 90/110 – standard pick-ups

90

2 men each side
300 kg total

2 x 205 lit drums
water – 450 kg

Space for 15 jerry cans

110

4 men each side
600 kg total

3 x 205 lit drums
water – 675 kg

5 x 20 lit jerry cans diesel between
wheelarch boxes – 110 kg

Space for 25 jerry cans

Defender 110/130 – High Capacity pick-ups

110 HCPU: 5 x 205 lit drums diesel – 1000 kg
5 x 205 lit drums water weigh 1125 kg
(*NB Space available for 6 drums but max
payload is 1087 kg*)

Defender 130 HCPU loadbed is
shorter. Takes 4 drums.

110 HCPU

2 x 1 m sq pallets (110 HCPU)

Between wheelarches:
1 x 1 m sq pallet or 6 x 20 lit jerry cans
(6 cans diesel – 132 kg)

Room for 10 jerry cans at tailgate

...continued

The Land Rover Experience

8.1. Loading – contd

Excessive roof rack load – above – increases risk of tipping. (NB Camel Trophy vehicles have internal roll-cages which increase roof strength.) Photographs below show Land Rover Parts approved roof racks – ideal for bulky, relatively light, items such as surf-boards, skis or ladders. Maximum recommended roof load is 75 kg (50 kg for Discovery). Internally stowed and lashed loads (see next spread) are preferable to roof racks like that above.

Weight distribution would be better termed weight concentration. Concentrate it low down and at the front of the load bed.

Weight distribution

Normal weight distribution. As the axle load table at Section 8.2 shows, all Land Rover products are designed to take a greater load on their springs and axles at the rear when fully laden because that is the inevitable nature of the easy-access bonneted design.

Low down, 50/50 fore and aft. However, a degree of control over weight distribution lies with the operator. From a handling and flotation point of view in the most demanding conditions, the nearer a vehicle can get to a 50/50 fore and aft axle load condition the better it will be. Except with the lightest loads, even front/rear distribution will not be possible but *keeping the main load ahead of the rear axle* and as low down as possible will enhance both handling and flotation.

In on-the-limit flotation conditions 50/50 front/rear axle loads is best. Keep main load ahead of rear axle.

Distribution within the load. Thus even within a given load which may get close to your vehicle's maximum GVW it is sensible to place high density items at the front of the load bed and as close to the floor as possible. A vehicle bogging in soft sand or in mud will all too often be seen to sink at the rear first due to less than ideal weight distribution; evening-out the fore and aft load will help.

Check weights for best tyre pressures. Users regularly operating in limiting flotation conditions at less than maximum payload where rear axle load is low, can benefit from a calculated assessment of how low rear tyre pressures can go. Where standard loads or load kits are involved it would pay, as suggested at

Avoid roof rack or anything that will increase vehicle's moment of inertia. If you really do need one, put only light loads on it.

Section 8.2, to have a vehicle weighed front and rear to determine what axle loads really are.

Roof racks, external bolt-ons. A natural corollary of this attention to weight distribution is the elimination, where possible, of roof racks or other external bolt-on paraphernalia. These items increase a vehicle's moment of inertia in pitch and roll and can be a safety hazard when mis-

Variation of axle load with load position – 250 kg load

A 250 kg
610 mm (24 in)

1114 kg
(Kerb + 195 kg)

1052 kg
(Kerb + 55 kg)

Defender 110 HCPU Tdi at kerb weight

919 kg

998 kg

NB. *Danger of exceeding axle weights.*
A 638 kg load positioned aft at B would increase rear axle load to the top limit of 1850 kg. Front axle load in this case would be 250 kg lighter than at kerb weight.

B
1016 mm (40 in)

250 kg

1260 kg
(Kerb + 341 kg)

907 kg
(Kerb – 91 kg)

CAUTION. Poorly distributed load – too far aft – can result in rear axle load being exceeded.

Count trailer nose-weight as payload and remember its effect on vehicle dynamics – see Sections 4.1, 6.4.

used. Many expedition Land Rover vehicles have been grossly overloaded on the roof rack – and some, unsurprisingly, have paid the price by tipping. There are many operators, however, for whom a roof rack is essential and in these cases remember that the maximum roof load recommended for a Defender and Range Rover is 75 kg (50 kg for Discovery). This is enough to accommodate light bulky items such as ladders, small-section timber, canoes and the like.

Effect of trailers. Remember that a trailer, with its appropriate trailer preponderance (see Section 4.1 and 6.4), will, for a given actual nose load, exert a disproportionately high download on the rear axle because the tow hitch is well aft of the axle line. This is another reason for keeping cargo forward.

...continued

The Land Rover Experience

8.1. Loading – contd

Lashing cleats – military vehicle shown above – may be fitted to any Land Rover. Part number is RRC 3588/3674 plus locknuts. Older, non-plated version (left) from 1-tonne, is 395104. Typical suitable lashing straps are shown above – 1-inch and 1.5-inch webbing with over-centre tensioners.

Securing the load

Eliminating rattles, good driving. A rattling, sliding load jars the nerves as much as it does the vehicle and those who have experienced both will attest the beneficial effects of a well-secured load (and the resultant reduction of noise) on their driving ability and general composure. Noisy, rattling vehicles tend to be driven without consideration and the converse is true – a quiet, rattle-free vehicle is driven smoothly and with mechanical sympathy.

Rattle-free load carriers get driven well; lash the load.

The pay-off for this in multi-vehicle fleet operations and also in overland expeditions is notable in terms of reducing the stress the vehicle undergoes in difficult conditions.

Tie-downs. In general, loads may be stabilised by using rope in the cleats around the periphery of the Defender pick-up cargo area. The ease with which the cargo area of virtually any Land

Load lashing in practice: nowhere is it more important than on overland expeditions of the kind shown here using the Land Rover military One Tonne. Though expedition routine makes load lashing second nature, it need not be a chore in give-and-take fleet operation if thought is given to placing of cleats and provision of the right kind of straps.

Lashed-down fuel

Light boxes netted

Lashed-down water drums

Mid-wheelbase stowage for scientific instruments gives best ride

Water drum

Nylon lashing strap with over-centre tensioner

Sand ladders stowed on vehicle sides for quick access

Rover product can be customised with tie-downs makes the securing of planned loads a very straightforward business. Robust-gauge aluminium alloy panels permit tie-down cleats to be bolted into position without the risk of corrosion causing subsequent damage; position them astride strengtheners where possible. Military versions of Defenders have usually got these cleats in position already but the same parts (RRC 3588/3674) may be obtained from Land Rover dealerships for tailored installations. Use lashing straps with hooks and non-slip tighteners.

Cargo nets. A simple, unfussy way to secure a mixed load, particularly of 'soft' items, is to use a cargo net over a small tarpaulin and roped to the hood-canvas cleats.

Install internal lashing cleats to suit your most-used cargo format and use built-for-purpose lashing straps.

The Land Rover Experience

8.2. Tyres

Tyres function optimally – ie at their very best – in only one set of conditions. Operators can maximise effectiveness – including COST-effectiveness – by careful choice of tyre type, tread type, pressures and driving technique. 'Africa-S' shown here is limited-production specialist tyre.

Specialist tyres exist for every use. The converse of that is that for any variation in vehicle use all tyres are a compromise.

Tyre types, axle loads
What this Section does. This Section:
• Gives an overview of generic tyre types, with for and against information – Table 1.
• Shows how, with a knowledge of axle loads and payload, to arrive at an optimum tyre pressure for your particular job using any tyre for which you have data. Tables 2 and 3.
• Gives 'ready-made' data for a wide range of approved OE tyres – Tables 4-10.

Tyre types – specialisation vs compromise. For optimum traction there is a specialist tyre for just about every type of terrain. The converse, of course, is also true: whatever tyres you have fitted will have disadvantages on ground other than that for which they were designed. This is a simple fact of life – and the laws of physics – and any attempt to produce a multi-purpose, compromise tyre results in exactly that; a compromise. So, for example, a good mud tyre will be noisy, have a reduced tread life and be not very grippy on wet tarmac in comparison with a road-optimised tyre which in turn would have poor traction in muddy conditions. Road oriented and even M+S tyres (see table opposite) will usually have an S or T speed rating (113 or 118 mph max) whereas a good mud tyre, with its heavier build will probably be L – 75 mph max (see tables at end of this Section).

Major-use compromise. In very general terms, most 4x4s spend more time on public roads with tarmac surfaces than they do off-road, however important or challenging their off road forays may be. All Land Rover products are supplied with original equipment (OE) tyres appropriate to the needs of these average model users since, in the same general terms, it is sensible to use tyres that retain the hard-road grip required for steering and braking. It is ultimately for you, as operator, to decide in which direction you wish to optimise your tyre performance. The information that follows gives a guide to the strengths and weaknesses of each specialist-use tyre type.

Table 1 – Tyre types and characteristics

Road oriented	Optimised for tarmac. Close tread, relatively smooth with sipes ('knife cuts')	**For:** Long life, quiet, smooth running, best braking. **Against:** Close tread susceptible to filling in mud, reducing traction.	
M+S tyre	M+S = Mud and Snow. Bolder tread version of road tyre. Quite a close, small bold tread. Sometimes provision for studs also.	**For:** As above but slightly less so. Good grip in snow and on grass. **Against:** Better in snow than mud. Close tread susceptible to filling in mud, reducing traction. (Note: Tread too bold to perform well on sand.)	
Mud tyre	Bold, open tread pattern, sharp right-angle edges. The best are quite narrow, have 'swept-back', self-cleaning tread pattern (illustration) designed for particular direction of rotation.	**For:** Very good in all types of mud and clay. **Against:** Grip on wet tarmac slightly impaired. 'Heel and toe' wear on tread blocks shortens life. Noisy. Limited speed rating. See also discussion at Section 4.7. (Note: The worst possible tyre for dry sand.)	
Multi purpose	Combination of mud tyre and road tyre build – usually a zig-zag centre band with bold transverse edge lugs. Wide variation in off-road performance among brands. Non-directional.	**For:** A good compromise for frequent on/off road use, eg farming. **Against:** Grip on wet tarmac slightly impaired on some multi-purpose tyres. Wears faster than road tyre, slightly noisy. See also discussion at Section 4.7. (Note: Poor on dry sand.)	
Sand tyres	Subtly shaped tread with shouldered blocks to compress sand in 'cups' (enhancing flotation and traction) rather than cut through it.Circumferentially grooved tyres look good but are ineffective in sand.	**For:** Very good for extracting last gramme of traction from sand. Robust enough for all desert terrain. **Against:** Poorer grip on wet tarmac must be allowed for. Some 'heel and toe' wear on tread blocks, some noise.Watch sidewalls on rock. (Note: Good flotation but poor performance in mud.)	
Tyres for rock	There are no tyres made specially for rock – by rock is meant any rough surface of large or small angular rocks or stones. The key to traversing rock lies with the driver – see Section 4.9. Clearly a robust tyre is best, in most cases a radial with a reinforced tread – but see below. The M+S, mud and multi-purpose types listed above would do well though the mud and multi-purpose tyres would have greater tread thickness. See below for special conditions applicable to sustained off-road operations in rocky conditions without on-road use*.		

*Cross-ply tyres. Where operations are almost exclusively off-road on rock or stone – such as fleet operations in quarries – the more damage-resistant qualities (at full inflation pressures) of cross-ply tyres could help keep operating costs down. It is essential, however, to consider and accommodate the following criteria:

a. Virtually all 7.50 x 16 cross-plies are – see table last page of this Section – 'L' speed rated, ie limited to 120 kph(75 mph), so should not be fitted to high powered vehicles operating on-road.

b. Cross-ply tyres have higher rolling resistance so will marginally reduce fuel economy.

c. Cross-plies have marginally less grip than radials on-road so handling affected.

Tyre designers have an impossible task trying to cater for all uses. Learn as much as you can about tyres and you will enormously enhance their effectiveness.

Land Rover OE (original equipment) tyres cover most operations. This Section guides you through choice, loads and pressures where you have special needs or re-supply problems....

.... and will in any case foster the requisite tyre-awareness!

... continued

The Land Rover Experience

8.2. Tyres – contd

If a fleet operator seldom runs his vehicles on road or at GVW, weighing representative vehicles to determine typical axle loads could establish an acceptably lower tyre pressure that would enhance off-road performance fleet-wide.

Tyre pressures and axle loads are interdependent – both affect sidewall deflection, a critical criterion.

Tables 4-9 give you pressures for Land Rover OE tyres at GVW and kerb weight on- and off-road. For other tyres follow the Table 3 example.

Tyre pressures – relevance of axle loads. Tyres give their optimum performance – the best combination of grip, handling response, operating temperature (important for structural reasons) and a degree of shock absorption – when their elements (tread, beads and sidewalls) are optimally disposed to one another. The main criterion in determining this is sidewall deflection and this is established by the load on the tyre and its internal pressure. There is thus a theoretically optimum tyre pressure for every change in axle load or payload within the vehicle; this is why front and rear tyre pressures are different. In practice (and to ensure you do not spend your whole life changing tyre pressures) there is some latitude and usually two sets (ie front and rear) of pressures are quoted for vehicles – one for the unladen and one for the fully laden condition. These, of course, are based on individual front and rear axle loads – the weight each axle carries. Because they will be of use in determining the pressures to be used with specialist tyres – ie any not shown on the following pages – a table of axle loads for all Land Rover vehicles is given on the facing page.

Vehicle type Maximum weights GVW and maximum individual axle loads. See notes 1 and 2. GVW/front/rear max	Body type and/or manual/auto	Axle loads at kerb weight – 2.5 petrol engine Front/rear Kg	Axle loads at kerb weight – V8 petrol engine Front/rear Kg	Axle loads at kerb weight – 2.5D or VM engine Front/rear Kg	Axle loads at kerb weight – Tdi engine Front/rear Kg
Defender 90 Std: 2400/1200/1380 Hi-load suspension: 2550/1200/1500	Soft top Pick up Hard top Station wagon	922/714 919/717 916/767 911/790	908/719 905/722 902/770 897/793	946/710 943/722 940/763 935/786	971/724 967/727 960/786 959/834
Defender 110 Levelled suspension: 2950/1200/1750 Unlevelled susp'n: 3050/1200/1850	Soft top Pick up Hi cap pick up Hard top Station wagon County	941/864 940/875 938/915 938/902 924/1019 935/1044	941/865 939/876 937/916 937/903 935/1009 935/1045	972/856 972/867 970/907 970/897 955/1014 966/1039	1004/868 1000/880 998/919 994/919 982/1036 993/1061
Defender 130 3500/1500/2200	Crew cab HCPU	-	1027/985	-	1070/1016
Discovery V8: 2720/1100/1650 Tdi: 2720/1200/1650	3 dr manual 3 dr auto 5 dr manual 5 dr auto	- - - -	921/998 921/998 921/1065 921/1065	- - - -	991/1017 - 1006/1047 -
Range Rover 3.9 V8: 2510/1100/1510 Tdi Diesel: 2510/1200/1510 4.2 LSE: 2620/1200/1620	2 dr manual 2 dr auto 4 dr manual 4 dr auto LSE	- - - - -	952/968 979/972 964/922 980/1020 1070/1080	1027/1004 1039/1027 -	1024/1028 1024/1028 -
New Range Rover All versions: 2780/1320/1840	manual auto		*4.0 V8* 1171/1081 1176/1086	*4.6 V8* 1171/1081 1176/1086	*2.5 diesel* 1187/1072 -

If you want the best tyre performance or want to save the time wasted in recovery in your fleet, check axle loads and tyre pressures.

NOTE 1: Gross vehicle weight (GVW), ie weight fully laden, is the maximum weight for which the suspension was designed so is constant for a given vehicle type. Only where the suspension itself has an alternative specification, as in the Defender 90 and Defender 110, or where heavier diesel engines are fitted, are different GVWs or GVW axle loads shown.

NOTE 2: Because it is not always easy to get weight distribution front/rear precisely correct, individual axles may be loaded to the 'max' figures shown so long as the *overall* GVW is not exceeded. Note that in most cases the sum of the front and rear 'max' figures would exceed the GVW so do not load both axles to max. The Defender 110 has max and actual axle loads at GVW that are the same.

NOTE 3: Kerb weight (sometimes 'EEC kerb'), is defined as unladen weight plus full fuel plus a 75 kg driver.

NOTE 4 – Using the figures. *Example:*

Defender 90
Std: 2400/1200/1380

This means the Defender with standard suspension (ie not fitted with the hi-load heavy duty springs) has a maximum loaded weight of 2400 kg. *Individual* axles can take a max of up to 1200 kg at front, 1380 kg at rear – but not at the same time (since 1200 +1380 = 2580 which would exceed the 2400 kg GVW maximum for standard suspension.)

NOTE 5 – Using the figures. *Example:*

Defender 90. Station wagon, Tdi engine, axle loads at kerb weight: 959/834

This means an *empty* Tdi Defender 90 Station Wagon has axle loads of 959 kg front and 834 kg rear. If you aim to carry a 300 kg payload in the rear (assume exactly over the rear axle), the rear axle load will be 1134 kg. So 959/1134 are the figures you would enter into the tyre pressures table on the next page.

... continued

The Land Rover Experience

8.2. Tyres – contd

Do axle loads really matter? In a word, yes. The reason you are reading this section at all is that you want the best flotation and performance from your tyres under specific conditions; clearly you do not want this if it will hazard your vehicles' safety or durability or damage your tyres. Applying the correct axle loads (accurate to 100 kg will do) to tyre data from a manufacturer will enable you to select a pressure that will yield best

flotation and performance without compromising safety and durability. The span of the figures is considerable; an unladen Defender 90 rear axle carries only 38% of the load that the rear axle of a laden Defender 110 does. That matters. The above table can be used to interpolate axle loads – between unladen and fully laden – for your particular type of operations. For precise further details contact the tyre manufacturer but they will need the axle loads given above. Axle load is greatly (and surprisingly) affected by load distribution – diagrams Section 8.1.

Axle load	Wheel load	On-road tyre pressures – bar										Off-road pressures – bar	
												Track	Sand/mud
kg	kg				Speed km/hr							65 kph	20 kph
		120	110	100	90	80	65	50	40	30	20		
2000	1000	3.75	3.8	3.8	3.5	3.4	3.4	3.4	3.3	3.3	3.1	3.1	1.7
1880	940	3.5	3.4	3.3	3.2	3.2	3.1	3.1	3.1	3.0	2.8	2.5	1.2
1800	900	3.3	3.2	3.1	3.0	3.0	3.0	3.0	2.9	2.8.	2.7	2.4	1.2
1600	800	2.8	2.7	2.7	2.6	2.6	2.6	2.5	2.5	2.4	2.3	2.1	1.0
1400	700	2.4	2.3	2.3	2.2	2.2	2.2	2.1	2.1	2.1	2.0	1.7	0.8
1200	600	2.0	1.9	1.9	1.8	1.8	1.8	1.8	1.8	1.7	1.6	1.4	0.6
1000	500	1.6	1.5	1.5	1.4	1.4	1.4	1.4	1.4	1.3	1.3	1.1	0.6
800	400	1.2	1.1	1.1	1.1	1.0	1.0	1.0	1.0	1.0	0.9	0.8	0.6

Table 3 – Pressures (on/off-road) vs wheel load, speed – example 7.50 x 16 Michelin XS

NOTE – Using the figures. *Example:* Take the Tdi Defender 90 Station Wagon on the previous page (Note 5) with front/rear axle loads of 959 and 1134 kg.
• *On-road.* Reading from the axle load column above, for a 120 kph road speed (interpolating or using next highest pressure), the vehicle should run at 1.6 bar front and 2.0 bar rear <u>minimum.</u>
• *Off-road.* Similarly the off-road figures that may be used, where you want the lowest pressures for reasons of flotation or ride, are 1.1 bar front and 1.4 bar rear *on tracks* at a <u>*speed not exceeding 65 kph*</u>.. If you got bogged in soft sand, the emergency soft would be 0.6 bar front and rear at <u>*at a speed not over 20 kph (12 mph)*</u>. (NB Here, for handling reasons, 0.6 bar not recommended; see Tables 4 and 10.)

Overall picture. Having chosen your tyre type from Table 1, and ascertained your axle load from Table 2 you would apply it to a manufacturer's data sheet like Table 3 above to get the operating pressures on and off-road. (Note incidentally that 65 kph on-road demands a higher pressure than 65 kph off-road due to heat dissipation problems). The next two spreads give you ready-access information for Land Rover approved OE tyres.

Optimum pressures

Tyre pressures – three conditions. To get the best out of your tyres and vehicle on:

- roads
- on tracks and poor roads and
- emergency flotation conditions

you need three sets of tyre pressures. As we have seen (Sections 4.7, 4.8, and in the adjacent diagram) lowering tyre pressures increases the size of the tyre 'footprint' and thus lowers the unit pressure on the ground. The ground is thus less stressed and will yield better traction and flotation, so assisting a vehicle in traversing difficult terrain or in self-recovery if it is stuck. But we have also seen that a tyre has an optimum operating pressure. This assumes given criteria of handling response and maximum speed.

Limit the speed when deflated. It follows, therefore, that if we reduce the tyre pressures we must also accept different handling characteristics and, for structural and safety reasons, also limit the maximum speed when at reduced pressures. The tables that follow list (at kerb weight and at maximum permitted laden weight – GVW), firstly, normal road pressures which assume best handling and unlimited speed; secondly, 'tracks and poor road' pressures which might be applicable to tracks with more difficult off-road diversions; and finally 'emergency flotation' is listed where the terrain requires the absolute maximum flotation and traction. This latter would be applicable to terrain at the limits of your vehicle's off-road capabilities or for self-recovery from a bogged situation; such use *must be followed by re-inflation to appropriate road or tracks pressures.*

Preliminary note: For reasons of simplicity of operation, Land Rover handbooks quote a single set of front/rear tyre pressures (shown underlined in the tables here) catering for all conditions up to maximum load on hard roads. However, where flotation, traction and/or comfort are important, operators should follow the lower pressure recommendations in the tables on the next spread. (Note that these pressures assume 'normal' ambient temperatures – about 15°C ±10°. Tyre pressure should always be checked 'cold', ie after the vehicle has been standing for an hour or more; never 'bleed' pressure from a warmed-up tyre. If ambient temperatures are high – around 30–45°C – increase all inflation pressures shown by 10% – eg 2.0 bar would be 2.2.)

Tyre footprint of Michelin XS at (left to right) road pressures, track pressure and emergency flotation pressure. Percentage increases in area are considerable.

Details count - even when you are having a difficult time. Always use tyre valve caps and replace them - without dirt and grit on the inside – when deflating and re-inflating tyres.

... continued

8.2. Tyres – contd

> **NB: Single, all-loads pressure underlined**

> *Different tyre pressures for different conditions. ESSENTIAL to keep within speed and load limitations and reinflate tyres when back on easier ground.*

Tyre no	Tyre name and size	Load index / speed symbol (See end of Section)	Vehicle weight	Hard-road pressures (to max speed) Front / rear	Tracks and poor roads 40 mph max Front / rear	Off-road emergency flotation. 12 mph max Front / rear

Table 4 – Defender 90 – tyre pressure in bars (bars to psi – see table end of Section)

Tyre no	Tyre name and size	Load index / speed symbol	Vehicle weight	Hard-road Front / rear	Tracks/poor roads Front / rear	Off-road Front / rear
1.	Michelin 205 R 16 X M+S	99Q	Kerb GVW	1.9 / 2.1 <u>1.9 / 2.4</u>	1.6 / 1.9 1.7 / 2.1	1.2 / 1.2 1.2 / 1.4
2.	Michelin 7.50 R 16 X 4x4 Michelin 7.50 R 16 X-CL * Michelin 7.50 R 16 XS * Michelin 7.50 R 16 XZL *	108N 112L 108N 108N	Kerb GVW	1.8 / 2.0 <u>1.9 / 2.9</u>	1.4 / 1.6 1.5 / 2.2	1.1 / 1.2 1.1 / 1.7
3.	Goodyear 7.50 R 16 G90	116N	Kerb GVW	1.8 / 2.0 <u>1.9 / 2.9</u>	1.4 /1.6 1.5 / 2.2	1.1 / 1.2 1.1 / 1.7
4. and....	Goodrich 265/75R16 Mud Terrain Goodrich 265/75R16 All Terrain	120Q 120Q	Kerb GVW	1.7 / 1.9 <u>1.9 / 2.4</u>	1.4 / 1.4 1.4 / 1.6	0.8 / 0.8 1.0 / 1.4

NB Can also be used with **Defender 110 and 130** (heavy duty wheel) to give softer footprint. Check with dealer.

Table 5 - Defender 110 – tyre pressure in bars (bars to psi – see table end of Section)

Tyre no	Tyre name and size	Load index / speed symbol	Vehicle weight	Hard-road Front / rear	Tracks/poor roads Front / rear	Off-road Front / rear
1.	Michelin 7.50 R16 X 4x4 Michelin 7.50 R16 X-CL * Michelin 7.50 R16 XS * Michelin 7.50 R16 X ZY Michelin 7.50 R16 XZL *	108N 112L 108N 112L 108N	Kerb GVW	1.8 / 2.0 <u>1.9 / 3.3</u>	1.4 / 1.6 1.5 / 2.5	1.1 / 1.2 1.1 / 2.0
2.	Avon Rangemaster 7.50 R16	108/106N	Kerb GVW	1.8 / 2.1 <u>1.9 / 3.3</u>	1.6 / 1.6 1.8 / 2.1	1.1 / 1.1 1.1 / 1.8
3.	Goodyear 7.50 R 16 G90	108N	Kerb GVW	1.8 /2.1 <u>1.9 /3.3</u>	1.4 /1.6 1.5 / 2.5	1.1 / 1.2 1.1 / 2.0

Table 6 – Defender 130 – tyre pressure in bars (bars to psi – see table end of Section)

Tyre no	Tyre name and size	Load index / speed symbol	Vehicle weight	Hard-road Front / rear	Tracks/poor roads Front / rear	Off-road Front / rear
1.	Michelin 7.50 R16 XZY Michelin 7.50 R16 X-CL * Michelin 7.50 R16 XS * Michelin 750 R16 X ZL *	112L 112L 108N 108N	Kerb GVW	1.9 / 2.1 <u>3.0 / 4.5</u>	1.6 / 1.6 2.4 / 3.6	1.2 / 1.3 1.8 / 2.8
2.	Goodyear 7.50 R 16 G90	108N	Kerb GVW	1.9 / 2.1 <u>3.0 / 4.5</u>	1.6 / 1.6 2.4 / 3.6	1.2 / 1.3 1.8 / 2.8

Table 7 – Discovery – tyre pressure in bars (bars to psi – see table end of Section)

Tyre no	Tyre name and size	Load index / speed symbol	Vehicle weight	Hard-road Front / rear	Tracks/poor roads Front / rear	Off-road Front / rear
1.	Michelin 205 R 16 XM+S 244 TL	104T	Kerb GVW	1.9 / 2.2 <u>1.9 / 2.6</u>	1.6 / 2.0 1.6 / 2.3	1.2 / 1.2 1.2 / 1.4
2.	Michelin 235/70 R 16 4x4 TL	105H	Kerb GVW	1.8 / 2.0 <u>1.8 / 2.3</u>	1.6 / 1.8 1.6 / 2.0	1.2 / 1.2 1.2 / 1.4
3.	Pirelli Akros 205 R 16	104S	Kerb GVW	1.6 / 1.8 <u>1.9 / 2.6</u>	1.3 / 1.4 1.6 / 2.2	1.1 / 1.2 1.4 / 1.9
4.	Goodyear Wrangler 205 R 16	104T	Kerb GVW	1.9 / 2.2 <u>1.9 /2.6</u>	1.6 / 2.0 1.6 / 2.3	1.2 / 1.2 1.2 / 1.4

Tyre no	Tyre name and size	Load index/ speed symbol (see end of Section)	Vehicle weight	Hard road pressures (to max speed) Front/rear	Tracks and poor roads 40 mph max Front/rear	Off-road emergency flotation 12 mph max Front/rear
Discovery (contd)						
5.	Goodyear Eagle GT+4 235/70R16 105H		Kerb	1.8 / 2.0	1.6 / 1.8	1.2 / 1.2
			GVW	1.8 / 2.3	1.6 / 2.0	1.4 / 1.4

Table 8 – Range Rover – tyre pressure in bars (bars to psi – see table end of Section)

1.	Michelin 205 R 16 XM+S 244 TL	104T	Kerb	1.9 / 2.1	1.6 / 1.9	1.2 / 1.2
			GVW	1.9 / 2.4	1.6 / 2.1	1.2 / 1.4
2.	Goodyear Wrangler 205 R16	104T	Kerb	1.9 / 2.1	1.6 / 1.9	1.2 / 1.2
			GVW	1.9 / 2.4	1.6 / 2.1	1.2/ 1.4

Table 9 – New Range Rover – tyre pressure in bars (bars to psi – see table end of Section)

1. and....	Michelin 235/70 R 16 4x4 TL Pirelli Scorpion II 235/70 R 16	105H 105H	Kerb GVW	1.9 / 2.2 1.9 / 2.6	1.6 / 2.0 1.6 / 2.3	1.2 / 1.2 1.2 / 1.4
2. and....	Michelin 255/65 R 16 4x4 TL Pirelli Scorpion II 255/65 R 16	109H 109H	Kerb GVW	1.9 / 2.2 1.9 / 2.6	1.6 / 2.0 1.6 / 2.3	1.2 / 1.2 1.2 / 1.4

NOTE – Table 10

Off-road tyres. Although low speeds are involved, Land Rover have imposed the lower limits of tyre pressures in Tables 4-9 for handling reasons and to reduce the possibility of dislodging a tyre. Certain of Michelin's off-road tyres – **indicated * above** – are, however, cleared by Michelin structurally and operationally to function at and benefit from exceptionally low pressures – down to 0.60 bar (9 psi) – where the absolute limit of flotation must be combined with the tyres' other unique features. Michelin stipulate only that 'track' and 'emergency flotation' speed limits (as above) are observed and that, in sand, tubes should be used in case sand gets between bead and seat. These tyres will perform magnificently but you must still treat them with care; beware of damaging sidewalls, beware of extreme lateral stress that could roll them off the rims. Observe the speed limits scrupulously, re-inflate when clear. Pressures, listed against axle load, for the various tyres are shown right. You may ascertain the likely axle load for your vehicle by consulting Table 2 on the second spread of this Section.

Table 10 – Michelin off-road tyres

Tyre type/size	Axle load kg	Tracks 40 mph max	Sand/mud 12 mph max
7.00 R16 XCL	1000	1.20	0.60
	1400	1.90	1.00
	1600	2.30	1.20
	1800	2.70	1.40
7.00 R16 XZL	1200	1.30	0.60
	1400	1.50	0.80
	1600	1.80	0.90
	1800	2.70	1.30
7.50 R16 XCL	1000	1.10	0.90
	1400	1.80	0.90
	1600	2.20	1.10
	1800	2.50	1.30
	2240	3.30	1.80
7.50 R16 XS	1200	1.30	0.60
	1600	1.90	0.90
	1800	2.20	1.10
	2000	2.60	1.30
7.50 R16 XZL (Also known as '4x4 O/R')	1200	1.40	0.70
	1400	1.80	0.90
	1600	2.20	1.10
	1800	2.50	1.30
	2240	3.30	1.80

... continued

The Land Rover Experience

8.2. Tyres – contd

Tyre pressures – speed warning. It is important to emphasise the speed limitations at reduced pressures shown in the columns on the previous spread. Never exceed the speed limits shown there. Driving too fast on under-inflated tyres will cause structural damage to your tyres through over-heating and possible de-lamination of the carcass; it will usually produce unacceptable handling and the possibility of rolling the tyres off the rims on corners. Be sure always to *be equipped with an accurate tyre pressure gauge and a re-inflation pump* if you are going off-road-ing.

Pressure gauges, re-inflation. It has often been shown that concern for and care of tyres can be set at naught by that weakest of weak links the tyre pressure gauge. The pen-type gauge is often inac-

Make it easy if you can. Re-inflation by muscle power is very hard work taking four tyres from emergency low to track pressures – especially in hot climates. Where there is a repeated heavy duty working requirement for re-inflation, using a line from the air brakes compressor (where fitted, see Section 4.1) or from a unit such as the ARB (opposite, top) fitted to one vehicle amongst a team may be more suitable. The ARB is actually designed for a locking axle differential but can inflate tyres as well. 12 volt electric pumps are probably best solution (opposite).

WARNING. A repeated warning about NEVER exceeding the speed and load limitations on tyres at reduced pressures.

curate and some dial gauges are not necessarily an improvement. Others, however, are good but should still be checked against one or more air hoses at service stations. In the UK such hoses and gauges have to be checked by law and can usually be relied upon. Once you have your accurate, proven tyre gauge, keep it in a dust-proof plastic bag in the vehicle at all

Obtain – and take care of – a good and accurate tyre pressure gauge.

Pen-type tyre gauges are better than no gauge but are not always accurate. Regularly checked against a calibrated source they are cheap and effective. Not all dial gauges are an improvement. Those shown are good.

tubed tyre, the same thing would not be possible with a tubeless tyre. A note, however, about alloy wheels which are designed with an internal AH (asymmetric hump) rim profile to enhance bead retention at very low pressures; these wheels are not recommended for use with tubes since low pressure flexing of the tyre can cause chafing of the tubes on the internal rim humps.

Small cheap electric pumps are surprisingly effective but get hot. It is worth having two – one cooling while the other is pumping. If using an electric pump be sure it cannot 'inhale' dust.

times. Re-inflation of the tyres after pressure reduction for-off road work is best done by an electric pump carried with you. Again you should be circumspect about the standard of unit you buy. Tyres fitted to Land Rover vehicles need a lot of air compared to car tyres so get a pump that is large, robust and can stand up to long periods of use without overheating.

Tubeless tyres. When severe off-road conditions are likely it is in most cases sensible, for two reasons, to fit tubes in your tyres. Firstly, encountering extreme conditions of roughness when inflation has been reduced to emergency soft could conceivably cause unseating of a tubeless tyre from the rim and thus cause total loss of pressure. Secondly, severe off-road conditions are often associated with operations away from full service facilities. Whilst changing or repairing a tyre by hand in the field is possible with a

Tubed tyres are best for remote-region off-roading as repair or replacement can be done by hand using low volume air supply. However, do not fit tubes to rims designed for tubeless tyres.

12 v electric tyre pumps are effective for in-the-field re-inflation.

... continued

The Land Rover Experience

8.2. Tyres – contd

Data on load and speed ratings, tyre construction and build are inscribed on the sidewall – see diagram opposite for full data and tables below for de-coding load index and speed symbol. Thus the Michelin X M+S 244 in the photographs, having a 99T load/speed rating is cleared to a maximum load per tyre of 775 kg up to 118 mph (at appropriate pressures).

Tyre nomenclature. A considerable amount of information is inscribed on the sidewall (and tread) of tyres, all of which is relevant to its specification – despite the assurances of those who would try to sell you tyres that are 'the same' as the one you specifically seek. The principal dimensions of a tyre are its width (not the depth between tread and bead) and the wheel diameter to which it is fitted. Thus

If you have to buy an unfamiliar tyre, everything you need to know about it will be written on the sidewall. If it isn't, don't buy it.

a '7.50 x 16' is a tyre designed for a 16 inch diameter wheel and having a normal inflated width – ie the external maximum width of the inflated, unladen tyre – of 7.50 inches; it is not necessarily the width of the tread itself. This width data can also be shown in millimetres (still allied to a rim size in inches) as in the 205 x 16. Other criteria, some of which are shown in the diagram opposite, are:

Manufacturer's generic name such as 'X'
Manufacturer's type number or name, eg XCL, Rangemaster, Wrangler
Metric width in mm, eg 205, 235
Aspect ratio (cross section height:width ratio percentage)
       - follows metric width when shown (would be 235/70).
'R' for radial
Overall tyre diameter (usually given in the US)
Load index/speed symbol – see tables opposite
Maximum load and pressure – in lb and psi in addition to load index (US requirement)
Sidewall and tread construction – plies and material, eg steel, rayon (US requirement)
Ply rating – (equivalent) sidewall plies in a crossply tyre
Wear indicators
Country of manufacture
Direction of rotation – sometimes shown
ECE and US Dept of Transport type approval mark

Tyre sidewall markings

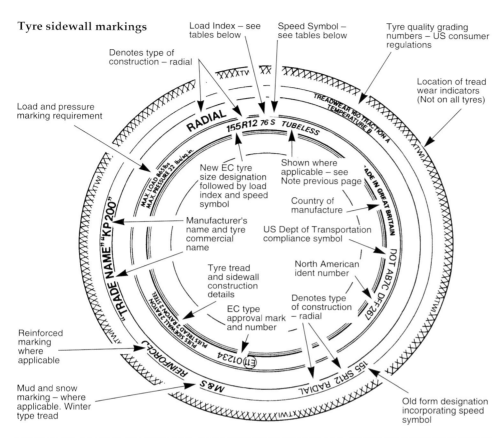

Load Index – see tables below

Speed Symbol – see tables below

Tyre quality grading numbers – US consumer regulations

Denotes type of construction – radial

Location of tread wear indicators (Not on all tyres)

Load and pressure marking requirement

New EC tyre size designation followed by load index and speed symbol

Shown where applicable – see Note previous page

Country of manufacture

Manufacturer's name and tyre commercial name

US Dept of Transportation compliance symbol

North American ident number

Tyre tread and sidewall construction details

EC type approval mark and number

Denotes type of construction – radial

Reinforced marking where applicable

Mud and snow marking – where applicable. Winter type tread

Old form designation incorporating speed symbol

Tyre Load Index			
(NB Max load per-tyre at full road pressures at speed shown by accompanying speed symbol)			
Index	kg	Index	kg
97	730	111	1090
98	750	112	1120
99	775	113	1150
100	800	114	1180
101	825	115	1215
102	850	116	1250
103	875	117	1285
104	900	118	1320
105	925	119	1360
106	950	120	1400
107	975	121	1450
108	1000	122	1500
109	1030	123	1550
110	1060	124	1600

Tyre Speed Symbol		
(NB Max speed at full road pressures at per-tyre load shown by load index		
Symbol	kph	mph
J	100	62
K	110	68
L	120	75
M	130	81
N	140	87
P	150	95
Q	160	100
R	170	105
S	180	113
T	190	118
U	200	125
H	210	130
V	240	150
VR	210/240	130/150

Tyre pressures – bars to (nearest whole) psi			
Bars	psi	Bars	psi
1.1	16	2.7	39
1.2	17	2.8	41
1.3	19	2.9	42
1.4	20	3.0	44
1.5	22	3.1	45
1.6	23	3.2	46
1.7	25	3.3	48
1.8	26	3.4	49
1.9	27	3.5	51
2.0	29	3.6	52
2.1	30		
2.2	32	4.3	62
2.3	33	4.4	64
2.4	35	4.5	65
2.5	36	4.6	67
2.6	38	4.7	68

Using the figures:
A load/speed index of 108N defines outer-limits ultimate capability: max load of 1000 kg per tyre ; max speed 87 mph. Having selected your tyre, then apply tyre pressures according to actual loads and speeds in tables 1-10.

Most good mud tyres and crossplies (heavy tread) have an L-rating – 75 mph maximum.

Section 9

Technical data

9.1. Technical data – Defender 90

Weights

Model	90 Soft Top				90 Pick-Up				90 Hard Top				90 County Station Wagon			
Engine	2.5P	3.5P	2.5D	2.5Tdi	2.5P	3.5P	2.5D	2.5Tdi	2.5P	3.5P	2.5D	2.5Tdi	2.5P	3.5P	2.5D	2.5Tdi
Gross vehicle weight kg	Standard suspension: 2400															
Kerb weight kg	1652	1643	1672	1686	1652	1643	1681	1686	1699	1688	1719	1733	1717	1706	1737	1751
Payload kg	748	757	728	714	748	757	719	714	701	712	681	667	683	694	663	649
Gross vehicle weight kg	High load suspension: 2550															
Kerb weight kg	1659	1646	1675	1689	1655	1646	1684	1689	1703	1692	1723	1737	1721	1710	1741	1755
Payload kg	891	904	875	861	895	904	866	861	847	858	827	813	829	840	809	795
Seating capacity	2 – 7				2 – 7				2 – 7				6 – 7			

Defender 90 comes in four body options, each with four engine options, standard or high load suspension, manual or power assisted steering, two tyre-size options.

Exterior dimensions – mm (ins)

Width overall (excl mirrors) 1790 (70.5)

Height 1963-2061max (tyre,suspension options) (77.3-81.1)

Lashing rings 144 (5.66)

Track 1486 (58.5)

Wheelbase 2360 (92.9)

Overhang 635 (25.0)

Length overall Soft top/pick-up 3722 (146.5) Hard top/stn wgn 3883 (152.9)

Lashing rings 293 (11.5) – plus spare wheel

Rear overhang Soft top/pick-up 727 (28.6) Spare wheel add approx 250 (9.80)

Wheelbase is 92.9 inches – the '90' name is wheelbase rounded to nearest 10 inches.

Interior dimensions – mm (ins)

See also Section 8.1– biggest slide-in box

Interior width: Station wagon 1400 (55.1) Others 1430 (56.3)

Wheel arch boxes height: 220 (9.2)

Interior height: Station wagon 1175 (46.3) Others 1205 (47.4)

Door aperture: Hard top/ station wagon 1080 (42.7)

Tailgate: 500 (19.7)

Door/tailgate width: 864 (34.0)

Width between wheel arch boxes: 925 (36.4)

Loadspace length: 1144 (45.0)

Length of load space times interior width gives load area of 1.63 sq metres.

Geometric limitations

Minimum under *axle*
204 (8.0) – 205R 16 tyres -
228 (9.0) – 7.50 x 16 tyres -

Min mid-chassis under *belly* – unladen
290 (11.4) approx
314 (12.4) approx

Tyres	Approach angle	Ramp angle (Kerb wt)	Departure angle
205R 16	48°	150°	49°
7.50 x 16	51°	146°	52°

Normal wading depth 500 (19.7). See Sec 4.10 re wading plugs

Max payloads of 649-904 kg give cargo 90s best power to weight ratio of the Defenders; best articulation of product range gives best off-road potential.

Longitudinal articulation angle: 7.51° (see Glossary)
Wheel movement at GVW, bump stops 50% compressed:
Front: 166 (6.5) up, 125 (4.9) down, total 291 (11.5)
Rear: 186 (7.3) up, 148.(5.8) down, total 334 (13.1)

Minimum kerb-kerb turning circle:
205R 16 tyres 11.7 m (38.4 ft)
7.50 x 16 tyres 12.3 m (40.4 ft)

Castor angle (kerb) 3°±0.5°
Swivel pin inclination 7°±0.5°
Ground offset 63.0 mm
Front wheel toe-out 0.60-1.80 mm
Turns, lock to lock. 4.0
Wheels. 5.50F x 16 in steel. 6.00JK x 16 styled, optional.
Tyres. See Section 8.2..

Beam axles and coil springs front and rear. Disc brakes front, and rear, servo assisted. Power assisted steering standard. (UK)

CHASSIS
Type. Box section, ladder construction. 2mm (14 swg) steel.
Paint treatment. Zinc phosphate, cathodic electro coat followed by waxing in rear cross member.

SUSPENSION
Standard suspension. Long travel single-rate coil springs, double acting hydraulic dampers. High-load rear springs (2550 kg GVW) are dual-rate

Front. Beam axle located by radius arms and Panhard rod.
Rear. Beam axle located by trailing links and central A-frame.
High load suspension. As above but with dual rate coil springs on the rear axle.

STEERING
Type. Power assisted, worm and roller (Adwest Varamatic).
Ratio (straight ahead).
Straight ahead – 19.1:1
On lock – 14.2:1
Camber angle (kerb wt) 0°

BRAKES
Type. Vacuum servo-assisted. 1-1 split dual-circuit hydraulic. Solid disc brakes front and rear.
Handbrake (parking brake). Drum type. Single drum operating on transfer box rear output shaft. Handbrake not for use while vehicle in motion. Cab warning light.

...continued

9.1. Tech data – Defender 90 – contd

ENGINE – PETROL V8
Type. V8-cylinder, aluminium construction with 5-bearing crankshaft and self-adjusting hydraulic tappets.
Bore. 88.9 mm (3.50 in)
Stroke. 71.12 mm (2.80 in)
Displacement. 3528 cc (215 in^3)
Compression ratio. 8.13:1
Max power. 134 bhp @ 5000 rpm (100 kw) 80/1269/EEC
Max torque. 187.0 lbf ft @ 2500 rpm (253 Nm).
(US spec: Fuel injected 3.9V8)

ENGINE – DIESEL Tdi
Type. 300 Tdi, 4 cylinder in-line, intercooled and turbo-charged high speed direct injection diesel. Cast iron with aluminium cylinder head. Rigidly-mounted auxiliaries with serpentine multi-ribbed belt and dynamic spring tensioner.
Bore. 90.47 mm (3.56 in)
Stroke. 97.00 mm (3.82 in)
Displacement. 2495 cc (152 cu in)
Compression ratio. 19.5:1
Max power. 111.3 bhp @ 4000 rpm (83 kw) 80/1269/EEC
Max torque. 195 lbf ft @ 1800 rpm (265 Nm).
Turbo-charger model. Garrett T25 BCI 15
Turbo operating pressure. 0.8-1.01 bar (0.81-1.05 kgf/cm^2, 11.6-14.9 lbf/in^2) @ 2500 rpm.

ENGINE – DIESEL N/A
(N/A = normally aspirated, ie not turbo-charged)
Type. 4 cylinder in-line. Cast iron block and cylinder head, 5 bearing crankshaft.
Bore. 90.47 mm (3.56 in)
Stroke. 97.00 mm (3.82 in)
Displacement. 2495 cc (152 cu in)
Compression ratio. 21:1
Max power. 67 bhp @ 4000 rpm (50 kw) 80/1269/EEC
Max torque. 114 lbf ft @ 1800 rpm (155 Nm)

ENGINE – PETROL 4 CYL
Type. 4 cylinder in-line, cast iron block and cylinder head, 5 bearing crankshaft.
Bore. 90.47 mm (3.56 in)
Stroke. 97.00 mm (3.82 in)
Displacement. 2495 cc (152 in^3)
Compression ratio. 8:1
Max power. 83 bhp @ 4000 rpm (62 kw) 80/1269/EEC
Max torque. 133 lbf ft @ 2000 rpm (181 Nm).

FUEL SYSTEM – PETROL V8
Carburettors. Two SU HIF44.
Fuel pump. Electrical, submerged in fuel tank.
Filters. In line.
Fuel tank construction. Mild steel, tin terne coated, seam welded. (US spec: high density polyurethane, blow moulded.)
Fuel. 91/93 RON leaded, 91/93 RON unleaded.

FUEL SYSTEM – DIESEL Tdi
Pump. Bosch R509.
Injectors: Bosch KBAL 90 P37 (2 spring).
Fuel pump. Bosch mechanical.
Fuel tank construction. Mild steel tin terne coated and seam welded.
Filters. In line filter.
Fuel. Derv class A1 or A2.

FUEL SYSTEM – DIESEL N/A
Type. Self governing DPA distributor type.
Fuel pump. Engine driven mechanical pump.
Fuel tank construction. Mild steel tin terne coated and stitch welded.
Filters. In line filter.
Fuel. Derv class A1 or A2.

FUEL SYSTEM – PET 4 CYL
Carburettor type. Weber 32/34 DM TL.
Fuel pump. Electrical, submerged in fuel tank.
Filters. In line.
Fuel tank construction. Mild steel, tin terne coated, stitch welded.
Fuel. 90 RON (2 star) leaded

90 RON unleaded.

COOLING SYSTEM
Type. Pressurised liquid with pump and mechanical fan.
Radiator
Except Tdi – copper and brass full face area type.
Tdi – copper and brass integral unit with oil cooler and aluminium intercooler.
Thermostat
Petrol 4 cyl, diesel N/A – 82°C.
V8 and diesel Tdi – 88°C.
Fan
V8 and diesel Tdi – 406 mm (16 in). Temperature sensitive viscous drive.
Petrol 4 cyl and diesel N/A – 390 mm (15.5 in), 4 blade.

ELECTRICAL SYSTEM
Battery (see also Glossary)
Petrol – 12v, 210/85/90.
Diesel and US spec petrol – 12v, 380/120/90.
Diesel N/A, cold climate – 12v, 490/170/90
Alternator
Petrol – 65 amp.
US spec petrol – 85 or 100 amp
Diesel – 65 amp.
Headlamps. 75/50 watt sealed beam units.

TRANSMISSION
Clutch
Hydraulic push, reduced-load clutch operation. Asbestos-free lining. Clutch plate diam:
V8 engine – 267 mm (10.5 in)
4-cyl engines – 235 mm (9.25 in)
(2.5P – 240 mm, 9.45 in)
Main gearbox. R380 manual gearbox: five forward speeds, one reverse. Synchromesh on all gears – triple cone 1st, 2nd and 3rd; large single cone on 4th and 5th. Synchronised constant-mesh reverse gear train. Integral oil pump with remote cooler in heavy duty derivatives.
Transfer gearbox. LT230T 2-speed reduction on main gearbox output. Front and rear drive permanently engaged via a third differential – locked mechanically by movement of the transfer lever to the left.

MAIN GEARBOX RATIOS – Defender 90, and mph per 1000 engine rpm

	Ratio	mph/1000 rpm 205 x 16 tyres		mph/1000 rpm 7.50 x 16 tyres	
		High	Low	High	Low
3.5.l V8 petrol					
5th	0.770:1	25.22	9.26	26.51	9.73
4th	1.000:1	19.42	7.13	20.41	7.49
3rd	1.397:1	13.90	5.10	14.61	5.36
2nd	2.132:1	9.11	3.34	9.57	3.51
1st	3.692:1	5.26	1.93	5.53	2.03
Rev	3.536:1	5.49	2.02	5.77	2.12
2.5 l petrol and N/A 2.5 l diesel					
5th	0.831:1	20.10	8.54	21.13	8.98
4th	1.000:1	16.71	7.10	17.56	7.45
3rd	1.507:1	11.09	4.71	11.65	4.95
2nd	2.301:1	7.26	3.09	7.63	3.24
1st	3.585:1	4.67	1.98	4.90	2.08
Rev	3.816:1	4.38	1.86	4.60	1.96
2.5.l diesel 300 Tdi					
5th	0.770:1	21.70	9.22	22.81	9.69
4th	1.000:1	16.71	7.10	17.56	7.46
3rd	1.397:1	11.96	5.08	12.57	5.34
2nd	2.132:1	7.84	3.33	8.24	3.50
1st	3.692:1	4.53	1.92	4.76	2.02
Rev	3.536:1	4.73	2.01	4.97	2.11

Defender 90 hard top

FINAL DRIVE
Axle ratios. 3.540:1
Transfer ratios

	V8	All 4-cyl engines
High	1.214:1	1.411:1
Low	3.308:1	3.320:1

Front axle. Spiral bevel crown wheel and pinion with fully enclosed constant velocity joints.
Rear axle. Spiral bevel crown wheel and pinion with fully floating shafts.

BODY
Material. All panels with the exception of the dash bulkhead are of aluminium alloy. Front wheelarches of galvanised steel.
Plating/painting. Zinc phosphate. Cathodic electrocoat, polyester surfacer. Colour coat – alkyd for solid colours.

CAPACITIES (litres, Imp gal)
Full fuel tank
54.5 lit (12 gal)
Cooling system
V8 petrol: 12.8 lit (22.5 pint)
4 cyl petrol: 10.8 lit (19 pint)
Diesel Tdi: 11.1 lit (20 pint)
Diesel N/A: 10.8 lit (19 pint)
Engine oil, including filter
V8 petrol: 5.66 lit (10 pint)
4 cyl engines: 6.85 lit
(12 pint), *300Tdi*: 6.65 lit (11.7)

Main gearbox
2.67 lit (4.7 pint)
Transfer gearbox
2.3 lit (4.0 pint)
Front differential
1.7 lit (3.0 pint)
Rear differential
1.7 lit (3.0 pint)
Swivel pin housing
0.35 lit (0.6 pint)
Power steering
2.9 lit (5.0 pint)
Windscreen washer reservoir
4.0 lit (7.0 pint), 5.5 lit (9.7 pt) if air conditioning fitted

9.2. Technical data – Defender 110

Pick-ups and soft-top

Weights

Model	110 Soft Top				110 Pick-Up				110 High Capacity Pick-Up			
Engine	2.5P	3.5P	2.5D	2.5Tdi	2.5P	3.5P	2.5D	2.5Tdi	2.5P	3.5P	2.5D	2.5Tdi
Gross vehicle weight kg	Unlevelled suspension: 3050											
Kerb weight kg	1821	1822	1844	1866	1821	1831	1855	1873	1869	1869	1893	1911
Payload kg	1229	1228	1206	1184	1229	1219	1195	1177	1181	1181	1157	1139
Gross vehicle weight kg	Levelled suspension: 2950											
Kerb weight kg	1845	1846	1868	1890	1845	1855	1879	1897	1893	1893	1917	1936
Payload kg	1105	1104	1082	1060	1105	1095	1071	1053	1057	1057	1033	1014
Seating capacity	2/3/11				2/3/11				2/3			

Exterior dimensions – *all* Defender 110 – mm (ins)

Defender 110 comes in six body options (see Sec 9.3 for full length hard-tops), each with four engine options, unlevelled or levelled suspension, manual or power assisted steering.

Overall width 1790 (70.5) (excl mirrors)

Lashing rings 165 (6.49)

Track 1486 (58.5)

Height 2060 (81.1) - max, all configurations, suspensions

Lashing rings 410 (16.1)

Wheelbase 2794 (110)

Overhang 730 (26.7)

Length overall 4438 (175) With door-mounted spare wheel – eg hardtop – 4599 (181)

Overhang 1010 (39.8)

Wheelbase is exactly 110 inches.

Interior dimensions – 110 std pick-ups, soft tops – mm (ins)

See also Section 8.1– biggest slide-in box

Interior width1430 (56.3)

Loadspace length 1900 (74.8) – reduce by 161 (6.3) for spare wheel

Tailgate 500 (20.0)

Tailgate aperture 864 (34.0)

Interior height (soft-top) 1205 (47.4)

Width between wheel arch boxes 925 (36.4)

Length of load space times interior width gives load area of 2.72 sq metres (3.36 sq metres on Hi Cap pick-up opposite).

Defender 110 High Capacity Pick-Up (HCPU) is cleared for slightly higher payload (about 38 kg) than standard version but its main strength is ability to accept far bulkier loads. HCPU left, standard 110 pickup, right.

Exterior dimensions – 110 High Capacity pick-up (HCPU)– mm (ins)

Dimensions differ from 110 standard pickup only in overall length, rear overhang, rear lashing rings, height.

Defender 110's max payloads of 1014-1229 kg (see Sec 9.3 for hard-tops) are higher than 90's and give best trade-off of power-weight ratio for load capacity. Hi Cap is optimised for lower-density bulky loads.

Height
Unlevelled: 2076 (81.7)
Levelled: 2052 (80.8)

Length overall 4631 (182.0)

Overhang 1202 (47.3)

Lashing rings 602 (23.7)

Loadspace – Defender 110 HCPU – mm (ins)

See also Section 8.1 – biggest slide-in box

Loadspace length 2010 (79.2) – NB Longer than Defender 130 HCPU

Interior width 1670 (65.75)

Width between wheel arches 1090 (43.0)

Tailgate 475 (19.0)

Tailgate aperture 1362 (53.6)

Beam axles and coil springs front and rear. Disc brakes front and rear, servo assisted. Power assisted steering standard.

...continued

9.2. Technical data – Defender 110
Pick-ups and soft top – continued

Geometric limitations

Hi Cap is designed for low-density loads, has full width tailgate, minimal intrusion of wheel arches and can accept 1-metre pallets.

110 Pick-up

50°

34.5°

152°

110 HCPU

34.5°

Minimum mid-chassis under *belly* 312 (12.3) approx

Minimum under *axle* 215 (8.5)

Minimum kerb-kerb turning circle 12.8 m (42.0 ft)

Normal wading depth 500 (19.7). See Sec 4.10 re wading plugs

Longitudinal articulation angle: 6.35° (see Glossary)
Wheel movement at GVW, bump stops 50% compressed:
Front: 166 (6.5) up, 125 (4.9) down, total 291 (11.5)
Rear: 186 (7.3) up, 148.(5.8) down, total 334 (13.1)

CHASSIS
As Defender 90 – Sec 9.1.

SUSPENSION
Type. Long travel coil spring, dual-rate front spring, single rate rear. Double-acting hydraulic dampers.
Front. Beam axle located by radius arms and Panhard rod.
Rear – unlevelled. (3050 kg GVW). Beam axle located by trailing links and central A-frame.
Rear – levelled. (2950 kg GVW). As above plus levelling unit and anti-roll bar.

STEERING
As Defender 90 – Sec 9.1
Wheels. 5.50F x 16 in steel. (Styled steel wheels from Defender 90 not suitable for 110 or 130).
Tyres. 7.50 x 16, see Sec 8.2.

BRAKES
As Defender 90 – see Sec 9.1.

ENGINES
Petrol V8, 3.5 ltr
Petrol 4 cyl, 2.5 ltr
Diesel Tdi, 2.5 ltr
Diesel N/A, 2.5 ltr
Engines as Defender 90, Sec 9.1

FUEL SYSTEMS
All fuel systems as Defender 90 according to engine type – see Sec 9.1. But see below regarding fuel tank capacity.

COOLING SYSTEMS
All cooling systems as Defender 90 according to engine type – see Sec 9.1.

ELECTRICAL SYSTEMS
All electrical systems as Defender 90 – see Sec 9.1 – except headlamps on County Station Wagon (Sec 9.3) which are halogen 60/55 w.

TRANSMISSION
Transmission system as Defender 90 – see Sec 9.1.

Defender 110 pick-up .. ... and HCPU (below)

MAIN GEARBOX RATIOS,
mph per 1000 engine rpm

Ratio	mph/1000 rpm 7.50 x 16 tyres	
	High	Low
3.5 l V8 pet, 2.5 l 300Tdi diesel		
5th	0.770:1	22.81	9.69
4th	1.000:1	17.56	7.46
3rd	1.397:1	12.57	5.34
2nd	2.132:1	8.24	3.50
1st	3.692:1	4.76	2.02
Rev	3.536:1	4.97	2.11
2.5 l petrol and N/A 2.5 l diesel		
5th	0.831:1	18.56	8.98
4th	1.000:1	15.42	7.46
3rd	1.507:1	10.23	4.95
2nd	2.301:1	5.71	3.24
1st	3.585:1	4.30	2.08
Rev	3.816:1	4.04	1.96

FINAL DRIVE
Axle ratios. 3.540:1
Transfer ratios

	V8, Tdi	Other 4-cyl
High	1.411:1	1.607:1
Low	3.320:1	3.320

Front axle, rear axle. As Defender 90 – see Sec 9.1.

BODY
Material and finish. As Defender 90 – see Sec 9.1.

CAPACITIES (litres, Imp gal)
All capacities as Defender 90 – Sec 9.1. – except the following:
Full fuel tank
Standard rear tank 79.5 lit (17.5 gal)
Side tank option – station wagon only – 45.5 lit (10.0 gal)
Side tank option – others – 68.2 lit (15.0 gal)
Rear differential
2.26 lit (4.0 pint)

9.3. Technical data – Defender 110, 130
Full-length hard-tops, 130 HCPU and crew cab

Weights

Model	110 Hard Top				110 Station Wagon				110 County				130 Crew Cab, HCPU	
Engine	2.5P	3.5P	2.5D	2.5Tdi	2.5P	3.5P	2.5D	2.5Tdi	2.5P	3.5P	2.5D	2.5Tdi	3.5P	2.5Tdi
Gross vehicle weight kg	Unlevelled suspension: 3050												3500	3500
Kerb weight kg	1856	1856	1883	1901	1959	1960	1975	2006	1970	1971	1996	2015	2066	2133
Payload kg	1194	1194	1167	1149	1091	1090	1075	1044	1080	1079	1054	1035	1434	1367
Gross vehicle weight kg	Levelled suspension: 2950												N/A	N/A
Kerb weight kg	1880	1880	1907	1925	1983	1984	1999	2030	1986	1987	2011	2031	N/A	N/A
Payload kg	1070	1070	1043	1025	967	966	951	920	964	963	939	919	N/A	N/A
Seating capacity	2/3/11				9/10/11/12				9/10/11/12				5/6/12	

Defender 130, as a production line vehicle, comes with a 6-man crew cab and slightly shortened Hi Cap pick up back end.

Exterior dimensions – Defender 130 (see Sec 9.2 for 110) – mm (ins)

Width overall 1790 (70.5) (Excl mirrors)

Lashing rings 165 (6.49)

Track 1486 (58.5)

Wheelbase 3226 (127.0)

Overhang 730 (28.7)

Length overall 5152 (202.8)

Height 2060 (81.1) - max, all configurations

Lashing rings 602 (23.7)

Overhang: 1192 (46.8). Spare wheel add approx 250 (9.80) on 110

It is also available, through Land Rover Special Vehicles as a chassis-cab – 3-man 2-door or 6-man 4-door – with almost any body a customer may require. Engines are V8 or Tdi only. Wheelbase is 127 inches.

Loadspace – Defender 130 Crew Cab HCPU – mm (ins)

See also Section 8.1– biggest slide-in box

Interior width 1670 (65.75)

Loadspace length 1670 (65.75) – NB Less than 110 HCPU

Width between wheel arches 1090 (43.0)

Tailgate 475 (19.0)

Tailgate aperture 1335 (52.5)

Length of load space times interior width gives load area (in the pick up portion) of 1.82 sq metres. Modular body options shown next spread.

Geometric limitations Defender 130 (all 110s at Sec 9.2) – mm (ins)

Minimum kerb-kerb turning circle
15.1 m (49.0 ft)

Minimum under *axle* clearance 215 (8.5)

Minimum mid chassis under *belly* clearance 390 (15.4) approx

50°   151°   34.5°

Normal wading depth 500 (19.7). See Sec 4.10 re wading plugs

Longitudinal articulation angle: 5.51° (see Glossary)
Wheel movement at GVW, bump stops 50% compressed:
Front: 166 (6.5) up, 125 (4.9) down, total 291 (11.5)
Rear: 186 (7.3) up, 148.(5.8) down, total 334 (13.1)

Defender 110 hard top, estates' payload is 919-1194 kg. Production Defender 130s' is over 1350 kg. Special Vehicles models share same 3500 kg GVW; payload will vary with body.

Interior dimensions – 110 hardtop (see also Sec 9.2) – mm (ins)

Dimensions similar to Defender 90 hardtop except for loadspace length

See also Section 8.1 – biggest slide-in box

Interior width: 1430 (56.3)

Wheel arch boxes height: 220 (9.2)

Loadspace length: 1900 (74.8)

Interior height: 1205 (47.7) [station wagon 1175 (46.3)]

Door aperture 1080 (42.7)

Door width 864 (34.0) – but see p 118 load-widths

Width between wheel arch boxes: 925 (36.4)

As with other Defenders, 130 has beam axles and coil springs front and rear. Disc brakes front, drums rear, servo assisted. Power steering is standard on 130.

...continued

9.3. Technical data – Defender 110, 130
Full-length hard-tops, 130 HCPU and crew cab – continued

Land Rover Special Vehicles Quadtec modular body
system for Defender 130

Quadtec 1 and 2 for 6-man crew-cab

Quadtec 1 – low profile

1155 (46)

1620 (64)

1550 (61)

Quadtec 2 – high profile

Quadtec 3 and 4 for 3-man cab

1155 (46)

Quadtec 3 – low profile

2450 (96)

1550 (61)

Quadtec 4 – high profile

*NB Technical data for hard-
top Defender 110 in this section
is the same as for 110 pick-ups
and soft top as shown in
Section 9.2. Written data here
mainly concerns Defender 130.*

CHASSIS
As Defender 90 – see Sec 9.1.

SUSPENSION
Defender 110 – see Sec 9.2.
Defender 130 – as below:
Type. Long travel coil springs.
Single rate front spring. Rear
springs comprise two sets of
single rate coil springs co-
axially mounted each side, one
within the other. Double-acting
hydraulic dampers.
Front. Beam axle located by
radius arms and Panhard rod.
Rear. Beam axle located by
trailing links and central A-
frame. Unlevelled, with anti-
roll bar.

STEERING
Defender 110 – see Sec 9.2.
Defender 130:
As Defender 90 – Sec 9.1
Wheels. 6.50F x 16 in steel.
Tyres. 7.50 x 16, (130 tyres must
be 12 ply rating).

BRAKES
As Defender 90 – see Sec 9.1.

ENGINES
Defender 110 – see Sec 9.2.
Defender 130:
Petrol V8, 3.5 ltr
Diesel Tdi, 2.5 ltr
Engine details as Defender 90 –
see Sec 9.1.

FUEL SYSTEMS
Fuel systems as Defender 90
according to engine type – see
Sec 9.1. But see below re fuel
tank capacity on 130.

COOLING SYSTEMS
Cooling systems as Defender 90
according to engine type – see
Sec 9.1.

CAPACITIES
As Defender 110 – see Sec 9.2.

ELECTRICAL SYSTEM
Defender 110 – see Sec 9.2.
Defender 130:
As Defender 90 – see Sec 9.1.

TRANSMISSION
As Defender 90 – see Sec 9.1.

**GEAR , FINAL DRIVE
RATIOS**
Defender 110 – see Sec 9.2.
Defender 130:
Defender 130 is only fitted with
petrol V8 or diesel Tdi engines.
Overall and final drive ratios
are as for Defender 110 with
these engines – see Sec 9.2.

BODY
Material and finish. As
Defender 90.
Defender 130: Special Vehicles
bodies mainly aluminium.

Defender 110 hard top and estates (main picture) share same overall dimensions; 3-door hard top is all cargo aft of driver. 130s (lower shot) are, from left, Land Rover Special Vehicles Quadtec 4, tipper and Quadtec 1.

Defender 110 County and (below) 130 HCPU crew cab

9.4. Technical data – Discovery

Weights

Model	3 door			5 door		
Engine	3.9V8	2.5Tdi	2.0Mpi	3.9V8	2.5Tdi	2.0Mpi
Gross vehicle weight kg	All models 2720					
Kerb weight kg	1919	2008	1890	1986	2053	1925
Payload kg	801	712	830	734	667	795
Seating capacity	5 (7 if optional rear seats fitted)					

Notes:
1. Options affect kerb weight as shown:
adjust payload to keep within GVW.
　　Air conditioning　　　　　+42 kg
　　Auto transmission, V8, Tdi　-7 kg
　　Catalyst on V8 (Std on Mpi)　+7 kg

Discovery comes as a 3-door or a 5-door, each with the option of 3.9V8 or 2.0 l petrol or 2.5 l diesel engines. Auto transmission available with V8 and diesel.

Exterior dimensions mm (ins)

Width overall
2189 (86.18)
(inc mirrors)

Lashing rings
440 (17.32)

Overhang
462 (18.2)

Track
1486
(58.5)

Wheelbase
2540 (100)

Length overall 4538 (178.6)

Height:(top of roof bars) 1968 (77.5)
Exc bars 1914 (75.4)

Lashing rings
500 (19.68)

Overhang
839 (33.0)
inc spare wheel

Wheelbase is 100 inches.

Interior dimensions – mm (ins)

See also Section 8.1– biggest slide-in box

Door aperture – 1055 (41.54)

Loadspace length
Rear seats up
870 (34.25)
Rear seats folded
1325 (52.16)

Door aperture – 1540 (60.63)

Luggage capacity is 1.29 cu m (45.8 cu ft) seats up, 1.97 cu m (69.8 cu ft) seats down.

Geometric limitations

Minimum under *axle* clearance 204 (8.0)

Minimum mid-chassis under *belly* clearance 307 (12.1) approx

34.3°

29.0°

Ramp angle
V8, Mpi 151°
Tdi 149°

Normal wading depth 500 (19.7). See Sec 4.10 re wading plugs

Payload varies between 667 and 830 kg according to body type and engine.

Longitudinal articulation angle: 6.98° (see Glossary)
Wheel movement at GVW, bump stops 50% compressed:
Front: 166 (6.5) up, 125 (4.9) down, total 291 (11.5)
Rear: 186 (7.3) up, 148.(5.8) down, total 334 (13.1)

Minimum kerb-kerb turning circle 11.9 m (39.0 ft)

CHASSIS
Type. Box section, ladder construction. 2mm (14 swg) steel. 'Crush-can' energy absorbers at front bumpers.
Paint treatment. Zinc phosphate, cathodic electro coat followed by waxing in the box sections.

SUSPENSION
Type. Long travel coil spring, single rate front, dual rate rear. Double acting hydraulic dampers.
Front. Beam axle located by radius arms and Panhard rod.
Rear. Beam axle located by trailing links and central A-frame.

Levelling and control. Front and rear anti-roll bars.

STEERING
Type. Power assisted, worm and roller (Adwest Varamatic). Tilt-adjustable steering column.
Ratio, geometry.
Straight ahead – 19.3:1
On lock – 17.2:1
Camber angle (kerb wt) 0°
Castor angle (kerb) 3°±0.5°
Swivel pin inclination 7°±0.5°
Ground offset 63.0 mm
Front wheel toe-out 0.0-2.0 mm
Turns, lock to lock. 3.375.
Wheels.
7.00J x 16 in styled steel (standard, 3 door)
Alloy wheels with asymmetric

safety-hump feature to aid tyre retention at blow-out (suitable for Land Rover Parts design snowchains.):
7.00J x 16 in 5-spoke alloy (optional 3 door, standard 5 door; special style with 'Freestyle Choice' option)..
Tyres. See Section 8.2; tubeless tyres on asymmetric-hump safety alloy wheels.

BRAKES
Type. Vacuum servo-assisted. IH split dual circuit hydraulic, solid disc brakes front and rear. (Ventilated front discs, certain markets.) Asbestos-free pads on all vehicles. Optional anti-lock facility (ABS) provides electronic 4-channel anti-lock braking system usable on- and off-road.
Handbrake (parking brake). Single drum operating on transfer box rear output shaft. Handbrake not for use while vehicle in motion.

Beam axles and coil springs front and rear. Disc brakes front and rear, servo assisted; ABS optional. Power steering standard.

...continued

9.4. Technical data – Discovery – contd

ENGINE – V8i 3.9 litre, petrol
Type. V8-cylinder, aluminium construction with 5-bearing crankshaft, self-adjusting hydraulic tappets. Electronic engine management with a fuel injector for each cylinder. Rigidly-mounted auxiliaries with serpentine multi-ribbed belt and dynamic spring tensioner.
Bore. 94.0 mm (3.70 in)
Stroke. 71.1 mm (2.80 in)
Displacement. 3947 cc (241 in³)
Low compression engine
Compression ratio. 8.13:1
Max power. 170.3 bhp @ 4750 rpm (127 kw) 80/1269/EEC.
Max torque. 220 lbf ft @ 2500 rpm (298 Nm).
High compression engine
Compression ratio. 9.35:1
Max power. 185.1 bhp @ 4750 rpm (138 kw) 80/1269/EEC.
Max torque. 235 lbf ft @ 2600 rpm (319 Nm).
High compression catalyst engine
Compression ratio. 9.35:1
Max power. 182 bhp @ 4750 rpm (135.5 kw) 80/1269/EEC.
Max torque. 230 lbf ft @ 3100 rpm (313 Nm).

ENGINE – Tdi 2.5 litre, diesel
Type. 300 Tdi, 4 cylinder in-line, intercooled and turbo-charged high speed direct injection diesel. Cast iron with aluminium cylinder head. Rigidly-mounted auxiliaries with serpentine multi-ribbed belt and dynamic spring tensioner.
Bore. 90.47 mm (3.56 in)
Stroke. 97.00 mm (3.82 in)
Displacement. 2495 cc (152 in³)
Compression ratio. 19.5:1
Max power. 111.3 bhp @ 4000 rpm (83 kw) 80/1269/EEC .
Max torque. 195 lbf ft @ 1800 rpm (265 Nm).
Turbo-charger model. Garrett T25 BCI 15
Turbo operating pressure. 0.8-1.01 bar (0.81-1.05 kgf/cm², 11.6-14.9 lbf/in²) @ 2500 rpm.

ENGINE – Mpi 2.0 litre, petrol
Type. 2.0 Mpi, 4 cylinder in-line. Iron block, aluminium head, 16 valves with self-adjusting hydraulic tappets. Twin overhead camshafts, belt driven. Distributor-less, breaker-less quad-coil electronic engine management system. Catalyst exhaust standard. Poly-V belt accessory drive.
Bore. 84.5 mm (3.33 in)
Stroke. 89.0 mm (3.50 in)
Displacement. 1994 cc (121 in³)
Compression ratio. 10.0:1
Max power. 134 bhp @ 6000 rpm (100 kw) 80/1269/EEC.
Max torque. 140 lbf ft @ 3600 rpm (190 Nm).

FUEL SYSTEM – PETROL V8
Fuel injection type. Lucas electronic fuel injection with 14CUX-ECU.
Fuel pump. Electrical, submerged in fuel tank.
Filters. In line.
Fuel tank construction. Blow moulded plastic – high density polyurethane.
Fuel. 97 RON leaded, 95 RON unleaded.

FUEL SYSTEM – DIESEL Tdi
Injector pump. Bosch KBEL 98 PVI 870398 (2 spring).
Fuel pump. Engine driven mechanical pump.
Fuel tank construction. Blow moulded plastic – high density polyurethane.
Filters. In line filter.
Fuel. Derv class A1 or A2.

FUEL SYSTEM – PETROL Mpi
As V8 system except:
Fuel injection type. Multi-point electronic fuel injection with MEMS 1.6 fuelling and ignition ECU.
Fuel. 95 RON unleaded.

COOLING SYSTEM
Type. Pressurised liquid with pump and mechanical fan.

Radiator
V8 engine – copper and brass full face area. No oil cooler.
Tdi engine – copper and brass integral unit with oil cooler and aluminium intercooler.
Mpi engine – copper and brass full face area type. No oil cooler.
Gearbox oil cooler
V8 engine – single air blast.
Tdi and Mpi engine – none.
Thermostat. 88°C.
Fan
V8 – 432 mm (17 in).
Tdi – 406 mm (16 in).
Temperature sensitive viscous drive.
Mpi – single electrically driven 290 mm (11.4 in) fan; twin units when air conditioning fitted.

ELECTRICAL SYSTEM
Battery (see also Glossary)
Petrol – 12v, 210/85/90.
Diesel – 12v, 380/120/90.
Alternator
All models – 100 amp.
Headlamps. 60/55 watt halogen bulbs.

TRANSMISSION
Manual transmission
Clutch
Hydraulic push, reduced-load clutch operation. Asbestos-free lining. Clutch plate diam:
V8 engine – 267 mm (10.5 in)
Tdi engine – 235 mm (9.25 in)
Mpi engine – 242 mm (9.35 in)

Main gearbox. R380 manual gearbox incorporating five forward speeds and one reverse. Synchromesh on all gears – triple cone 1st, 2nd and 3rd; large single cone on 4th and 5th. Synchronised constant-mesh reverse gear train. Integral oil pump with remote cooler.
Automatic transmission
Automatic gearbox. Available on V8 and Tdi engines only. ZF type 4HP22 with four forward and one reverse speed. Incorporates automatic torque converter lock-up on 4th.
Manual and auto transmission
Transfer gearbox. LT230T 2-speed reduction on main

gearbox output. Drive to front and rear propeller shafts permanently engaged via a third differential which may be locked mechanically by movement of the transfer lever to the left.

MAIN GEARBOX RATIOS, mph per 1000 engine rpm

	Ratio	mph/1000 rpm High	Low
V8i manual			
5th	0.730:1	26.60	9.75
4th	1.000:1	19.50	7.12
3rd	1.397:1	14.00	5.10
2nd	2.132:1	9.07	3.34
1st	3.321:1	5.84	2.14
Rev	3.429:1	5.64	2.08
300 Tdi manual			
5th	0.770:1	25.30	9.24
4th	1.000:1	19.50	7.12
3rd	1.397:1	14.00	5.10
2nd	2.132:1	9.07	3.34
1st	3.692:1	5.24	1.93
Rev	3.429:1	5.64	2.08
Mpi manual			
5th	0.791:1	21.20	7.95
4th	1.000:1	16.80	6.30
3rd	1.396:1	12.00	4.50
2nd	2.131:1	7.90	2.96
1st	3.321:1	5.10	1.91
Rev	3.429:1	4.90	1.84
V8i and 300 Tdi automatic			
4th	0.728:1	26.80	9.79
3rd	1.000:1	19.50	7.14
2nd	1.480:1	13.20	4.82
1st	2.480:1	7.90	2.87
Rev	2.086:1	9.23	3.40

Discovery 5-door

FINAL DRIVE RATIOS
Axle ratios. 3.540:1
Transfer ratios

	All models
High	1.214:1
Low	3.308:1

Front axle. Spiral bevel crown wheel and pinion, enclosed constant velocity joints.
Rear axle. Spiral bevel crown wheel and pinion with fully floating shafts.

BODY
Construction. Steel monocoque frame with aluminium alloy body panels (roof panel steel). Side intrusion beams in front doors.
Aluminium panels. Front wings, bonnet, body sides, rear quarters, door outer panels.
Plating/painting. Zinc phosphate. Cathodic electrocoat, polyester surfacer. Colour coated either clear over metallic or alkyd solid colours.

CAPACITIES (litres, Imp gal)
Full fuel tank
88.6 lit (19.5 gal)
Usable fuel
81.7 lit (18.0 gal)
Low fuel warning
12 lit approx
Cooling system
V8 – 11.3 lit
Diesel Tdi – 11.5 lit
Mpi – 10 lit
Engine oil, including filter
V8 – 5.66 lit
Diesel Tdi – 6.75 lit
 Mpi – 4.5-5.5 lit (min-max)
Main gearbox (manual)
V8 – 3.17 lit
Diesel Tdi and Mpi – 2.67 lit
Main gearbox (auto)
9.8 lit
Transfer gearbox
2.8 lit
Front differential
1.7 lit
Rear differential
1.7 lit
Swivel pin housing
0.36 lit
Power steering
2.9 lit
Windscreen washer reservoir
7.4 lit

9.5. Technical data – Range Rover

Weights

Model	4 door 100 inch		4 door LSE 108 inch
Engine	3.9 V8	2.5Tdi	4.2 V8 Auto
Gross vehicle weight kg	All 100 inch models: 2510		2620
Kerb weight kg	2070	2110	2185
	440	400	435
Seating capacity	All models 4/5 seats		
To kerb wt add 42 kg for air conditioning. Reduce payload to keep within GVW.			

Exterior dimensions – mm (ins)

Range Rover comes as a 4-door; also available in long wheelbase format. The long (108 inch) wheelbase (known as Vogue LSE or County LWB – US Spec) has a 4.2 l engine, auto transmission and air suspension as standard.

External dimensions the same for LSE except :
Wheelbase: 2743 (108)
Overall length: 4676 (184.1)

Width overall 2080 (81.8) (inc mirrors)

Air suspension. To height shown, add or subtract figures shown on p 151 to obtain height in various EAS modes.

Lashing rings 320 (12.60)

Track 1486 (58.5)

Overhang 757 (29.8)

Wheelbase 2540 (100.0)

Standard levelled height 1792 (70.6)

Lashing rings 450 (17.72)

Length overall 4478 (176.3)

Overhang 1153 (45.4)

The Vogue and Vogue SE Range Rover has a 100 inch wheelbase. It is available with a 3.9 l petrol engine or a 2.5 l Tdi diesel. Both versions available with auto transmission and air suspension.

Interior dimensions – mm (ins)

See also Section 8.1- biggest slide-in box

Loadspace length
Rear seats up
870 (34.25)
Rear seats folded
100 inch – 1445 (56.9)
LSE – 1545 (60.8)

Tailgate aperture height – 870 (34.2)

Tailgate width – 1313 (51.7))

Luggage capacity is 1.02 cu m (36.2 cu ft) seats up; with seats down it is 2.00 cu m (70.8 cu ft) on the 100 inch, 2.16 cu m (76.3 cu ft) on the 108 inch.

Geometric limitations

Minimum under *axle* 204 (8.0)

108 in wheelbase (LSE)

Minimum mid-chassis under *belly*, approx:
Air Standard 305 (12.0))
Air High profile 345 (13.6)

EAS posn (see Glossary)	Approach angle	Ramp angle	Departure angle
Standard	35°	153°	30°
High profile	37°	150°	32°
Extended	39°	147°	33°

100 in wheelbase

Minimum under *belly*:
Air suspension as LSE
Coils as 'Standard' above

Payload varies between 400 and 440 kg according to body style and engine.

EAS posn (Glossary)	Approach angle	Ramp angle	Departure angle
Standard	35°	151° (Tdi 150°)	30°
High profile	37°	147°	32°
Extended	39°	145°	33°

Normal wading depth 500 (19.7)
With EAS: 540 (21.3)
See Sec 4.10 re wading plugs.

Minimum kerb-kerb turning circle
100 in wheelbase 11.9 m (39.0 ft)
108 in wheelbase (LSE) 12.9 m (41.8 ft)

Longitudinal articulation angle (see Glossary, Section 10.1)
100 inch wheelbase: 6.98°
108 inch wheelbase: 6.47°
Wheel movement at GVW, bump stops 50% compressed:
Front: 166 (6.5) up, 125 (4.9) down, total 291 (11.5)
Rear: 186 (7.3) up, 148.(5.8) down, total 334 (13.1)

Beam axles front and rear with coil springs or air suspension, both self-levelled. Disc brakes front and rear, with ABS and ETC option. Power steering standard.

CHASSIS
Type. Box section, ladder construction. 2mm (14 swg) steel. 'Crush-can' energy absorbers at front bumpers.
Paint treatment. Zinc phosphate, cathodic electro coat followed by waxing in the box sections.

SUSPENSION
Type. Long travel single rate coil springs (standard), or (optional) electronically controlled, variable-height air suspension. Double acting hydraulic dampers.
Front. Beam axle located by radius arms and Panhard rod.
Rear. Beam axle located by trailing links and central A-frame.
Levelling and control
Standard suspension
Self-energising Boge ride-levelling unit fitted to rear axle. Front and rear anti-roll bars standard on Vogue.

Air suspension (LSE, SE , option on Vogue). See Glossary - 'EAS'. Variable rate air springs. System activated by electric air compressor with pressure reservoir and modulated by an electronic control unit (ECU). Four selectable ride heights – standard, low, high and access. Auto selection of low above 50 mph (unless manually inhibited), automatic reversion to normal setting at given speeds. Automatic self levelling

...continued

9.5. Technical data – Range Rover – contd

front and rear. Ride height sensors fitted to radius arms. Front and rear anti-roll bars.

STEERING
Type. Power assisted, worm and roller (Adwest Varamatic).
Ratio.
Straight ahead – 19.3:1
On lock – 14.3:1
Camber angle (kerb wt) 0°
Castor angle (kerb) 3°±0.5°
Swivel pin inclination 7°±0.5°
Ground offset 63.0 mm
Front wheel toe-out 0.0-2.0 mm.
Turns, lock to lock. 3.375.
Wheels.
6.00JKJ x 16 in styled steel (standard model)
7.00J x 16 in alloy (Vogue, and SE).
Tyres. See Section 8.2; tubeless tyres on alloy wheels.

BRAKES
Type. Vacuum servo-assisted. IH split dual circuit hydraulic brakes, ventilated discs front, plain discs rear; asbestos-free pads.
Anti-lock brakes (ABS). Electrically driven hydraulic pump and reservoir provide power for electronic 4-channel anti-lock braking system usable on and off-road. ABS standard on Vogue SE and LSE models, optional on others.
Handbrake (parking brake). Single drum operating on transfer box rear output shaft. Handbrake not for use while vehicle in motion.

ENGINE – V8 4.2 litre
Type. V8-cylinder, aluminium construction with 5-bearing crankshaft, self-adjusting hydraulic tappets and fuel injection. Exhaust catalyst standard.
Bore. 93.98 mm (3.70 in)
Stroke. 77 mm (3.03 in)
Displacement. 4278 cc (261 in^3)
Compression ratio. 8.94:1
Max power. 200 bhp @ 4750

rpm (149 kw) 80/1269/EEC.
Max torque. 250 lbf ft @ 3250 rpm (340 Nm).

ENGINE – V8 3.9 litre
Type. V8-cylinder, aluminium construction with 5-bearing crankshaft, self-adjusting hydraulic tappets and fuel injection. Exhaust catalyst standard.
Bore. 94.0 mm (3.70 in)
Stroke. 71.1 mm (2.80 in)
Displacement. 3947 cc (241 in^3)
Compression ratio. 9.35:1
Max power. 181.6 bhp @ 4750 rpm (135.5 kw) 80/1269/EEC.
Max torque. 231.5 lbf ft @ 2600 rpm (314 Nm).

ENGINE – DIESEL Tdi
As Discovery – Sec 9.4.

FUEL SYSTEM – PETROL
As Discovery – Sec 9.4.

FUEL SYSTEM – DIESEL Tdi
As Discovery – Sec 9.4.

COOLING SYSTEM
Type. Pressurised liquid with pump and mechanical fan.
Radiator, oil coolers
V8 auto – copper and brass full face area type with twin oil coolers and single air blast gearbox oil cooler.
V8 manual – copper and brass full face area type with single oil cooler and single air blast gearbox oil cooler.
Tdi engine – copper and brass integral unit with oil cooler and aluminium intercooler.
Thermostat. 88°C.
Fan
V8 – 432 mm (17 in).
Tdi – 406 mm (16 in).
Temperature sensitive viscous drive.

ELECTRICAL SYSTEM
Battery (see also Glossary)
All models – 12v, 380/120/90.
Alternator
All models – 100 amp.

Headlamps. 60/55 watt halogen bulbs.

TRANSMISSION
Manual transmission
Clutch
Hydraulic push, reduced-load clutch operation. Asbestos-free lining. Clutch plate diam:
V8 engine – 267 mm (10.5 in)
Tdi engines – 235 mm (9.25 in)
Main gearbox. R380 manual gearbox incorporating five forward speeds and one reverse. Synchromesh on all gears – triple cone 1st, 2nd and 3rd; large single cone on 4th and 5th. Synchronised constant-mesh reverse gear train. Integral oil pump with remote cooler.
Automatic transmission
Automatic gearbox. Available on V8 engines only. ZF type 4HP22 with four forward and one reverse speed. Incorporates automatic torque converter lock-up on 4th.
Manual and auto transmission
Transfer gearbox. Borg Warner type 13-61-000-003 2-speed reduction on main gearbox output. Front and rear drive permanently engaged via a third differential – locked automatically by a viscous coupling unit (VCU) when front/rear prop shaft speed differences are sensed.
Electronic traction control – ETC
ETC is available on vehicles fitted with ABS. A spinning rear wheel is pulse braked to restore overall traction.

Differences between conventional coil springs and air suspension are shown above – viewed beneath rear axle looking forward. Note anti-roll bars in both cases, secured transversely between chassis members, curving forward to pick up beneath axle.

Range Rover 100 inch wheelbase 4-door (108 inch above)

MAIN GEARBOX RATIOS,
mph per 1000 engine rpm

	Ratio	mph/1000 rpm High	Low
V8 and Tdi automatic			
4th	0.728:1	26.91	10.00
3rd	1.000:1	19.59	7.28
2nd	1.480:1	13.24	4.92
1st	2.480:1	7.90	2.94
Rev	2.086:1	9.51	3.54
Tdi manual			
5th	0.770:1	25.45	9.46
4th	1.000:1	19.59	7.28
3rd	1.397:1	14.03	5.21
2nd	2.132:1	9.19	3.41
1st	3.692:1	5.31	1.97
Rev	3.429:1	5.71	2.12
3.9 l V8 manual			
5th	0.731:1	26.79	9.96
4th	1.000:1	19.59	7.28
3rd	1.397:1	14.03	5.21
2nd	2.132:1	9.19	3.41
1st	3.321:1	5.90	2.19
Rev	3.429:1	5.71	2.12

FINAL DRIVE
Axle ratios. 3.540:1
Transfer ratios
High   1.205:1
Low   3.245:1
Axles. As Discovery – Sec 9.4.

BODY
Construction. Steel monocoque, bonnet, tailgate, and rear lower quarter panels. **Aluminium panels.** Both front wings, roof, body sides, decker and upper rear quarters. All door outer panels. Side intrusion beams in doors.
Plating/painting. Zinc phosphate. Cathodic electrocoat, polyester surfacer. Colour coated either clear over metallic or alkyd for solid colours.

CAPACITIES (litres, Imp gal)
As Discovery – Sec 9.4 – except:
Engine oil, including filter
V8 – 6.66 lit
Diesel Tdi – 6.85 lit
Transfer gearbox
1.7 lit

9.6. Technical data – New Range Rover

Weights

Model	4 door				
Engine	4.0 V8	4.0 V8 Auto	4.6 V8	4.6 V8 Auto	MIX 2.5 diesel
Gross vehicle weight kg	2780				
Kerb weight	2252	2262	2252	2262	2259
Payload	603	593	603	593	596
Seating capacity	All models 4/5 seats				

New Range Rover comes as a 4-door with air suspension as standard.

Exterior dimensions – mm (ins)

Width overall
1889 (74.4)
(Excl mirrors)

Air suspension. To height shown, add or subtract figures shown Section 10.1 (Glossary – 'EAS') to obtain height in various EAS modes.

Lashing rings
388 (15.2)

Track
1540
(60.6)

Standard levelled
height 1803 (80.0)

Overhang
862 (33.9)

Wheelbase
2745 (108.0)

Rear track
1530 (60.24)

Length overall 4715 (185.6)

Overhang
1106 (43.5)

Lashing rings
359 (14.1)

The New Range Rover has a 108 inch wheelbase. It is available with a 4.0 l or 4.6 l V8 petrol engine or a 2.5 l 6 cylinder diesel. The petrol versions are available with auto transmission.

Interior dimensions – mm (ins)

See also Section 8.1- biggest slide-in box

Loadspace length
Rear seats up
1010 (39.8)
Rear seats folded
1841 (72.5)

Tailgate aperture
height – 960 (37.8)

Tailgate width –
1240 (48.8))

Luggage capacity is 522 litres seats, parcel shelf in use; with seats down it is 920 litres stacked to window line, 1643 litres stacked to roof .

Geometric limitations

Minimum under *axle* 214(8.43)

Normal wading depth 500 (19.7)

Minimum mid-chassis under *belly*, approx:
Air Standard 302 (11.9))
Air High profile 342 (13.4)

Ride height (see Glossary 'EAS')	Approach angle (to spoiler/bumper)	Ramp angle (235/70 or 255/65 tyres)	Departure angle to exhaust (pet/diesel)
Crawl/access	24 / 28°	160°	19-20°
Low	28 / 32°	156°	21-22°
Standard	30 / 34°	154°	23-24°
High	34 / 37°	151°	25-26°

Minimum kerb-kerb turning circle
235/70 x 16 tyres: 11.85 m (38.9 ft)
255/65 x 16 tyres: 11.89 m (39.0 ft)

Longitudinal articulation angle: 6.51° (see Glossary)
Wheel movement at GVW, bump stops 50% compressed:
Front: 159 (6.3) up, 135 (5.3) down, total 294 (11.6)
Rear: 178 (7.0) up, 153.(6.0) down, total 331 (13.01)

CHASSIS
Type. Box section, ladder construction. 2mm – 4mm steel; refined crash-collapse characteristics. Provision for detachable, stowable towing swan-neck using wheel nut wrench. Towing recovery eyes (one each front/rear). Lashing provision (2 each front/rear). 'Crush-can' energy absorbers at front bumpers.
Paint treatment. Zinc phosphate, cathodic electro coat followed by waxing in the box sections.

SUSPENSION
Type. Electronically controlled, variable-height air suspension – EAS (electronic air suspension). (See Section 10.1) Double acting hydraulic dampers.

Front. Beam axle located by cranked radius arms and Panhard rod; anti-roll bar.
Rear. Beam axle located by composite trailing link and Panhard rod.
Levelling and control
Automatic ride-levelling front and rear; periodic re-levelling when parked. Automatic control of normal and high speed ride height. Manual control of arduous off-road/wading, low profile and access height. Recovery from chassis-grounding off-road by automatic selection of 'extended' ride height position when wheel off-loading sensed. 'Crawl' (on the bump-stops) facility at access height up to 20 mph (alert warning at 10 mph). Fascia-mounted control switch,

Composite material trailing links for rear axle, clamped under axle and lateral-axis bolted to chassis, inhibit axle twisting so also function as an anti-roll bar. Note Panhard rod (upper left) for lateral location of axle (see Glossary).

...continued

The Land Rover Experience

9.6. Technical data – New Range Rover – contd

display and manual override; interface with message centre to provide suspension information. See Glossary under EAS, Section 10.1 for more detail. Ride height sensors fitted to radius arms.

STEERING
Type. Linear power assisted, recirculating ball with positive on-centre feel, hydraulic and mechanical lock stops. (PAS pump: ZF7691 petrol versions, ZF7681 diesel). Adjustable steering column (78 mm axial and 5-position tilt, 28° total); on-steering wheel options include cruise and radio controls, airbag.
Ratio, geometry.
Ratio, constant – 15.2:1
Camber angle (kerb wt) 0°
Castor angle (kerb) 4°±0.5°
Swivel pin inclination 8°±0.5°
Ground offset 17.0 mm
Front wheel toe-out 0.60-1.80 mm
Turns, lock to lock. 3.16.

Wide-span swivel pins (king-pins) and new design put front hub further into wheel, thus reducing ground offset for improved steering.

Wheels and tyres.
Alloy wheels with asymmetric safety-hump feature to aid tyre retention at blow-out. Suitable for Land Rover Parts design snowchains.
7.00J x 16 in 3-spoke, (standard), or 7.00J x 16 in 5-spoke New and Prestige style. Stainless steel capped wheelnuts. Steel spare wheel. Tubeless tyres, H-rated, 235/70 x 16 or 255/65 x 16 – see Section 8.2.

BRAKES
Type. Power-assisted, hydraulically activated disc brakes with permanently engaged dual circuit anti-lock facility (ABS). Electrically driven hydraulic pump and reservoir provide power for electronic 4-channel anti-lock braking system usable on and off-road. Optional traction control (ETC) controls wheel-spin on rear wheels (see Transmission in next spread) using ABS system. Ventilated discs front, solid discs rear.
Handbrake (parking brake).
Single drum operating on transfer box rear output shaft. Handbrake not for use while vehicle in motion.

ENGINE – V8 4.0 litre, petrol
Type. V8-cylinder, aluminium construction with 5-bearing crankshaft, self-adjusting hydraulic tappets. Crankshaft-nose mounted oil pump, high-output water pump. Rigidly-mounted auxiliaries with serpentine multi-ribbed belt and dynamic spring tensioner. Fully programmed closed-loop Sagem/Lucas GEMS engine management system with double-ended coils and knock sensing. Champion RN11YCC spark plugs with 30000 mile life. Exhaust catalyst standard.
Bore. 94.0 mm (3.70 in)

Stroke. 71 mm (2.79 in)
Displacement. 3950 cc (241 cu in)
Compression ratio. 9.34:1. Low compression 8.2:1 available.
Max power. 186 bhp @ 4750 rpm (139 kw) EEC1256.
Max torque. 236 lbf ft @ 3000 rpm (320 Nm).
Rev limiter. Fuel cut-off point 5500 rpm; re-introduced 5400.

ENGINE – V8 4.6 litre, petrol
Type. Details 4.0 litre except:
Bore. 94.0 mm (3.70 in)
Stroke. 82 mm (3.23 in)
Displacement. 4554 cc (278 cu in)
Compression ratio. 9.34:1. Low compression 8.4:1 available.
Max power. 221 bhp @ 4750 rpm (164.6 kw) EEC1256.
Max torque. 278 lbf ft @ 3000 rpm (376.6 Nm).

ENGINE – BMW 2.5 litre diesel
Type. 6 cylinder in-line, intercooled and turbo-charged high speed indirect injection diesel with hydraulic self-adjusting tappets. Cast iron block with aluminium cylinder head.
Bore. 80.00 mm (3.12 in)
Stroke. 82.8 mm (3.26 in)
Displacement. 2497 cc (152 cu in)
Compression ratio. 22.0:1
Max power. 134 bhp @ 4400 rpm (100 kw) EEC1256.
Max torque. 199 lbf ft @ 2300 rpm (270 Nm).
Turbo-charger model. Mitsubishi TD04-11G4.
Maximum operating pressure. 1.2 bar (1.26 kgf/cm^2, 18.0 lbf/in^2).

FUEL SYSTEM – PETROL V8
Fuel injection type. Lucas electronic fuel injection with GEMS-ECU.
Fuel pump. Electrical, submerged in fuel tank.
Filters. In line.
Fuel tank construction. Blow moulded plastic – high density polyurethane.
Fuel. 95 RON unleaded, 91 RON unleaded on low-

compression models.
Inertia switch. Collision or sudden impact cuts off fuel supply. May be re-set via access flap in right hand footwell.

FUEL SYSTEM – DIESEL
Injection system. Bosch fully electronic control DDE 2.5.
Fuel pump. Electrical pump submerged in fuel tank, engine driven injection pump.
Fuel tank construction. Blow moulded plastic – high density polyurethane.
Filters. In line filter.
Fuel. Derv class A1 or A2. (Or fuel not exceeding 1% sulphur content.)
Inertia switch. Collision or sudden impact cuts off fuel supply. May be re-set via access flap in right hand footwell.

COOLING SYSTEM
Type. Pressurised liquid with pump and mechanical fan.
Radiator. Aluminium radiator with remote plastic header tank and bottom-hose thermostat for improved heater performance and progressive warm-up. Separate engine oil cooler. Diesel post-turbo-charger intercooler matrix mounted ahead of radiator. Diesel has 'two-pass' coolant radiator.
Gearbox oil cooler (manual and auto)
V8 engine – mounted in front of radiator.
Diesel – mounted in front of radiator.
Thermostat. 82°C.
Fan
V8 – 425 mm (16.7 in) sickle-bladed ring-fan.
Diesel – 432 mm (17 in). Temperature sensitive viscous drive.

New Range Rover

ELECTRICAL SYSTEM
Message centre and warning system. Comprehensive driver information, system functions, diagnostic and electrical system monitoring (eg any bulb or fuse failure) are shown and graded on the instrument cluster alpha-numeric message centre and also on the warning light panel. Under-bonnet fusebox housing fuses, fusible links, control relays. Seat base fuse box with BCM (Body Control Module - EAS, ABS, Message Centre.)

Battery (see also Glossary)
V8 engine – 12 v, 380/120/90.
Diesel – 12 v, 490/170/90.
Alternator
4.0 l V8 engine – 100 amp.
4.6 l V8 engine – 120 amp.
Diesel engine – 95 amp.
Headlamps. 60/55 watt halogen bulbs.

9.6. Technical data – New Range Rover – contd

TRANSMISSION
Manual transmission
Clutch
V8 engine – AP, 267 mm (10.51 in) diam.
Diesel engine – Valeo, 242 mm (9.53 in) diam.
Hydraulic pull, reduced-load clutch operation. Asbestos-free lining.
Main gearbox. R380 manual gearbox incorporating five forward speeds and one reverse. Synchromesh on all gears – triple cone 1st, 2nd and 3rd; large single cone on 4th and 5th. Synchronised constant-mesh reverse gear train. Integral oil pump with remote cooler.
Automatic transmission
Automatic gearbox. Available on V8 engines only. ZF type

H-gate shift controls on automatic version of New Range Rover enable selection of low range gears to be achieved by moving selector lever to plane farthest from driver. See Section 2.3.

4HP24 fitted to 4.6 litre variants, otherwise ZF 4HP22. Four forward and one reverse speed. Incorporates automatic torque converter lock-up on 4th. H-gate selector – driver side of H is high range, passenger side is low range. Plus forward/aft mode selections in each plane: high range – Normal and Sports; low range – Normal and Manual. (Manual gives select-and-hold facility on gear selected.)
Manual and auto transmission
Transfer gearbox. Borg Warner chain-drive 2-speed reduction on main gearbox output with high, low and neutral positions electrically switched and selected. Transfer box range on manual vehicles controlled by in/out (lo/hi) button on fascia;

auto vehicle range controlled via 'H-gate'. (NB Transfer box neutral can only be selected – eg for towing – by adding a 5 amp fuse to position 11 in the seat-base fuse box.) Front and rear drive permanently engaged. Third differential between front/rear shafts, locked by viscous control unit when shaft speed differential sensed.

MAIN GEARBOX RATIOS, mph per 1000 engine rpm

	Ratio	mph/1000 rpm	
		High	Low
4.0/4.6 V8 manual			
5th	0.730:1	26.56	9.87
4th	1.000:1	19.44	7.23
3rd	1.397:1	13.92	5.18
2nd	2.132:1	9.12	3.39
1st	3.321:1	5.85	2.17
Rev	3.535:1	5.50	2.04
V8 automatic			
4th	0.730:1	26.7	9.93
3rd	1.000:1	19.4	7.22
2nd	1.480:1	13.14	4.89
1st	2.480:1	7.84	2.92
Rev	2.090:1	9.30	3.45
BMW 2.5 l diesel manual			
5th	0.730:1	26.56	9.87
4th	1.000:1	19.44	7.23
3rd	1.397:1	13.92	5.18
2nd	2.132:1	9.12	3.39
1st	3.692:1	5.27	1.96
Rev	3.535:1	5.50	2.04

FINAL DRIVE RATIOS
Axle ratios. 3.540:1
Transfer ratios

	All models
High	1.216:1
Low	3.271:1

Front axle. Spiral bevel crown wheel and pinion. Separate ball-joint swivel pins; external, gaitered constant velocity joints.
Rear axle. Spiral bevel crown wheel and pinion with fully floating shafts.

BODY

Construction. Inner steel monocoque, steel bonnet, roof, tailgate and door inners, and rear lower quarter panels; all exterior panels double-sided zinc coated. Side intrusion rail. Rear floor has provision for flush-fitting load-lashing cleats. **Aluminium panels.** Both front wings (bolt-on), all door outer panels and lower tailgate skin. **Painting.** Zinc phosphate. Cathodic electrocoat, polyester surfacer. Colour coated either clear over metallic or alkyd for solid colours.

CAPACITIES (litres, Imp gal)
Full fuel tank
Petrol:100 lit (22.0 gal)
Diesel: 90 lit (19.8 gal)
Usable fuel
Petrol: 93 lit (20.4 gal)
Diesel: 83 lit (18.2 gal)
Low fuel warning
9 lit (2.0 gal) approx
Cooling system
V8 and diesel – 11.3 lit
Engine oil, including filter
V8 – 4.9 lit (0.85 lit min to max)
Diesel – 9.5 lit (1.0 lit min to max)
Main gearbox (manual)
2.7 lit initial fill; 2.4 lit top-up to filler plug after draining.
Main gearbox (auto)
ZF4HP22 – 9.7 lit
ZF4HP24 – 11.0 lit
Transfer gearbox
2.4 lit
Front differential
1.7 lit
Rear differential
1.7 lit
Swivel pins
N/A - packed for life
Power steering
1.65 lit
Windscreen washer reservoir
6.0 lit

Section 10

Reference

10.1. Glossary

Assembly. Diagram shows concept of assembly exemplified on Discovery. Start is with box section chassis lowered onto axle/suspension sub-assemblies. Engine, gearbox and transfer gearbox – as a single unit – is then lowered onto chassis to pick up on four mounts, two aft and two at mid-point of engine. Body shell – wired, trimmed, furnished on another line – is then lowered (the 'body-drop') onto engine-chassis unit to pick up on ten rubber body mounts (six of which highlighted here with arrows). Doors are actually trimmed and furnished off-body and meet the vehicle some time after the body-drop.

One of ten rubber body/chassis mounts (6 arrow-highlighted here).

Aft body/chassis mount

Aft engine/gearbox mount

'A-frame', ball-jointed to top of axle. Forward ends reach up to chassis cross-member to effect axle lateral location.

Trailing links locate axle longitudinally.

'C-spanners', the leading links that locate the front axle longitudinally. They also provide anti-dive geometry under braking.

Panhard rod, attached to chassis via vertical forging (left) and to axle (lower right), locates axle laterally.

ABS. Anti-lock braking system; prevents wheels locking under maximum braking. Works on the principle of braking a wheel until it just begins to skid (this is the point where braking efficiency would drop off dramatically) and then releasing the brake pressure and re-applying the brakes. Wheel speed sensors identify the skid point and trigger a release in brake pressure. The cycle is repeated many times a second – with appropriate 'cobblestone' feed-back on the brake pedal to indicate you are in ABS mode. See also 'Cadence braking'.

A-frame. The means of effecting lateral location of the rear axle. Acting with the trailing links it also controls axle rotation. See diagram left and at 'Levelled suspension'.

Air suspension. – see EAS.

Anti-lock brakes. See ABS above.

Anti-roll bar (ARB). A large, U-shaped bar of steel (about 25 mm diameter) anchored to each side of the chassis in pivoting rubber mounts at the bottom of the U. The free ends of the U are attached to a front or rear axle to limit roll of the body relative to that axle. If the chassis/body is called on to move up and down parallel to the axle the ARB offers no interference; if, however body roll forces are induced by cornering, the twisting moments on the ARB tend to inhibit roll. In an off-road vehicle an ARB must be carefully designed not to limit axle articulation excessively and thus affect off-road performance. (See photos of rear axle anti-roll bars on Range Rover at Section 9.5). New Range Rover's composite trailing arms function as anti-roll bars as well as locating the axle longitudinally – 'Composite trailing arms' below.

Approach angle. In side-view, the angle between the ground and a line, ahead of the vehicle, joining the periphery of the front wheel and (typically) the front bumper or other low component. It represents the size or steepness of a slope or obstacle that can be approached or

climbed without striking bodywork. See diagram (right) and Sec 3.3.

Articulation. The ability of one axle to move – left wheel up, right wheel down or vice versa – relative to the chassis or its fellow axle. It is a measure of the ease with which wheels can stay in contact with the ground – and thus retain traction – on very 'twisty' off-road terrain. See Sec 3.3, 5.1.

Articulation angle, longitudinal. See 'Longitudinal articulation angle', p 199.

Assembly. See opposite.

Axles, one-piece, live. Also referred to as rigid or beam axles, in which the drive shafts to the wheels run within rigid casings without joints to allow vertical hinging as with independent suspension. See Sec 1.2.

Battery designation. Three figures define battery designation by encapsulating performance criteria. A '380/120/90' battery thus has a maximum rapid-discharge current at -18°C of 380 amp; it can maintain a discharge of 25 amp at 25°C for 120 minutes before reaching a terminal voltage of 10.2 volts; and its rate of voltage drop at max rapid-discharge of 380 amp (at -18°C) will be such that 5-7 seconds after commencement of discharge, voltage will have dropped to 9.0 volts. This is multiplied by 10 to give 90.

BCM. Body Control Module: and electronic module on New Range Rover, positioned under the front seats of the vehicle in which are contained the ECUs for the EAS and ABS. See p 194.

Boge unit. Self-levelling unit fitted to the rear axle of Range Rover and on Defenders fitted with optional self-levelling suspension. Unit has the function of 'self-pumping' the suspension up to a pre-determined height after the vehicle has travelled a certain distance. See diagram at 'Levelled suspension', p 199.

Bridle. A rope or cable attached to

...continued

The Land Rover Experience

two points – typically the right and left chassis members – of a vehicle and converging to a point of attachment for a tow rope. See Sec 5.2.

'C-spanner'. See 'Trailing/leading link' and diagram at 'Assembly', p 188.

Cadence braking. A method of manual braking with the foot brake to simulate the action of ABS brakes – see above. Very effective in slippery conditions where brake locking has occurred or might otherwise occur, the driver applies the footbrake in a series of very rapid jabs at the pedal taking the wheels up to the point of brake locking and then releasing them before the inevitable fall-off in braking efficiency takes place. Effects improved braking in any extremely slippery conditions such as ice, snow, wet mud, or rain. See Sec 3.2, 4.11, 6.3..

Camber. Angle at which, when viewed from the front, the front wheels of a vehicle splay out (positive camber) from the vertical – as shown in diagram; in some layouts it varies with position of suspension. Camber affects lateral control and ideally should be zero at all times. With Land Rover products, equipped with beam axles, camber angle is always zero.

Front axle

Camber angle

Capstan winch. A winch, generally mounted on or just behind the front bumper, usually run from an engagable extension to the engine crankshaft. The active component is usually a slowly revolving drum, about 15 cm in diameter, round which a rope may be wound to effect a winching operation. Has the advantage of being powered by the engine at idling speed and being a very low-stress unit that may be used all day without overheating or high electrical load. See Sec 5.4.

Castor (or caster) angle. When the front wheels are moved right or left to steer the vehicle they each move about a steering axis. The aft inclination of this steering axis from the vertical (when viewed from the side) – about 3° in the case of most Land Rovers – is the castor angle. Like casters on a tea trolley or office chair, this puts the ground contact point of the wheels behind the pivot axis and the result is a self-centring action tending to keep the front wheels pointing forward when in forward motion. Note that in deep sand with a 'bow wave' build-up of

sand ahead of the wheels the effective ground contact point moves ahead of the steering axis and can give the effect of negative castor with 'runaway' steering. The same thing happens when vehicle is travelling in reverse – the ground contact point being 'ahead' of the steering axis and again tending to make the front wheels 'run away' to full lock – see Sec 4.4, (failed climbing of steep off-road inclines). Also see 'Steering feel', p 202.

Castor action. Tendency of front wheels to self-centre when the steering wheel is released with the vehicle going forward. NB Opposite action takes place when in reverse – see Castor angle above. Castor action is a basic ingredient of steering feel – see 'Steering feel', p 202.

Centre differential. A differential gear device – diagram Sec 1.3 – installed at the point where the transfer box splits engine power between the front and rear axles via the front and rear propeller shafts. Working in the same way as the conventional rear axle differential on a two-wheel drive car, it allows differential rotation of front and rear shafts to accommodate the small rotational differences encountered in normal running, going

Main gearbox (manual)

Forward

Transfer gearbox

Clutch bell housing

Rear prop shaft

Front prop shaft

Transmission brake

Centre differential

round sharp corners etc. Such a device is essential in a vehicle having – for use on-road as well as off-road – full-time or permanent 4x4. Vehicles (currently by other manufacturers) fitted with part-time or selectable 4x4 are not fitted with centre differentials and thus cannot be used in four wheel drive on hard roads. See Sec 1.3, 2.5, also 'Diff lock', p 196.

Chott. Local name for salt flat or sebkha in Tunisia, Algeria and Morocco.

CLA. Coefficient of longitudinal articulation (superseded term) – see 'Longitudinal articulation angle'. A measure of 'twisty ground' capability.

Composite trailing arm. The new Range Rover rear axle uses composite material trailing arm links and a Panhard rod to locate the rear axle longitudinally and laterally (respectively) – see photo Sec 9.6. The composite trailing arm, by reason of the way it is attached to the chassis and clamped to the axle, also acts as an anti-roll bar. See also 'Trailing link'.

Continuous rolling contact. Description of a wheel in steady rolling contact with the ground without slip, wheel-spin or slide (as with locked brakes). Should be the aim at all times both on and off road. See Sec 3.2. Also see 'Discontinuity of rolling contact' below.

Co-ordinated tow. When recovering a stuck vehicle, the process by which the engine power of both the tug and the stuck vehicle are co-ordinated – usually by a signal from an external marshaller – and the clutches of both vehicles are engaged at the same time. See Sec 5.2.

Corrugations. Deformation of an unsurfaced track taking the form of transverse, close-pitch undulations – ie at right angles to the direction of the track. Often referred to as 'washboard'. See Sec 4.9.

Coupled brakes. Brake system installed with certain large trailers whereby the trailer brakes are applied at the same time as are the brakes of the towing vehicle. Vehicles must be specifically modified to operate this system – with appropriate trailers. See Sec 4.1.

Cross-axled. See 'Diagonal suspension'.

Cross ply tyre. Tyre in which the sidewall reinforcement plies run diagonally from the bead towards the tread – each layer of textile at a different angle to its adjacent layer. Generally superseded by radial-ply tyres whose thinner, more flexible sidewalls and braced tread yield better grip and lower rolling resistance. Because of thicker, multi-ply sidewalls, not so prone to sidewall damage as radials and – see Sec 4.9, 8.2 – can have low-cost applications when operating continuously on rock. However, reduced pressures in soft going can, due to the thick sidewalls, cause overheating and possibly de-lamination of the tyre. See diagram at 'Radial ply tyres' on p 200.

De-coupled prop shaft. Feature introduced for 1995 model year on Discovery to reduce transmission of NVH (noise, vibration and harshness). Normal Hookes universal joint at aft end of rear prop shaft is replaced by a rubber doughnut joint designed to isolate vibration from the chassis.

Alphabetical sequence of Glossary items resumed on p 196 after four page insert for Electronic Air Suspension.

...continued

The Land Rover Experience

EAS: <u>AUTOMATIC</u> AIR SUSPENSION ACTIVATION – ALL RANGE ROVERS (WHERE SPECIFIED) ...contd →

NOTES

1. This sequence does not occur every time you use the vehicle. Chart shows criteria that will trigger automatic suspension changes from given start points.
2. Manually selected suspension changes, see charts facing page.
3. If you are in the condition shown at the beginning of an arrow, end of arrow is the automatically selected condition if the activation criteria shown in columns occur.

Use of diagram, examples:

a. Parked vehicle starts in 'Standard'. When it reaches 50 mph and exceeds it for 30 sec (col 8) it moves to 'Low'.

b. If it then drops to 35 mph or less for 30 secs (col 2), it automatically rises to 'Standard' .

c. If you have manually selected 'High', suspension will automatically return to 'Standard' when 35 mph exceeded (col 7).

4. 'High' and 'Access' can only be selected manually though an auto-sensed change to 'Extended' (cols 3, 4) will (if speed still under 35 mph) automatically revert to 'High' after 10 min. (col 5). Col 6, 7 if 35 mph exceeded.

5. '**Freezes**':

a. 'Footbrake freeze'. Use of foot-brake *during height change* inhibits attainment of any new position for 1 min (3 min New Range Rover) unless speed 1-5 mph. This obviates front/rear dip under braking in mid-change.

b. 'Door freeze'. Opening door or tail-gate freezes movement to/from 'Access'. If freeze lasts more than 30 sec, further button selection required.

CHANGE CRITERIA →	AUTOMATIC SUSPENSION ACTIVATION – NO DRIVER INPUT							
	Drive off or handbrake released or auto out of Park	Under 35 mph			Exceed 35 mph		Over 50 mph 30 sec
		for 30 secs	Wheel(s) off-loaded for 7 secs	After 10 mins			
	1	2	3	4	5	6	7	8

Height levels (top to bottom): Extended · High profile · **Standard** · Low profile · Access

Height differences shown: 30 mm, 40 mm, 20 mm, 60 mm

New Range Rover, if 'Access' originally selected with Inhibit button pressed.

NB. New Range Rover 'Low' and 'Access' (Crawl) are 25 and 65 mm below 'Standard', not 20 and 60 mm as on diagram.

SELECTION OF 'ACCESS' REQUIRES:
1. Vehicle stationary
2. Handbrake on or selector in 'Park' with automatic transmission
3. Doors closed
4. Footbrake off
5. Engine running or has been in previous 15 secs (40 secs, New Range Rover)

EAS – electronic air suspension. A complete summary of automatic and manual operation on both models of Range Rover is contained in the diagrams above – automatic functions on this page, manual overrides on the facing page. Introduced in the 1993 model year on certain Range Rover models and further refined as the standard fit for 1995 new Range Rover, EAS enhances standards of road noise insulation, ride and handling and off-road versatility. It substitutes air springs and a pneumatic system, (ie an electrically driven compressor, air pressure reservoir and associated controls) for the steel coil springs used on the rest of the Land Rover model range. Logic-controlled by an electronic control unit (ECU), height sensors and driver controls, the system maintains front and rear self-levelling in the five height modes shown above. These notes show details of the system and and its operating mode change criteria. However, for the casual driver, new to the vehicle, no prior knowledge or expertise is required; so

EAS: <u>MANUALLY CONTROLLED</u> AIR SUSPENSION ACTIVATION

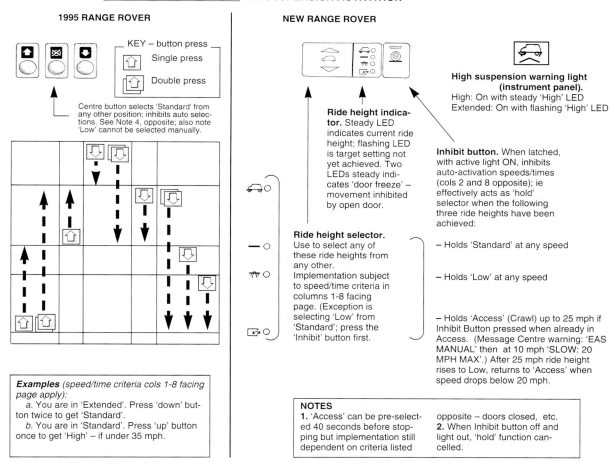

1995 RANGE ROVER

KEY – button press

Single press

Double press

Centre button selects 'Standard' from any other position; inhibits auto selections. See Note 4, opposite; also note 'Low' cannot be selected manually.

Examples *(speed/time criteria cols 1-8 facing page apply):*
a. You are in 'Extended'. Press 'down' button twice to get 'Standard'.
b. You are in 'Standard'. Press 'up' button once to get 'High' – if under 35 mph.

NEW RANGE ROVER

Ride height indicator. Steady LED indicates current ride height; flashing LED is target setting not yet achieved. Two LEDs steady indicates 'door freeze' – movement inhibited by open door.

Ride height selector. Use to select any of these ride heights from any other. Implementation subject to speed/time criteria in columns 1-8 facing page. (Exception is selecting 'Low' from 'Standard'; press the 'Inhibit' button first.

High suspension warning light (instrument panel).
High: On with steady 'High' LED
Extended: On with flashing 'High' LED

Inhibit button. When latched, with active light ON, inhibits auto-activation speeds/times (cols 2 and 8 opposite); ie effectively acts as 'hold' selector when the following three ride heights have been achieved:

– Holds 'Standard' at any speed

– Holds 'Low' at any speed

– Holds 'Access' (Crawl) up to 25 mph if Inhibit Button pressed when already in Access. (Message Centre warning: 'EAS MANUAL' then at 10 mph 'SLOW: 20 MPH MAX'.) After 25 mph ride height rises to Low, returns to 'Access' when speed drops below 20 mph.

NOTES
1. 'Access' can be pre-selected 40 seconds before stopping but implementation still dependent on criteria listed

opposite – doors closed, etc.
2. When Inhibit button off and light out, 'hold' function cancelled.

long as the 'Inhibit' button on '95 model is not pressed (diag, facing page), EAS will cycle automatically through appropriate modes according to basic programming. The driver need not even know EAS is fitted. On engine start-up EAS assumes the last selected ride height.

1. *Standard ride height* – similar to that of coil springs; normal road use – and offroad use, keeping High in reserve. Can be 'held' as an Inhibit mode (eg for towing) cutting out automatic height changes.

2. *Low profile;* automatically activated

to drop ride height by 20 mm (25 mm new Range Rover) if 50 mph is exceeded for 30 seconds. Reduces aerodynamic drag and tunes steering for high speed use by slightly increasing castor angle. If less than 35 mph is held for more than 30 seconds, standard ride height will be resumed automatically. In new Range Rover this ride height can, like Standard, be held as an Inhibit mode at any speed.

3. *High profile;* manually selected by ride height selector buttons, it raises ride height by 40 mm for occasional use off-

...continued

The Land Rover Experience

road or when wading; auto-reversion is to Standard ride height when 35 mph exceeded. Manually de-selectable. In both '95 model year Range Rover and New Range Rover, 'high suspension' warning lights show when in this mode – steady light indicating 'High' mode and flashing indications showing 'Extended' mode (see item **5.** below)

'High suspension' warning indicators on '95 Range Rover (above) and New Range Rover (below)

4. *Access;* manually selected by ride height buttons when stationary and doors closed. Drops ride height by 60 mm (65 mm new Range Rover) from standard. Mode cancelled and standard ride height resumed automatically when handbrake released or the automatic transmission shifter moved from 'Park' and vehicle driven away. Various requirements – see diagram – before Access position can be assumed. Opening a door during descent/ascent to/from Access position will freeze the suspension at that point. New Range Rover has Crawl mode in which Access can be 'held' up to 25 mph (see previous page). Purpose of Crawl is for manoeuvring in height-limited conditions such as multi-storey carparks. In

Access/Crawl, vehicle is actually lowered to bump stops – hence the need for speed-related automatic reversion to an air spring-supported condition when moving or moving above a certain speed.

5. *Extended;* raises ride height up to 20 mm above High Profile. Selected automatically when one or more wheels is off-loaded (eg when vehicle is bellied on a mound) for more than 7 seconds. Cannot be selected manually. Suspension reverts to High profile automatically after 10 minutes or reverts to standard ride height if 35 mph is exceeded. May be de-selected manually by one or two presses of suspension Down button which will respectively lower it to the High profile or Standard position.

EAS – basic system function. The plan-view diagram below gives a conceptual indication of the electronic air suspension (EAS) function; front of vehicle is to the right. An electrically driven air compressor supplies air at up to 10 bar (145 psi) to a reservoir mounted outboard of the left main chassis member (inboard right chassis member, New Range Rover) and thence to air springs at each corner of the vehicle. Actual air spring pressure varies between 3 bar and 7 bar according

Electronic air suspension – system operation concept

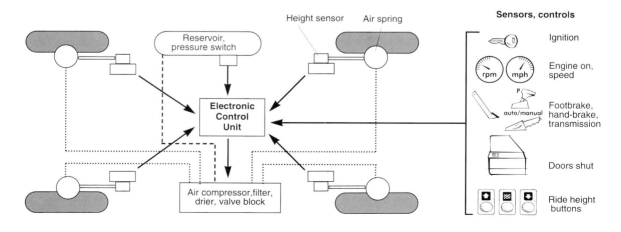

to load. An electronic control unit (ECU) housed under the front seat controls a valve block which apportions air to each spring as required. A height sensor on each longitudinal suspension link is the prime information feed to the ECU but, as shown on the diagrams overleaf, information on speed, door position, brakes-on etc are also needed and the ECU gets these from appropriate sensors as shown below. The ride height control buttons also feed direct to the ECU which puts commands through a logic check before implementing them.

EAS – functionality. Not surprisingly, the detailed functionality of the EAS, taking care of every possible combination of event and interruption by various inhibit interlocks, is very complex. The complexity need not concern an owner and is aimed only at the elimination of danger, damage or possible inconvenience – a vehicle with open doors descending to 'Access' over a high kerb that could damage the doors, ride-height changes that could cause temporary dazzle to oncoming traffic through a tail-first height change.

'Odd sensations' (and their elimination) are also catered for: a common one being arrival at traffic lights in 'Low' ride height. If you are at the lights over 30 seconds you might expect (Column 2 previous spread) the peculiar sensation of rising to 'Standard' in a stationary vehicle. This rise is postponed until the vehicle is moving. On the new Range Rover it is also postponed for a *further* 30 seconds so that, should you re-establish a speed above 35 mph in that time, the vehicle will actually remain in 'Low' – as you were when you approached the lights.

EAS – messages and faults. An 'intelligent' self-checking and fault logging system is built into the ECU to differentiate between faults that are temporary, important, those that require driver speed limitation, those that need logging for subsequent recovery and analysis by spe-

cialist equipment and those that are 'volatile' – ie will go ('evaporate') after the system has 'powered-down' (engine stopped) for two minutes or more. The main indications on the Message Centre in the New Range Rover are:

1. 'EAS MANUAL' on the Message Centre , as noted on the previous page, indicates that you have manually selected 'Access/crawl'. When your speed rises to 10 mph in this mode, since the vehicle is riding on the bump stops, the Message Centre will warn: 'SLOW: 20 MPH MAX'. If you ignore this the ride height will rise to 'Low' at 25 mph, returning to 'Access' when speed drops below 20 mph.

2. 'EAS FAULT' on the Message Centre accompanied by a bleep and return to 'Standard' ride height. If unaccompanied by further indication it is in order to continue without further action and it may well be a 'volatile' fault that on the next power-up has disappeared.

3. 'EAS FAULT' that alternates in 4 second cycle with 'SLOW: 35 MPH MAX' indicates the suspension is trapped in a position above 'Standard' or below 'Low' and the speed limit should be observed.

In cases 2 or 3 it is worth stopping, switching off and starting up again after two minutes in case the fault is a volatile one. If it is not, keep within the speed limits indicated and contact your Land Rover dealer who will use diagnostic equipment to establish detail cause.

EAS – uses of 'Inhibit'. A quick guide to the uses of 'Inhibit":

1. *Towing.* On both types of Range Rover, set suspension to 'Standard' and then select 'Inhibit' to keep it there.

2. *Sporty handling.* On new Range Rover, you may prefer the feel of the vehicle in 'Low' – taut ride and enhanced high speed steering. If not already in 'Low', select "Inhibit' first, then "Low'.

3. *'Access/crawl'.* On new Range Rover when, for example, manoeuvring in a low-roof multi-storey car park select 'Access', then 'Inhibit'.

...continued

Alphabetical sequence of Glossary items resumed here from p 191 after four page insert for Electronic Air Suspension.

Departure angle. In side view, the angle between the ground and a line, aft of the vehicle, joining the periphery of the rear wheel and (typically) the rear chassis member or other low component. It represents the size or steepness of a slope or obstacle that can be approached or climbed in reverse without striking bodywork. See Sec 3.3.

Diagonal suspension. A manifestation occurring off-road when a vehicle is, for example, diagonally crossing a small but well-defined ridge. When the ridge is so severe that, say, the right front wheel and the rear left wheels are on full 'bump' (ie fully up in the wheel arches) and the other wheels are hanging down to the full extent of wheel travel, the vehicle may be described as being diagonally suspended or on diagonal suspension. Some also refer to this state as being 'cross-axled'. See Sec 4.3.

Diagonal wheel-spin. The wheel-spin that can take place on the fully extended (or off-loaded) wheels in a condition of diagonal suspension as described above. The presence of slippery ground under these wheels can provoke the condition. Can also occur crossing ditches diagonally; see Sec 4.3.

Diff-lock. See first 'Centre differential' above. Locking of the centre differential, activated by moving the transfer gearbox lever to the left and confirmed by illumination of the 'DIFF-LOCK' indicator light, puts the differential function on hold. Where traction conditions or grip are different front and rear there would be a tendency for the centre differential to permit the front wheels, say, to spin ineffectively while they are on wet clay and cause the rear wheels, on grippier ground, to stop rotating. The diff-lock locks the centre differential, thus locking front and rear prop shafts together, ensuring they revolve at the same speed and enhancing traction. Diff-lock is usually engaged for difficult off-road conditions but should never remain engaged on hard grippy roads. See also 'Centre differential lock', Sec 2.5. See also 'Viscous coupling', p 205.

Differential casing. Not to be confused with the centre differential, each axle, of course, has a normal cross-axle differential at the point where the propeller shaft from the transfer gearbox meets the axle. The size of the crown wheel and pinion plus differential demands a bulge in the axle casing – referred to as the diff casing. It has special significance in off-road vehicles because it is the lowest point of the axle and thus the point of least ground clearance – Sec 3.3.

Discontinuity of rolling contact. Generic term for wheel-spin and wheel slide – as on locked brakes. See Sec 3.2 and 'Continuous rolling contact' above.

Divergent. A dynamic condition that 'gets worse of its own accord' – eg an oscillation of ever-increasing amplitude or a turn that, once initiated, tightens up on its own. See also 'Oversteer, divergent'.

EAS. See p 192.

Electric range change. Method of shifting transfer gears on the New Range Rover by pressing button or use of H-gate lever position instead of by manual lever.

Electronic air suspension. See p 192.

Electronic traction control – ETC. ETC is a standard/optional feature, available only on ABS-equipped Range Rovers. It inhibits wheel-spin by applying brake to a spinning rear wheel and thus enhances traction on ice, snow or in severe off-road conditions. It is an entirely automatic function and has no driver control or override. It utilises ABS sensors for wheel speed determination and brakes the spinning wheel to apply, through the axle differential, torque to the stationary wheel. Like ABS, it is especially effective in maintaining control when one side of the vehicle is on a more slippery surface than the other – a so-called 'split-μ' surface. A dashboard light illuminates when the system is operating. The function is inhibited above 50 kph to preclude over-heating, a speed above which unintentional wheel spin is unlikely to occur. See Sec 2.1, 3.2..

Engine braking. Vehicle retardation derived from engaging a low gear and taking your foot off the throttle. See also Sec 4.5, 6.3.

Emergency flotation (tyre pressure). Very low tyre pressure (about 60% of normal road pressures), always associated with a low maximum permitted speed (20 kph or 12 mph) used for traversing or recovery from very soft ground. Such low pressures cause extreme tyre sidewall flexing – hence the speed limitation. See Sec 4.7, 8.2..

Emergency soft. Another name for emergency flotation tyre pressure – see above.

ETC . See 'Electronic traction control' above.

Fatigue life. Number of specified load reversals at which a metal component will fail. In the context of this book see fatigue life of nylon snatch-towing ropes – 'Recovery – snatch-towing', Sec 5.3.

'Fesh-fesh'. Desert terrain comprising a thin crust of fine gravel or wind-blown sand laid over deep very fine dust of powder consistency. Can be bad enough to bog a vehicle. Difficult to spot due to overlay of normal-looking sand.

Flotation. Characteristic of a vehicle, by reason of large softly inflated tyres, not to sink on soft going such as mud or sand. See Sec 4.7 and 'Optimum pressures', Sec 8.2.

Four-wheel drive (4x4). Vehicle transmission system in which engine power is applied to all four wheels. The term 4x4 (four by four) has the specific connotation that it is a four (wheeled vehicle driven) by four (wheels). See Sec 1.1.

Full-time 4x4. A transmission system on a four-wheeled vehicle in which all four wheels are driven by the engine all the time. (As opposed to a vehicle that is normally in two-wheel drive with four-wheel drive selected by a separate lever when required.) See Sec 1.1, 2.1.

Geometric limitations. A term coined for this book to describe the limitations and extent of approach and departure angles, ramp angle, steering lock, articulation and – an even newer term – longitudinal articulation angle. See 'Geometric limitations', Sec 3.3, and throughout Sec 9.

Ground clearance. Space between the ground and a given mechanical part of the vehicle. Usually, when quoted for a vehicle, taken as the least for any component on the vehicle – the space under the differential casing. But note difference between under-axle and under-belly clearance – see Sec 3.3.

Ground offset. Sometimes also called 'steering offset'. The lateral distance between the point where the extension of the steering swivel pin (or king pin) axis touches the ground and the centre line of the front wheel – also at ground level – when viewed from the front. Offset influences amount of 'drag' present at each front wheel. These cancel out, side-to-side in normal straight, hard-road driving but when cornering causes weight transfer to one side or one wheel goes through thick 'draggy' mud off-road, steering feel and feedback of shock can be affected – hence need for damper and worm/roller steering box. Zero offset is the ideal but very hard to achieve with

Swivel pin inclination – about 8°

Front axle

Swivel pin

Ground offset

...continued

complexities of all-wheel drive and brakes to cram into a small space; New Range Rover has reduced ground offset to 17 mm, enabling use of recirculating ball steering system. See picture Sec 9.6.

Ground stress. Term coined for this book to indicate how much strength is being asked of a particular piece of ground in terms of flotation or lateral shear to accommodate traction, braking or acceleration. See Sec 1.2, 4.7.

GVW. Gross vehicle weight – the maximum permitted laden weight of a vehicle including payload, fuel and driver.

H-gate. New Range Rover with automatic transmission uses twin selection quadrants for high and low range gears separated by centre bar at the neutral position – hence 'H-gate'. See Sec 2.3.

Handbrake. See 'Transmission brake'.

Harmonics. Here taken as relating to the natural frequency of a vehicle's suspension system that can influence the formation of transverse surface corrugations on unsurfaced tracks. See Sec 4.9.

Heel and toe wear. Jargon for the uneven front to rear wear on individual blocks of a bold off-road tyre tread when used on roads. See Sec 8.2, 'Mud tyre' and 'Sand tyre'.

High box. Transmission status when the two-speed transfer gearbox lever is in the high ratio position – for normal, on-road, day-to-day use. See Sec 1.2.

High ratio. Term to describe the transmission when the transfer gearbox lever is in the high position – high box above.

Hi-lift jack. Versatile lever-operated mechanical bumper jack capable of a lift of about a metre. See Sec 5.1.

Hi-lo lever. Term sometimes used to describe the transfer gearbox range change lever. See Sec 1.2.

High Load suspension. An option on the Defender 90 (stronger, dual-rate rear springs) enabling payload to be raised by about 150 kg – see Sec 9.1.

Hydraulic tappets. Method of operat-

ing the engine cylinder valves incorporating what is in effect an oil-filled section of the operating rod. Method is 'self-adjusting', eliminates need for and noise emanating from 'valve clearances' associated with normal actuation method.

Hydraulic winch. Winch with rotational function actuated by a hydraulic motor. Power source is hydraulic pump mounted on power take off at rear of gearbox. See Sec 5.4.

Kerb weight. Empty vehicle plus full fuel plus 75 kg driver.

KERR. Kinetic Energy Recovery Rope. Descriptive term coined to describe specially specified nylon ropes capable of stretching during snatch tow. See 'Recovery – snatch-towing', Sec 5.3.

Kinetic energy. Energy of motion, proportional to total weight of the vehicle and the square of its speed. Thus if a vehicle's weight doubles its KE also goes up two times; but if its speed doubles its KE increases by two squared, ie four times. See 'Recovery – snatch-towing', Sec 5.3.

King pin. See 'Swivel pin'.

Laden. Vehicle carrying some or full payload. See also GVW above concerning loading to maximum permitted weight.

Leading link. See 'Trailing/leading link'.

Levelled suspension. (See diagram opposite page.) A means of eliminating the 'squat' of the rear suspension under load using a hydraulic self-levelling unit (see also 'Boge unit') between the chassis and the centre of the rear axle. Standard on coil sprung Range Rovers, Defender 110 Station Wagons and County; special order other Defender 110. See 'Unlevelled suspension', p 205. (Range Rovers with EAS have auto levelling front and rear.)

Longitudinal articulation angle. A single number, taking account of both wheel movement and wheelbase, that conveys the off-road, 'twisty ground' potential of an off-road vehicle. It is the angle between the ground and a line joining the front and rear hubs (or tyre

Longitudinal articulation angle

Unlevelled rear suspension

A-frame

Trailing link

Ball joint

Direction of travel

Self-levelling (Boge) unit

Direction of travel

Levelled rear suspension
(See opposite page, right hand column.)

periphery) when one wheel is on full bump and the other fully extended. A given max wheel movement enhances this capability more on a short wheelbase than on a long wheelbase vehicle. Higher values mean better articulation; small differences in articulation angle make quite large differences to performance. Vehicle values Sec 9.1 – 9.6.

Low box. Low range; when the transfer gearbox lever is in the low position – for difficult off-road conditions demanding greater traction or low speed control. See 'Traction – extra gears', Sec 1.2, and 'Low range – when and how', Sec 2.4.

Low range. Term to describe the transmission when transfer gearbox lever is in the low position. See Sec 2.1, 2.4, 2.5.

Low ratio. See 'low range'.

Marshalling. ('Marshaller' derived from ground-crew who marshal aircraft at airports.) In the context of off-road operations, taken to mean the detailed direction of a vehicle by a marshaller outside the vehicle who is able to see all four wheels and also the difficult ground being traversed. Marshalling should be undertaken when there is the danger of damaging tyre sidewalls or the underside of the vehicle on rocks or other obstacles. See 'Look before you leap', Sec 3.4.

Mechanical sympathy. In the context of this book, concern for and empathy with the structural stress, durability of, and possible damage to mechanical components of your vehicle. In a phrase, caring about your Land Rover. See 'Mindset – mechanical sympathy', Sec 3.1.

Message centre. Alpha-numeric information readout on New Range Rover instruments showing systems status, faults, fuse/bulb failures, suspension and transmission status. See Sec 9.6, 2.1, 2.3.

M+S tyres. Mud and snow tyres. A generic term for 4x4 tyres with a road-oriented, not especially bold, tread pattern suitable for mild snow and mud conditions. See Sec 8.2, 'Tyres'.

Mode. Method or regime of operation of a system – eg fast or slow, high or low, manual or auto. Hence its use in the context of (and see) 'EAS' (p 192-195) and 'H-gate automatic transmission' (Sec 2.3).

Mud tyres. Bold, open-tread tyres optimised for mud with disadvantages on hard roads. See Sec 8.2, 'Tyres'.

Multi-purpose tyre. Combination/compromise between on-road and mud tyres. See Sec 8.2, 'Tyres'.

...continued

NATO towing hook. Large, robust, four-bolt attachment towing pintle with top-closure originally specified for NATO 7.5 tonne military vehicles. Suitable for off-road towing ; noisy, due to trailer towing eye not being a close fit over the hook. See 'Towing – on-road', Sec 4.1 and 'Towing off-road', Sec 6.4.

Nose load. Trailers should be nose heavy; the nose-load is the amount of nose-heaviness measured at the tow-hitch and must be considered part of the towing vehicle's payload. See 'Towing – on-road', Sec 4.1.

NVH. Abbreviation for 'noise, vibration and harshness', an affliction the chassis and engine engineers try very hard to eliminate by the likes of carefully tuned power train mounts, suspension isolation pads, de-coupled prop shafts and air suspension.

OE. Abbreviation for 'original equipment', usually referring to tyres as supplied on a vehicle when bought from the factory.

On-foot recce. Inspecting a difficult off-road obstacle on foot before committing your vehicle to it. See 'Look before you leap', Sec 3.4.

Overrun brakes. Trailer brakes activated by the tendency of the trailer to overtake – or overrun – the towing vehicle when the vehicle brakes or slows down. See 'Towing- on-road', Sec 4.1.

Oversteer, divergent. Tendency for an initiated steering command to 'run away' toward full lock or (Sec 4.1) for an extremely nose-heavy trailer to cause this condition on a fast, sharp bend.

Over-torque. Used in this book to convey the concept of applying too much torque (or power) to the wheels so that they break their grip with the ground and spin.

Panhard rod. A suspension component, of the order of 30 mm diameter and a metre long, that laterally locates a front or rear axle relative to the chassis. One end is attached and pivoted to the (say,

right hand) chassis member and the other end to the (in this case, left hand) end of the axle. The arrangement permits vertical movement of the axle, and articulation, whilst constraining lateral movement. See diagram at 'Assembly' (p 188), and photo of New Range Rover at Sec 9.6. Panhard rods are used for front axle lateral location on all Land Rover products and, on New Range Rover, for the rear axle too. (For rear axles on other models, see 'A-frame'.) Together with the trailing or leading links, the Panhard rod is thus part of a linkage system that locates an axle fore and aft as well as laterally.

Part-time 4x4. See 'Selectable four-wheel drive' next page.

Permanent four-wheel drive. See 'Full-time 4x4' above.

Power take off. Attachment to rear of gearbox for running accessories such as hydraulic pumps or shaft drives to winches and saws. Approved versions available for Land Rover products.

PTO. See power take off.

Radial ply tyre. A type of tyre construction in which sidewall structural plies run radially out towards the tread

Cross ply tyre

Radial ply tyre

instead of criss-cross diagonally. With their thinner, more flexible sidewalls, radial tyres have lower rolling resistance than cross-ply tyres (yielding better fuel consumption) as well as giving longer tread life. They can accommodate the use of low inflation pressures without over-heating, due to their flexible sidewalls, but are sometimes more prone to sidewall damage when operating in rocky or stony conditions. Because radial tyres invari-ably also have a braced tread area of great dimensional stability, they 'track-lay' the tread (like a bulldozer), do not suffer from 'tread shuffle' and so achieve more traction in limiting off-road conditions. See also Sec 4.7.

Ramp angle. A measure of vehicle under-belly clearance or the ability to drive over a sharp ridge or ramp without touching the underside of the vehicle on the obsta-

cle. The ramp angle is the angle measured from the lowest part of the chassis at mid-wheelbase down to the periphery of front and rear wheels. Obviously a short wheelbase vehicle with large wheels will have the smallest ramp angle and best under-belly clearance; a Defender 90 will be better than a Defender 130 in this respect. See Sec 3.3.

Ramp breakover angle. The fuller title of 'Ramp angle ' above.

Range change. Term sometimes used for the transfer gearbox lever. See Sec 2.1.

Reduced inflation. Lowering tyre pressures to increase flotation in soft ground conditions such as mud or soft sand. See Sec 4.7 and Sec 8.2, 'Tyres'.

Rolling contact – see 'Continuous rolling contact'.

Sand ladders. A pair of aluminium ladders, about 170 cm long, specially made with rungs closer than normal, to lay beneath the vehicle wheels in soft sand to give grip and flotation. See 'Self-recovery', Sec 5.1.

Sand tracks. Generic name sometimes given to any item fulfiling the role of a sand ladder. May be PSP (pierced steel planking). See 'Self-recovery' and dia-gram Sec 5.1.

Sand channels. Term often inter-changeable with sand tracks, derivative from the days when metal channels were used for this purpose. Can include articu-lated sand planks, see 'Self-recovery' and photo Sec 5.1.

Sand tyres. Term often used to mean desert tyre – which implies an ability to cope with desert rock and stones as well as sand. These tyres are characterised by tread blocks of a gentle, shouldered pro-file with no bold, right-angled edges such as a mud tyre would have. Radial con-struction is far more suited to the low inflation pressures sometimes used in sand. Despite their appearance, 'balloon' tyres with circumferential groove treads are considerably less effective in sand than a radial such as the Michelin XS. See Sec 4.8 and Sec 8.2, 'Tyres'.

Salt flat. Salt marsh (also known as 'chott' or 'sebkha') of very unreliable con-sistency and bearing strength found in desert regions and characterised by a top crust of varying thickness and strength with soft salt mud of great depth beneath it. See Sec 4.8.

Sebkha. See Salt flat above.

Selectable four-wheel drive. A four-wheeled vehicle which proceeds normally in two-wheel drive but on which, by means of a lever control, four-wheel drive may be selected. It is important to remem-ber that such vehicles in four-wheel drive do not have the benefit of a centre differ-ential (see p 190 above) so should not be used on hard roads or firm grippy sur-faces in this mode. See Sec 1.3.

Self centring. The characteristic of front (steered) wheels to resume the

...continued

straight-ahead position due to castor angle (See 'Castor angle', p 190 above) when the steering wheel is released. This characteristic can be utilised to enhance safety when driving in deep wheel ruts on slippery ground. See 'Driving on tracks', Sec 4.2 and 'Steering feel' this page.

Self-levelling suspension. See 'Levelled suspension' p 198.

Sidewall. The external 'walls' of a tyre between the tread and the bead or wheel rim. This area is particularly vulnerable on radial ply tyres to damage in off-road operations from oblique rubbing contact with side-swiping sharp rocks. Driver awareness essential. See Sec 4.9.

Sidewall awareness. Awareness by sensitive drivers of the susceptibility to damage of the tyre sidewall. An attribute worth developing. See 'Rocks, stones, corrugations', Sec 4.9.

Sidewall deflection. Outward movement of the tyre sidewall in the region of the ground contact patch due to low infla-

Top section

Ground level section

tion pressures or hitting a sharp bump with excess speed. It is important not to run tyres at less than recommended inflation pressures for given maximum speeds and loads (see Sec 8.2, 'Tyres') since by doing so you will exceed the manufacturer's specified limits for sidewall deflection and thus cause overheating and serious damage to the tyre.

Shock loading. In the context of this book, taken to mean the arrest of mechanical motion in an excessively abrupt way or the application of sharp load reversals in a such a way as to risk structural fail-

ure. For example, the application of the handbrake whilst the vehicle is in motion – important, see 'Traction controls', Sec 2.1 – can cause unacceptable shock loading of the rear axle half-shafts. (See 'Transmission brake' next page.) Engaging diff lock whilst one or more wheel is spinning could also result in severe and damaging shock load to the transmission (See also 'Viscous coupling' p 205 and 'Mechanical sympathy', p 199.)

Small gear lever. Don't be embarrassed if you can't remember the name for the transfer gear lever..! (See p 204.)

Snatch tow. A method of recovering a stuck vehicle in which the towing vehicle is in motion before taking up the slack in the tow rope. Use only special-purpose stretch ropes and specified procedures for this, See 'Recovery – snatch towing', Sec 5.3.

Steering lock. The extent to which the steering wheel may be moved to the right or left. Thus 'full lock' implies movement of the steering wheel as far as it will go right or left.

Steering feel. Steering feel is a vital and safety-relevant ingredient of the feedback between vehicle and driver. The communication is achieved almost entirely by assimilating the amount of self-centring or castor action present and how it compares with normal on-road conditions. (See first Castor action and Castor angle above – p 190.) It is important for drivers always to be alert to variations in steering feel and to know what may cause them. A very brief summary follows:

1. *Power steering.* On Land Rover products this is power assisted steering so feel is retained at all times. The centre 6°, ie 3° either side of straight ahead, is not power assisted and this aids straight-ahead feel. Be alert to the possibility of inexperienced mechanics having adjusted this out.

2. *In slippery ruts* accurate feel will be lost and you will find it hard to know exactly which way your wheels are pointing. It is essential to check visually until back on normal ground – see Sec 4.2, Railway lining effect.

3. *In soft sand*, as noted above, the effective ground contact point may well be ahead of the pivot axis and this can give 'negative castor action' effect – ie a tendency for the wheels to run away to full lock. This will be particularly – and dangerously – apparent when descending the slip face of a sand dune. Grip the steering wheel firmly with both hands and, down a sand-fall, have a marshaller guide you: and watch the marshaller – he is the only one who can tell which way your front wheels are pointing.

4. *Rock or rough ground.* Whilst the worm and roller steering design and power assisted steering of Land Rover vehicles is ideally suited to off-road driving, be aware of the potential for serious kick-back from the steering when traversing rough ground, rocks and boulders. Grip the steering wheel firmly and keep your thumbs outside the rim so that sudden, unexpected kickback does not cause injury.

5. *Range Rover with electronic air suspension.* One of the additional benefits of EAS is that variations in suspension height also cause slight variations in castor angle. Low profile, automatically selected above 50 mph, increases castor angle by just over 1° and produces exceptional stability and enhanced self-centring – exactly what is required for high speed motorway driving. Conversely, when on high profile or extended suspension settings, steering castor is reduced, making the steering inherently lighter over difficult ground.

6. *Ice, snow, slippery conditions* – on road. This will be well-enough known to experienced 4x2 drivers but is still worth mentioning here since the same laws of physics apply to 4x4s. When grip is at a premium obviously the self-centring of the front wheels will be dramatically diminished and the heart-sinking 'lightness' of the steering wheel will be experi-

enced. As in a surprising number of off-road situations, delicate 'finger-tip' steering and 'the midwife's touch' are the order of the day.

Stretch limit (KERR ropes). The extent to which a kinetic energy recovery rope or strap will stretch before it is in danger of breaking. A guide for the Marlow Ropes Recovaline is 40% stretch; this limit should never be approached. See 'Recovery – snatch towing', Sec 5.3.

Survey on foot. Inspect before you drive. See On-foot recce above and 'Look before you leap', Sec 3.4.

Swivel pin. Sometimes known as king pin. The axis about which a front wheel pivots in order to effect steering. Swivel pin axes are invariably inclined aft to achieve a castor angle or trail thus providing self-centring. When viewed from the front, the lower end is further outboard than the top end which helps reduce ground offset and improves steering in other respects. See diagram at entry for 'Ground offset', p 197.

Swivel pin inclination. See above and Sec 9.1 – 9.6 for individual vehicle values.

Toe-in / toe-out. Amount by which front wheels, in plan view, are not parallel to each other. This is a designed-in feature that affects handling and steering feel and there are defined limits for each vehicle.

Traction. In the context of this book the concept of achieving grip between the wheels and the ground without slip, skid or sinkage. See Sec 1.2, 3.2.

Traction Control. See 'Electronic Traction Control, ETC'.

Traction controls. Here taken to mean the lever controlling the transfer gearbox and centre differential lock, see 'Traction controls', Sec 2.1.

Tractive effort. The amount of 'pull' exerted by a vehicle as a result of traction.

Trailer preponderance. Sometimes used to denote down-load on the vehicle towing hitch – see 'Nose load' p 200 above and 'Towing – on-road', Sec 4.1.

...continued

Trailer nose-load. See 'Nose load' p 200 above.

Trailing link / leading link. Trailing links, fitted to all current Land Rover vehicles, are structural members of the order of a metre long each side of the chassis linking (at their forward end) the chassis to (at their aft end) the rear axle. They thus locate the axle fore and aft relative to the chassis, allowing it to rise and fall as required whilst also transmitting braking loads and thrust from the wheels. See diagram at 'Levelled suspension'. Forward-pointing *leading links* do the same thing for the front axle; here they are forgings – often referred to as 'C-spanners' because of their shape and each bolted to the front axle by two rubber-bushed bolts (see diagram at 'Assembly'.)

Transfer gearbox. Originally the name implied the transfer of power from the main gearbox to the front axle as well as the rear axle on a four-wheel drive vehicle. In all Land Rover products a two-speed transfer box is fitted so it has the additional role of permitting power from the gearbox to go to the axles at normal 1:1 gearing (high ratio) or geared down by nearly 2:1 (low ratio). See 'Traction – extra gears', Sec 1.2, 'Low range – when and how', Sec 2.4 and diagram below.

Gearbox, transfer box, hand brake

Main gear lever
Main gearbox (manual)
Transfer gearbox
Rear prop shaft
Transfer gear lever
Forward
Front prop shaft
Centre differential
Transmission brake

Transfer gear lever. The 'small gear lever', in the cab next to the main gear lever. It controls whether the transmission is in 'high ratio' or 'low ratio' in the transfer box. The same lever also controls the engagement of the diff lock – see above – except in the Range Rover where a viscous coupling fulfils this requirement automatically. See 'Traction controls', Sec 2.1 and 'Viscous coupling' opposite.

Transmission brake. The handbrake on all Land Rovers operates by gripping the rear propeller shaft at the point where it leaves the transfer gearbox and is thus called a transmission brake. It should be used as a parking brake only and should never be operated whilst the vehicle is in motion except in emergency - see 'Traction controls', Sec 2.1 and drawing left.

Transmission wind-up. Read first 'Centre differential', p 190 above. A 4x4 with no centre differential or one driven with the centre diff locked (ie in both cases the front and rear propeller shafts locked together) is unable to accommodate the small differences in distance normally travelled by the front wheels compared to the rear wheels. The diff-lock ensures both propeller shafts rotate exactly the same amount despite the small differences in distance actually travelled. This results in some wheel slip and skid which, on loose ground, can take place without any harm. On hard roads, however, the superior wheel grip makes it difficult for the wheels to slip much and in the process of trying to do so considerable torsional stress builds up in the transmission. This is known as transmission wind-up and can sometimes exert so much stress that the diff-lock gears will not disengage when so selected. You will also sense very heavy steering. If this occurs due to your forgetting to de-select diff-lock on hard ground (or at any other time) and the diff lock will not disengage, the solution is to reverse the vehicle some distance until the diff-lock warning light extinguishes.

Tyre nomenclature. Details of all information inscribed on the sidewalls of tyres is contained in Sec 8.2, 'Tyres', final page.

'Two-pass' radiator. Engine coolant radiator type fitted to diesel version of New Range Rover; radiator is effectively split vertically by an internal baffle forcing coolant to follow a U-shaped path. Coolant enters upper left, passes down the left half, across the bottom and up the right side to exit upper right.

Unladen. Vehicle carrying fuel, driver but no payload or other load – see 'Kerb' above.

Unlevelled suspension. Defender 110 rear suspension without the self-levelling option as described at 'Levelled suspension', p 198 above.

Viscous coupling unit (VCU). A unit fitted as standard to all Range Rovers across the centre differential (not instead of it) automatically to effect locking of the differential when a significant speed difference between front and rear propeller shafts is sensed. Conceptually it comprises a cylinder attached to the rear prop shaft into which an extension of the front prop shaft is introduced. Discs are attached alternately to the front prop shaft and the inside of the cylinder so that

they interleave very closely within the cylinder. The cylinder is sealed at both ends and is filled with a special silicone fluid which has the characteristic of markedly increasing its viscosity when stirred. Thus when one prop shaft rotates relative to the other one – the situation of front (or rear) axle wheel-spin – the fluid increases its viscosity enough to lock the shafts together. When relative rotation ceases the viscosity changes back to its original value and the shafts are unlocked. The viscous coupling unit (VCU) has the advantage of being automatic on both engagement and disengagement and its action is gradual and without shock-loading to the transmission.

Wading plugs. Oil drain holes are provided in the bottom of the clutch housing (and the camshaft drive-belt housing on Tdi and 2.5D engines) to preclude the possibility of the clutch or cam belts becoming contaminated in the event of oil leaks from the adjacent bearings. Wading plugs should be fitted to block these holes when driving through water over 30 cm deep and subsequently removed. See 'Wading' and photo, Sec 4.10 (covers R380 gearbox).

Wheel-slide. See above 'Discontinuity of rolling contact' p 196. A condition in which one or more wheels slide over a slippery surface rather than rolling over it; can be provoked by brake lock up or excessive engine braking. See 'Gentle right foot', Sec 3.2.

Wheel-spin. See Discontinuity of rolling contact p 196. A condition in which a stationary or moving vehicle has power applied to the transmission in conditions of poor grip and one or more wheels spins without associated forward motion (or rearward if in reverse). See 'Gentle right foot', Sec 3.2.

10.2 Index

...continued

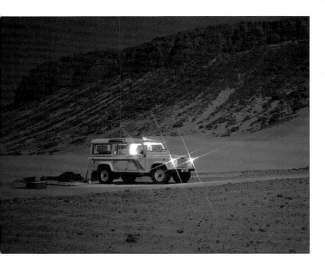

A Defender 110 County on an expedition in the Sahara desert. There are few regions where meticulous vehicle operation and mechanical sympathy could be more important.